Taylor's Guides to Gardening

Rita Buchanan, Editor

Frances Tenenbaum, Series Editor

HOUGHTON MIFFLIN COMPANY

Boston • New York

Taylor's Guide to Herbs

For information about permission to reproduce selections from
this book, write to Permissions, Houghton Mifflin Company,
215 Park Avenue South, New York, New York 10003.

Taylor's Guide is a registered trademark
of Houghton Mifflin Company.

Library of Congress Cataloging-in-Publication Data
Taylor's guide to herbs / Rita Buchanan, editor.
     p.   cm.
  Includes index.
  ISBN 0-395-68081-6
  1. Herb gardening. 2. Herbs. I. Buchanan, Rita.
SB351.H5T36 1994
635'.7—dc20   94-44241

Printed in Hong Kong

DNP 10 9 8 7 6 5 4 3 2

Cover photograph © 1992 by Dency Kane

Contents

Contributors

Peter Borchard and his wife, Susan, are the owners of Companion Plants, an herb nursery in Athens, Ohio. He grows hundreds of different culinary, medicinal, and fragrant plants and supplied extensive information for the plant encyclopedia in this guide.

Rita Buchanan was general editor of this guide and wrote several of the essays. A freelance editor and writer, she has contributed to other volumes in the Taylor's Guide series, including *Taylor's Master Guide to Gardening,* which she also coedited. She has also contributed to *Fine Gardening, The Herb Companion, Garden Design, Country Living Gardener,* the Brooklyn Botanic Garden *Handbooks,* and other publications. She grows a wide variety of hardy and tender herbs in her garden and greenhouse in Winsted, Connecticut.

Steve Buchanan did the illustrations for this book, as he has for other volumes in the Taylor's Guide series. He specializes in drawings of gardens and natural history subjects, and his illustrations appear regularly in gardening books and magazines such as *Fine Gardening, The Herb Companion, Garden Design,* and the Brooklyn Botanic Garden *Handbooks.*

Steven Foster wrote the essay on medicinal plants and supplied information on medicinal uses of plants for the plant encyclopedia. He has written seven books, among them *A Field Guide to Medicinal Plants,* in Houghton Mifflin's Peterson series. He is special publications editor for the American Botanical Council and makes his home in the Arkansas Ozarks.

Louise Hyde and her husband, Cyrus, own Well-Sweep Herbs, an herb nursery in Port Murray, New Jersey. She consulted on the plant list for this book and supplied descriptions of several herbs for the plant encyclopedia.

Debra Kirkpatrick wrote the essays on designing a traditional, formal herb garden and integrating herbs into the landscape. A Registered Landscape Architect with a special interest in herbs, she is the author of *Using Herbs in the Landscape,* published by Stackpole Books. She studied horticulture at Pennsylvania State University and landscape architecture at the University of Virginia. She lives in Dillsberg, Pennsylvania.

Tovah Martin is a horticulturist at Logee's Greenhouses in Danielson, Connecticut. She consulted on the plant list for this book and supplied descriptions of many tender herbs for the plant encyclopedia. She is a frequent contributor to gardening magazines and has written several books, including *The Essence of Paradise: Fragrant Plants for Indoor Gardens,* published by Little, Brown, and *Tasha Tudor's Garden,* published by Houghton Mifflin.

Jerry Parsons is curator of the herb collection at the University of California Botanic Garden in Berkeley, California. He consulted on the plant list for this book and supplied descriptions of several herbs for the plant encyclopedia.

Holly Shimizu was general consultant on the list of herbs to include in this book and supplied specific information on roses. She was the original curator of the National Herb Garden at the U.S. National Arboretum and is now Horticulturist at the U.S. Botanic Garden in Washington, D.C.

Kae Snow-Stephens supplied information on growing herbs in the South for the plant encyclopedia in this book. She tends an extensive collection of plants in her own garden in Shreveport, Louisiana; works at a large nursery; and participates in regional herb society events.

Chris Utterback wrote the essay on cooking with herbs. She is editor and publisher of the bimonthly newsletter *Herban Lifestyles* and has written for *The Herb Companion* and other herb magazines. She is active in the Connecticut Horticultural Society and the Connecticut chapter of the Herb Society of America.

Andrew Van Hevelingen and his wife, Melissa, own a wholesale herb nursery in Oregon's Willamette Valley and maintain a large demonstration garden where they grow hundreds of herbs and hardy perennials. He is a regular contributor to *The Herb Companion* and supplied information about lavenders and other fragrant herbs for this guide.

Hardiness Zone Map

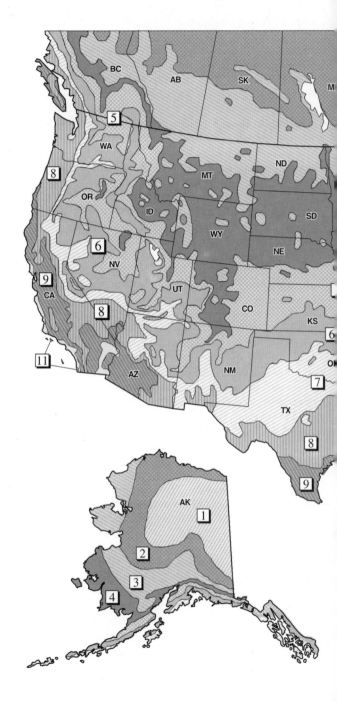

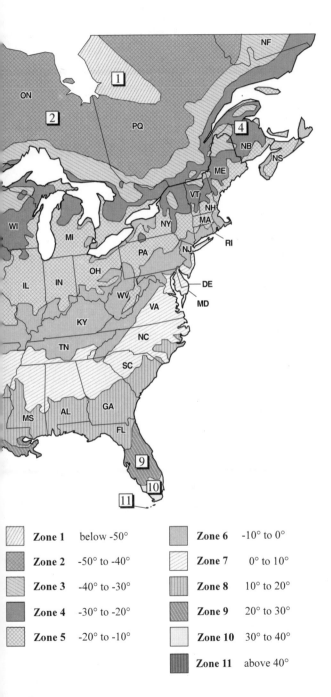

	Zone 1	below -50°		**Zone 6**	-10° to 0°
	Zone 2	-50° to -40°		**Zone 7**	0° to 10°
	Zone 3	-40° to -30°		**Zone 8**	10° to 20°
	Zone 4	-30° to -20°		**Zone 9**	20° to 30°
	Zone 5	-20° to -10°		**Zone 10**	30° to 40°
				Zone 11	above 40°

Introduction: What Is an Herb?

When gardeners talk about herbs, they're often thinking about a particular group of shrubby perennials that grow wild on rocky hillsides in countries around the Mediterranean Sea. This group includes rosemary, garden sage, hyssop, winter savory, catnip, horehound, lemon balm, and various kinds of thymes, oreganos, and lavenders. All of these plants have fragrant leaves; they all belong to the mint family; all require full sun and well-drained soil to grow well.

These Mediterranean plants are some of the most popular herbs, but they are just one group among many. The term "herbs" encompasses a wide assortment of plants. Herbs come from several parts of the world and from several plant families. Many are perennial plants, but others are annuals, biennials, shrubs, or trees. Different herbs are adapted to a variety of growing conditions, ranging from sun to shade, on dry or wet sites, with lean or fertile soil.

The plants themselves are diverse, but herbs have one thing in common: people use them in some way. By one definition, "An herb is a useful plant." That definition, however, is subject to interpretation. An enthusiast might say that all plants are herbs, because they absorb carbon dioxide from the atmosphere and release vital oxygen. Most gardeners take a narrower view. Tomatoes, apples, and wheat are certainly useful plants, but they're usually thought of as food, not herbs. Trees harvested for lumber, firewood, and paper pulp are very useful, but who would call them herbs? Ornamental plants are useful in the sense that they improve the appearance of our home gardens and public landscapes, but it would be broad-minded to label them herbs. To bypass these plants that are used in a general way, we can focus the definition and say that an herb is a plant with some particular use(s), because it provides some particular kind(s) of chemical compounds or raw materials. For example, chili peppers are good for making hot, spicy food because they contain an especially pungent compound called capsaicin.

We turn to herbs for many reasons. Some herbs give flavor to food or beverages. Others act medicinally, as home remedies for common ailments or as sources of powerful drugs used in modern medicine. Many herbs produce delightful fragrances that can perfume our homes, our clothing, and our bodies. Others have pungent aromas or poisonous properties that can repel or kill insect pests. Some herbs provide colorful pigments used in textile dyes, food coloring, and cosmetics. Others produce gums, resins, and waxes used in art, medicine, and industry. Herbs have been used in these ways for thousands of years, and they are still valuable commodities. Home gardeners tend to think in terms of individual plants, but on a worldwide scale, herbs are grown or collected by the acre or the ton, and millions of dollars worth of dried herbs or herb extracts are sold each year.

Even in today's world, there's no substitute for herbs. A few of the chemical compounds produced by herbs have been studied by chemists and duplicated in the laboratory, so we now have a limited number of synthetic flavorings, fragrances, drugs, insecticides, dyes, and other products that copy natural compounds. In most cases, though, the various compounds produced by a single herb haven't even been isolated and identified, let alone reproduced. The task is too difficult and expensive, because most herbs produce a complex mix of dozens of different compounds. A chemist could spend years studying the presence of these different compounds, their relative concentrations, their individual properties and effects, the interactions between them, and how the plant's chemistry was affected by genetics and growing conditions. Most of the research that is being done is centered on medicinal herbs, particularly plants that show potential to control cancers. In modern medicine, understanding the specific chemistry of an herb can be vitally important. On the other hand, we can enjoy the tastes and aromas of culinary and fragrant herbs without knowing the details of their makeup, and the complexity that challenges a researcher simply delights a gardener, who appreciates that each herb is unique and irreplaceable.

The scientific approach to studying herbs by identifying their chemistry is relatively new. Traditionally, people have described herbs in more poetic ways, by referring to their powers or properties. There is a vast amount of occasionally enlightening, sometimes entertaining, and often contradictory folklore on herbs. Different authors have written about the same herbs since the days of the ancient Greeks, Romans, and Chinese, repeating old ideas, adding new observations, and praising or refuting each other. For many gardeners, this reservoir of lore and legends is an important reason for growing herbs—reciting the folklore is a lot of fun, and it gives you a feeling of connection to the generations of people who grew and used the same plants in other times and other places. More than any other group of plants, herbs are plants with stories.

As modern gardeners, we don't necessarily use the herbs we grow. We choose plants for their appearance, or because we are curious about them or have some reason to care for them. But whether or not you use a particular herb yourself, it's always fascinating to learn how it has been used or could be used. Most of the herbs in this book fit into the three main categories of culinary herbs, medicinal herbs, and fragrant herbs; others provide dyes, soaps, insecticides, resins, or other useful materials. But herbs defy categorization. Although some herbs have just a single use, many are complex plants with several different uses, as mentioned below.

Culinary Herbs

Culinary herbs are used to season all kinds of food—meat and poultry, fish, cheese, vegetables and salads, rice and pasta, breads, fruits, cakes and desserts, candies, and beverages. Dozens of different herbs are used in different cuisines to provide a variety of flavors, ranging from hot to cool, sweet to sour, biting to soothing, or pungent to mellow. Various parts of the plants are used—the leaves, stems and bark, flowers, seeds and fruits, roots and rhizomes. Traditionally, American gardeners have been most familiar with the flavors of culinary herbs from Europe and the Mediterranean region, such as bay, rosemary, thyme, sage, oregano, garlic, dill, fennel, caraway, mustard, and horseradish. But in the last decade or so, herbs from other parts of the world have become very popular, too, and many cooks have expanded their gardens to include "ethnic" herbs such as lemon grass, perilla, and cilantro.

Sometimes it's difficult to answer the question, "What is an herb?" For example, it's hard to distinguish between herbs and spices. If you try to separate them on the basis of whether the plants are herbaceous or woody, or whether it's the leaves or some other plant part that is used, you soon think of exceptions. Both basil and rosemary are generally considered herbs, but basil is herbaceous and rosemary is woody; coriander seeds are often considered a spice, but dill seeds are usually counted as an herb. The distinctions seem so illogical that some people group herbs and spices together, just as they are on the grocery store shelf. One way to sort them out, though, is to think in terms of history and geography. Centuries ago, when European explorers set off around the globe, they weren't looking for herbs. They could grow herbs at home. They were looking for spices—exotic products from tropical plants such as vanilla, cinnamon, allspice, and ginger—and they had to go to Asia, Africa, and the New World to find them. If we think in these terms, culinary herbs are hardy plants (herbaceous or woody) native to Europe and the Mediterranean region, and spices come from tender plants (herbaceous or woody) native to warmer climates. That's a difference that makes sense to gardeners. This book doesn't distinguish between herbs and spices, but the color plates are grouped according to whether the plants are hardy (at least to USDA zone 6) or tender (surviving outdoors in USDA zone 7 and warmer regions).

Another gray area is the distinction between herbs and vegetables. The premise in this book is that herbs are consumed in small quantities, mostly for their flavor, whereas vegetables are eaten in larger amounts, for flavor and nutritive value. Old-fashioned books about herbs mention a category called pot herbs—herbs to put in the cooking pot. These typically were weedy plants, such as dandelion, mustard, nettles, or purslane; their tender new leaves, picked in early spring, made a vitamin-rich spring tonic that would have been a welcome contrast to a winter's diet of stored root crops and dried food. Now that refrigeration and long-distance trucking make it possible to buy fresh produce year-round, people don't crave pot herbs as much, and if they gather these greens at all, they're more likely to call them vegetables than herbs and to eat them raw in salads rather than boiling them.

Herbs for beverages

Many plants are used to flavor beverages such as teas, soft drinks, wines and beers, and liqueurs. Some of these beverages are globally popular and are produced in huge quantities by commercial growers and brewers. Others are local favorites, drunk only in certain regions or countries. Many herbal beverages can easily be prepared on a small scale, one batch at a time, at home.

The fragrant fruit clusters of hops add a thirst-quenching bitterness to beer. Other herbs have also been used to flavor beer, and soapwort commonly was used to increase the foaminess of the brew. Juniper berries give the characteristic fragrance to gin. Some beverage flavorings that were popular in the past are not allowed or recommended now. Wormwood, formerly used in absinthe, can cause narcosis and nerve damage. Sweet grass, used to flavor vodka in Russia, and sweet woodruff, added to white wine in Europe, both contain coumarin, which has a wonderful vanilla fragrance but may be carcinogenic.

The various soft drinks known as colas contain caffeine from the seeds of an African tree, *Cola acuminata*. Ginger ale is flavored with the rhizomes of ginger. Root beer is named for the spicy roots such as sarsaparilla and sassafras that were traditionally used to flavor it.

Tea (from the leaves of *Camellia sinensis*), coffee (from roasted seeds of *Coffea arabica*), and maté (from the leaves of *Ilex paraguariensis*) are valuable because they contain the stimulant caffeine. By contrast, teas made from betony, chamomile, cowslip, mint, passionflower, valerian, and several other herbs are valued because they have a soothing or calming, rather than stimulating, effect. Many of the herbs used to flavor beverages have medicinal properties. These may be of minor consequence or have some advantage when the beverage is consumed in small doses, but large doses of the same herb could have unpleasant or dangerous effects.

Medicinal Herbs

Much of the history of herbs involves their use in medicine. For thousands of years, people around the world have relied on herbs to relieve pain, heal wounds, increase stamina, stimulate digestion, expel parasites, resist infection, stop bleeding, reduce fever, promote or avoid conception, simplify childbirth, and cope with all the other normal and accidental conditions of human life. Herbs can do the job: they provide a vast spectrum of medicinal compounds with many charted and many more uncharted effects on the human organism.

It's hard to overstate the importance of medicinal herbs. Even today, a surprising number of prescription and over-the-counter drugs contain ingredients derived from plants, and government agencies and pharmaceutical companies alike are engaged in major programs to screen plants from the tropical rain forests for potential new drugs. It's just as important, however, to acknowledge the difficulties of using medicinal herbs. The success (and safety) of a treatment usually depends on dosage, but the concentration of active ingredients in an herb can vary from plant to plant, from place to place, and from time to time. Traditional herbal healers have to learn just what to pick and where and when to pick it, as well as how to prepare and administer it, in addition to assessing a patient's symptoms and choosing a suitable remedy. It takes years of training and apprenticeship, and a certain aptitude for understanding both plants and people, to become an herbal healer.

The safe, proper, and effective use of most medicinal herbs requires expert knowledge—it's not something to treat casually, as you would experiment with different herbs in cooking. Only a few herbs are mild enough to recommend as home remedies for minor ailments, such as using aloe vera gel to soothe a sunburn or drinking peppermint tea to settle an upset stomach. However, herb gardeners often grow medicinal plants in their garden, out of respect for their traditional importance, curiosity about their growth and appearance, or appreciation for their beauty. This book includes several examples of interesting and attractive medicinal herbs, such as foxglove, the source of the heart medicine digitalis; meadowsweet and willow, important precursors to aspirin; echinacea, Joe-Pye weed, and black cohosh, wildflowers that were all used in Native American traditions; and blackberry lily and balloon flower, popular perennials that are grown as ornamentals in America but are important medicinal herbs in their native land, China. Two categories of medicinal herbs that are not featured in this book are dangerously poisonous herbs and psychoactive or hallucinogenic plants.

Gardeners are often surprised to learn that familiar ornamentals such as butterfly weed and passionflower have medicinal properties. Cooks are just as surprised to learn that many culinary herbs such as garlic, sage, and mustard have therapeutic uses. Sometimes the question "What is an herb?" has to be restated as "Is this herb a food or a drug?" Deciding whether an herb is a food or a drug may seem like an arbitrary distinction, but it's a major issue to the U.S. Food and Drug Administration (FDA), the agency that regulates how herb products are labeled and sold. Products sold as foods must meet minimum standards of safety and purity, but products sold as drugs must also have demonstrated their efficacy—they must pass clinical trials to confirm that they fulfill whatever claims are made for their benefits, to establish recommended dosage, to identify any risks or side effects, and so on. Product testing is expensive, and new laws that impose stricter standards for labeling will probably curtail the supply of herb extracts and other commercial herb preparations in this country. Home gardeners will, however, still be free to grow and use herbs as they choose, and to call them what they like.

Fragrant Herbs

Today we take it for granted that products such as laundry detergent, bathroom tissue, hand lotion, and floor polish will have some kind of fragrance. From morning 'til bedtime, each product we use adds yet another layer to the cocoon of perfumes that surrounds our bodies and our homes. This is a notably modern phenomenon. Throughout history, humans have not been enveloped in a cloud of pleasant aromas. More often, the atmosphere was a rank stew of foul odors arising from infrequent washing and poor sanitation. Only fragrant herbs could provide relief from the miserable stench of everyday life, or create an exotic setting for special occasions.

Many plants are fragrant, but not all count as herbs. For example, plants with sweet-scented flowers such as apple blossoms or jonquils are not herbs, because there's no practical way to capture and use their fragrance. When the flowers fade, the fragrance is lost. What distinguishes fragrant herbs is that their fragrance can be preserved, either by drying the plant (or the part of it that is fragrant) or by extracting or distilling the fragrance into a concentrated fluid form. Dried or extracted, the perfumes from fragrant herbs can last for months, years, or decades. Different plant parts are used—the flowers of lavender and sweet violets, the leaves of balsam fir and eucalyptus, the seeds or fruits of sweet cicely and bayberry, the roots or rhizomes of orrisroot and sweet flag. Surprisingly, the fragrance isn't always noticeable in the growing plant—patchouli leaves, sweet woodruff leaves, and orrisroot rhizomes don't begin to smell good until after they have dried.

Fragrant herbs are used many ways, singly or in blends. Dried herbs are used to make sachets and potpourris for scenting the clothes and bedding stored in drawers, chests, and closets or to perfume whole rooms. Fragrant oils and extracts are used directly as perfume or added to soaps, cosmetics, lotions, candles, and other products. Fragrant woods such as eastern red cedar and leaves such as sweet grass are used to make special boxes, baskets, and treasure chests. Fragrant waxes and resins are used to make polishes and burned as incense.

Many herbs are used both for fragrance and in cooking;

for example, rosemary is used to season meats and also to perfume shampoos. Other fragrant herbs are used medicinally, in a practice called aromatherapy. Inhaling small doses of particular aromas has been shown to produce various effects, such as stimulating mental activity, renewing physical energy, calming nervous irritation, or inducing restful sleep. Aromatherapy is an ancient tradition that lately has become quite popular again.

Other Useful Plants

The uses of herbs go on and on. All parts of soapwort, the roots of yuccas, and the seed oil of jojoba make natural soaps, shampoos, and cleansers. Balsam fir, balsam poplar, sweet gum, and various pine trees yield saps, resins, and gums used in paints, varnishes, adhesives, finishes, and confections. Madder and lady's bedstraw roots, indigo and weld leaves, and dyer's coreopsis and safflower blossoms yield bright-colored dyes for yarns and fabrics. Pyrethrum flowers and Indian tobacco leaves produce compounds that actually kill insects. Pennyroyal, tansy, southernwood, and several other strong-scented herbs can help repel or deter flying insect pests.

Some people limit the term "herbs" to plants that produce useful compounds, but others think that plants that produce useful materials are herbs, too. Fiber sources such as flax and cotton, and other useful plants such as fuller's teasel, basket willow, broom corn, and gourds have found a place in many herb gardens. Wherever you draw the line, you'll find plenty of plants to grow and enjoy once you enter the wonderful world of herbs.

Getting Started with Herbs

Growing your own herbs is a fascinating and satisfying process. The plants are attractive in your garden, useful in your home, and interesting to know. Getting started is as simple as buying a few common herb plants, caring for them, and learning how to use them. Later, you may want to visit specialty nurseries or order by mail to obtain a wider selection of plants. As your interest develops, you'll need to become familiar with Latin names, so you can identify herbs with confidence and precision. You may decide to specialize in a particular group of plants, such as lavenders, or a certain category of use, such as dye plants or herbs used in Mexican food. In any case, you'll find dozens of plants to grow, plenty of information to read, activities and events to attend, and organizations to join.

Planting Your First Herb Garden

Although you don't need an herb garden to grow herbs—you can include them in any vegetable garden, flower bed, or border—it's fun to choose a site and make a special herb garden. The site can be quite small; an area only 3 by 5 feet can hold a dozen or so herb plants, enough to give you plenty of flavor and enjoyment.

Select a site that gets full sun for at least 6 hours a day during the growing season, but locate the garden as close to your house as possible. The more you see it, the more you'll enjoy it, and you're much more likely to use the herbs if it's convenient to step outside and gather them near the doorstep than if you have to walk across the property to get to them. It's handy if the garden is next to a path or walkway. You might transform one of those narrow spaces where it's hard to keep a lawn—the strip between the sidewalk and the street, between the driveway and the property line, or around the edge of a sunny patio.

Use stakes to mark the outline of the herb garden, and dig or till the area, removing any sod, stones, roots, and debris. Loosen the soil to a depth of 6 to 8 inches. Unless the soil has already been improved for previous use as a vegetable or flower garden, it's usually a good idea to improve it now by adding some organic matter, gritty sand, ground limestone, aged manure, and/or other amendments (see pp. 22–24). Install an edging of some kind—boards, timbers, bricks, or stones look good—to define the garden and separate it from adjacent lawn or other plantings. After filling the garden with herbs, choose one kind of mulch—cocoa or rice hulls, small pine bark chips, and coarse sand are all desirable and easy to get—and use it to cover the soil between all the plants, to discourage weeds, reduce watering, and make the garden look neat.

Labels are important in an herb garden. Don't take a chance on getting confused about which herb is which—the consequences could be distasteful or even dangerous. The plants you buy almost always come with a little plastic label; keep track of it. When you set herbs into the garden, you can either use the labels that came with the plants or replace them with larger, more permanent markers made of thick plastic, wood, or metal. For something really special, check herb shops and magazines for handmade ceramic markers that are lettered with the names of the most popular herbs.

Recommended herbs for beginners

Although you can raise many kinds of herbs from seeds, it's easier to start by buying plants. Herb plants are fairly inexpensive (usually about $2 to $3 apiece), and there's little point in buying a whole packet of seeds if you want only one or two plants of each herb.

Most garden centers sell a few kinds of culinary herbs in spring or early summer, along with the vegetables and bedding plants. Common or sweet basil has very fragrant leaves that taste good in combination with tomatoes. Dill has very fine, threadlike leaves and tall stalks topped with yellow flowers; its leaves, flowers, and seeds all make tasty season-ing for cabbage and cucumbers. Parsley forms a mound of dark green leaves that are rich in vitamins and full of flavor. Grow these three herbs as annuals, like tomatoes.

Some of the best and easiest culinary herbs are perennials that come back year after year. One clump of chives will give you a steady supply of mildly onion-flavored leaves from early spring to late fall, with a pretty show of rosy lilac flowers in May or June as a bonus. Lemon balm has crisp heart-shaped leaves that release a wonderful lemony fragrance when you touch them. They add a refreshing flavor to a fruit salad or a glass of iced tea. Peppermint, spearmint, and other forms of mint make excellent hot or iced tea, alone or in combination with regular black tea. Mints don't need wet soil—they grow fine in ordinary soil if watered regularly, but their runners do spread fast, so it's a good idea to bury a bottomless container and plant the mint inside that, to confine it.

Oregano, sage, and thyme are also perennials. Rub a leaf and sniff it before you buy an oregano plant. Be sure it has a strong, penetrating, pizzalike aroma. (Some kinds of oregano are pretty but flavorless.) Sage has pebbly-textured gray leaves that are good for seasoning turkey and pork, and lots of blue-purple flowers in June. Common thyme is a bushy little plant with tiny evergreen leaves on wiry stems and masses of pale lavender flowers in midsummer. Its leaves are tasty in soups, casseroles, and salad dressings.

Any garden center or nursery that sells perennials will have some herbs, too, because many popular perennials have herbal uses. You may already have some of these plants in your garden. Yarrow, purple coneflower, bee balm, and but-terfly weed and many other perennial wildflowers were all used as medicinal plants by Native Americans. Sweet wood-ruff is a traditional flavoring for white wine, and it makes fragrant sachets, too. The flowers of clove pinks, sweet violets, and lavender are all used in making perfumes. Certain old-fashioned shrub roses are also used in perfumery, and their dried petals are fragrant and colorful in potpourri.

Finding a Wider Variety of Herb Plants

As you watch your first herbs grow and discover how tasty, fragrant, and interesting they are, you'll soon want to add more plants to your collection. It's a good idea to look for a local nursery that specializes in herbs. There are hundreds of herb specialists around the country, in both rural and urban areas. Commonly these nurseries are quite small, so they can't afford big signs or splashy advertisements, but you can find them by word of mouth or by watching for small advertisements or announcements in the local newspaper. An advantage to buying from a local nursery is that the owner has probably chosen plants that are well suited for your climate and can give you specific advice on how to care for each one—whether it needs special soil amendments, frequent watering, shade from the summer sun, a protective mulch in winter, and so on. Also, when you choose a plant in person, you can select the one you want—smaller or larger size, straight or branched stems, symmetrical or with "character."

Another place to find herbs locally is at plant sales sponsored by botanic gardens, historic sites, or nature centers. These institutions often host plant sales in spring and/or fall as fund-raising events. The prices are reasonable, sometimes a bargain, and you can support a good cause at the same time as you stock up on herbs. Some of the plants may be just ordinary garden varieties, but many institutions go out of their way to offer something unusual, such as heirloom varieties, new introductions, or native plants. You may not find anyone to answer questions about the plants, especially if the staff is overwhelmed with customers, but if you find something interesting to buy, you can always try to learn about it later.

Ordering by mail from specialty nurseries gives you the widest selection of herb plants. Nationwide, there are several nurseries that list hundreds of different herbs in their catalogs. See p. 436 in the appendices for a list of company names and addresses, and check the classified advertisements in gardening magazines for more listings. Mail-order nurseries are excellent sources for hardy herbs to plant in your garden, and they are the main suppliers of unusual tender or tropical herbs, such as camphor tree, henna, vetiver, and a wonderful assortment of scented geraniums. Herbs for mail order are usually grown and sold in small plastic pots, and they tolerate the packing and shipping process surprisingly well. The majority of nurseries avoid shipping during extremely hot or cold weather, but they fill orders over a long season in spring and again in fall.

Most local herb nurseries sell annual, biennial, and hardy perennial herbs. Mail-order herb nurseries emphasize hardy perennials, tender perennials, and tender trees and shrubs. If you want an annual or biennial herb that you can't find at a local or mail-order nursery, you can probably grow it from seed. Many herb nurseries sell seeds as well as plants. See the list on p. 437 for other mail-order seed suppliers. The hardy trees and shrubs that are included in this book generally are not sold by herb nurseries. These plants usually are available at all-purpose nurseries and garden centers in regions where they grow well.

Calling Herbs by Name

For most people, the easiest way to talk about herbs is to use their common names. Nearly all herbs have a common name, and ordinarily common names are short and easy to pronounce. Even beginners are comfortable with names such as dill, lemon grass, wintergreen, and peppermint. Common names work pretty well for identifying most of the herbs in this book, but there can be problems. Sometimes the same plant has more than one common name, and sometimes the same name is used for two or more different plants. Obviously, this can cause confusion.

To be more precise, herb enthusiasts learn to identify plants by using their scientific or Latin names. Using Latin names is a reliable way to distinguish between herbs that might otherwise be confused because they look similar, smell alike, or have something else in common. It's the only way to be sure you're getting exactly what you want when you shop for a plant that you've read about in a book or magazine.

The Latin name for any plant consists of two or more words. The first word is the name of the genus, and this is a good starting place for understanding how the system of Latin names works. A genus (plural: genera) is a group of plants that have several attributes in common, and it's often a familiar grouping. For example, all roses belong to the genus *Rosa,* all lavenders belong to *Lavandula,* and all thymes belong to *Thymus.* In print, the name of a genus is always capitalized (and Latin names are always written in italics or underlined, to set them apart). In print and in conversation, gardeners often use the name of a genus as a common name. Thus you might hear someone talk about growing some interesting new salvias (plants in the genus *Salvia*) or agastaches (genus *Agastache*).

Most genera include several different kinds of plants, often with different common names such as lemon thyme, woolly thyme, creeping thyme, or French thyme. In general, these different forms are described as different species. The name for a species includes the name of the genus, followed by a second word called the specific epithet, which distinguishes that species from others in the genus. For example, *Viola odorata* is the sweet violet ("odorata" means sweet-scented). Each genus in the plant kingdom has a unique name, but some specific epithets have been used repeatedly for plants in different genera. Along with *Viola odorata,* you might grow *Galium odoratum,* sweet woodruff, or *Myrrhis odorata,* sweet cicely. In every case, it takes two words to give the full name for the plant.

Special cases

Biologists define a species as a group of individuals that share many characteristics and interbreed naturally, producing fertile offspring that resemble their parents. This definition works well for most animals and many wild plants but not as well for garden plants, including many popular herbs. There are two kinds of exceptions.

First, sometimes an individual plant shows an unusual characteristic, something not typical of the species. It may have variegated leaves, or white instead of pink flowers, or better than average flavor. Gardeners are keen to spot these special plants and propagate them by cutting, division, grafting, or even seed, if the seedlings show the desired trait (more often, seedlings turn out like the ordinary form of the species). Identifying a special plant adds a word to its name. A variant that occurs in nature is called a subspecies or a variety, abbreviated "subsp." or "var.," as in *Origanum vulgare* subsp. *hirtum* (Greek oregano, a form with especially good flavor) or *Salvia azurea* var. *grandiflora* (a sage with beautiful blue flowers). An unusual form that occurs only in cultivation is called a cultivar, abbreviated "cv." or enclosed in single quotes, as in *Artemisia absinthium* 'Lambrook Silver', a selection of wormwood with particularly silvery leaves.

The second exception to the species concept is that plants from different species often interbreed or hybridize, producing new plants that don't belong to either of the parent species. Hybrids can show traits from either or both parents, and they are frequently vigorous and desirable plants. They are sometimes infertile but often can be propagated by cutting or division. Hybrids are sometimes indicated by a multiplication sign in the name. For example, lavandin, *Lavandula* × *intermedia,* is a hybrid between *L. angustifolia* and *L. latifolia* (the generic name can be abbreviated to its first letter if it has already been written in full). Sometimes a hybrid just has a generic name and a cultivar name, such as *Pelargonium* 'Mabel Gray', a kind of scented geranium.

Name changes

The system for assigning plant names has been developed over time by botanists around the world, and like the rules of a game, there are rules for how the system works. From time to time, eminent botanists gather to reconsider, revise, and amend the rules, which are called the International Code of Botanical Nomenclature and the International Code of Nomenclature for Cultivated Plants. Although the rules are very logical and orderly, nature is not. Plants don't fall into neat categories, and sorting them into species and genera takes information and judgment. Most of the herbs in this book were first assigned Latin names in the 1700s or 1800s. Since then, botanists have decided to change some of the names. Some of the changes reflect new information and ideas and follow detailed study of a group of plants that sheds new light on their differences and similarities. Other changes are more procedural, made to correct errors that were published in the past—as, for example, when two botanists, unbeknownst to each other, have given the same name to two different plants. Gardeners groan when plant names are changed. It's hard enough to learn one name for a plant, let alone to forget it and learn a different one. But name changes are inevitable. Try to accept them as a sign of progress and increased understanding.

The meaning of names

Latin names are easier to remember and make more sense if you learn what they mean or where they come from. The name for a genus often derives from a Latin or Greek word or from a person's name. *Anethum* (dill) is the Greek name for dill, *Saponaria* (soapwort) comes from the Latin word for soap, and *Nicotiana* (tobacco) is named for Jean Nicot, who introduced tobacco to France. Specific epithets usually describe some attribute of a plant, such as *graveolens,* heavy-scented; *tinctorius,* used for dyeing; *aureus,* golden; or *officinalis,* sold in pharmacy shops (that is, medicinal). The *Dictionary of Plant Names for Gardeners,* by William T. Stearn (New York: Sterling, 1992), and *Gardener's Latin,* by Bill Neal (Chapel Hill, N.C.: Algonquin Books, 1992), are dictionary-type references that define thousands of plant names. The *Pronouncing Dictionary of Plant Names* (Chicago: Florists' Publishing Company, 1990) is a handy booklet that defines about 2,000 names and—unlike the other references—indicates how to pronounce them, too.

Plant families

A plant family is a larger grouping that includes as few as one or as many as hundreds of genera. Plant families also have both common and Latin names. Many herbs—mints, thymes, calamint, catnip, catmint, lavenders, rosemary, salvias, savories, mountain mints, and more—belong to the mint family, or Labiatae. Plants in the mint family typically have square stems, simple opposite leaves, hairs or glands filled with aromatic oils, and two-lipped flowers with nectar that attracts bees, butterflies, hummingbirds, or other pollinators. Other families that include many herbs are the Umbelliferae or carrot family (dill, parsley, lovage, coriander, anise, fennel, caraway, asafoetida, and sweet cicely); and the

Compositae or daisy family (pearly everlasting, southern-wood, wormwood, French tarragon, costmary, pyrethrum, feverfew, elecampane, Mexican mint marigold, sweet golden-rod, and tansy). Plants in the carrot family all have small 5-petaled flowers arranged in clusters called umbels, with stalks that radiate from a central point like the spokes of an umbrella. Plants in the daisy family have tiny flowers grouped in dense clusters (each "petal" of a daisy is actually a separate flower). Knowing which family an herb belongs to helps you associate it with other herbs that may require similar growing conditions or have similar properties.

Learning More About Herbs

There are many ways to pursue an interest in herbs. On pp. 430–435 at the back of this book is a bibliography of recommended books on various aspects of growing and using herbs, as well as a list of magazines or periodicals that feature articles about herbs. One thing leads to another. If you buy a magazine about herbs, you'll find advertisements for several herb nurseries and shops that sell herbal products. The catalogs of those nurseries and shops often list other magazines, books, and publications.

Magazine listings and announcements are also the best place to find out about major conferences, seminars, or workshops that are sponsored by national or regional herb societies and associations. These frequently are two- or three-day events, usually scheduled on weekends, and held in different parts of the country from one year to the next. There are also hundreds of herb festivals, celebrations, special events, and short classes each year, sponsored by herb nurseries and businesses and local herb societies. To find out about these events and organizations, watch local bulletin boards and newspapers, and get on the mailing list of any herb businesses in your area.

Finally, to see what plants look like and how big they grow, and to get new ideas for how to arrange them in your garden, there's nothing better than visiting other herb gardens. Most herb nurseries have a demonstration garden featuring the plants they grow. Many public gardens, parks, and botanic gardens have special areas devoted to herbs. Historic sites and nature centers sometimes have herb gardens also. Take a notebook to write down the names of plants that catch your attention, and take your camera, too, to record ideas that you can try at home.

Growing Herbs in the Garden

Growing herbs is like growing any other kind of plants: there are two main roads to success. One approach is to study your growing conditions—your climate's temperature and precipitation patterns, the soil and exposure at the garden site—and try to choose plants that are adapted to those conditions. The other approach is to select plants you particularly want to grow, learn what they require, and do your best to provide those conditions. Most gardeners do some of each, choosing well-adapted plants for low maintenance and long-term satisfaction over most of their landscape but taking the extra trouble to pamper some special favorite plants.

This chapter will discuss these two approaches to gardening and will outline basic techniques for growing healthy plants. Of course, the plants we call herbs are so diverse that it's difficult to generalize about their requirements, so the entries in the encyclopedia section supplement this chapter by giving specific information for each plant. Learn all you can by reading, but don't hesitate to experiment and to make your own observations about how different herbs grow in your garden. There's no substitute for trial and error. With experience, any gardener learns three important lessons: (1) Plants often surprise you by growing where they aren't "supposed" to; (2) if a plant doesn't grow well where you first set it, you can usually dig it up and move it someplace else; and (3) if a plant dies, you can always get another one to replace it.

Temperature

The growth and survival of any plant are influenced by several factors—some you can control, and some you can't. The most important of these factors are the temperature, the intensity and duration of sunlight, and the moisture and fertility of the soil. Of these factors, temperature plays the major role in determining which herbs you can and cannot grow. Cold in the winter, heat in the summer, and abrupt temperature changes at any time of the year are all stressful to plants. A gardener can provide some shelter or protection from the worst extremes, but even so, there's a limit to what any plant can tolerate. Too much cold or heat can stunt a plant or even kill it.

A plant's ability to endure cold weather is indicated by its hardiness zone rating. The U.S. Department of Agriculture (USDA) has divided the country into 11 hardiness zones that correspond to the average low temperatures in winter (see map on pp. viii–ix). For example, USDA zone 5 has average winter lows of –10° to –20° F. An herb that is rated as hardy to zone 5 should normally survive the winters in that zone, and also in warmer zones, but is liable to freeze and die in colder zones. It's a good idea to find your home on the map to determine what hardiness zone you live in and to use that as a guideline when choosing trees, shrubs, or perennials that you want to keep from year to year.

In cold climates, there are several steps you can take to increase the winter survival of marginally hardy herbs. Shelter tender plants from cold, dry winter winds by siting them next to a wall, fence, or hedge. Transplant them in the spring or early summer so that they have several months to establish good root systems before freezing weather sets in. Be sure the soil drains well so that water doesn't collect around the roots in winter. Don't prune or fertilize after midsummer; new top growth that forms late in the season is especially liable to freeze. Apply a winter mulch of pine boughs, hedge trimmings, or other coarse material in late fall to keep the soil temperature constant and prevent repeated freeze/thaw cycles, and don't remove the mulch until spring is well under way.

Annual herbs usually aren't assigned USDA ratings, but they do differ in their sensitivity to cold. The individual entries indicate which annuals you can plant outdoors in early spring and which you should protect or not plant until danger of frost has passed. Hardy annuals such as dill and calendulas can tolerate several degrees of frost in spring (and again in fall). Tender annuals such as basil and chili peppers turn black and don't recover from frost; even night temperatures around 40° F are cold enough to stunt these tender plants. In the fall, listen for frost warnings on the weather forecast. Often the first frost is followed by a return to mild weather. If you cover tender herbs with a blanket, sheet, or cardboard box to protect them from the first frost, you can continue picking for several weeks before later frosts kill the plants.

Many perennial and shrubby herbs that are tender to cold, such as gotu kola, lemon verbena, pineapple sage, scented geraniums, and Mexican mint marigold, can be treated like annuals in the garden. Plant them outdoors in spring, enjoy them all summer, give a sigh when they freeze in fall, and replace them the next year. Or, if you have room to fit them indoors on a sunny windowsill, you can grow them as houseplants in winter.

There's no rating system for tolerance of summer heat, but herbs differ greatly in their ability to take moist or dry heat. Some herbs, such as ginger, chaste tree, and lemon grass, thrive in hot, humid conditions that would melt pearly everlasting or lamb's-ears into oblivion. Others, such as Cuban oregano, horehound, and crimson-spot rock rose, bask in hot, arid weather that would dry angelica or balsam fir to a crisp. The encyclopedia entries note herbs that are especially sensitive to hot weather, damp or dry.

Gardeners across the southern United States who want to experiment with heat-sensitive plants should try planting them in part shade, with protection from the midday and afternoon sun. Expect some perennials to slow down or go dormant in summer and to resume growth when the weather cools off. Where summers are hot, plant fast-growing annuals such as borage and cilantro in early spring or fall, not in summer.

Sun and Shade

All plants need light to grow, but some require more light than others in order to grow well. To keep it simple, gardeners generally talk about three lighting conditions—full sun, part sun (or part shade), and shade—and describe plants as adapted to or tolerant of these different light levels.

In gardening talk, "full sun" usually means direct, unblocked exposure to the sun for at least 6 hours a day during the growing season. Six hours is the minimum; many sun-loving plants do better with full sun from dawn to dusk. Of course, full sun means one thing in Dallas and something else in Minneapolis. But in any location, you can judge if plants are getting enough light by looking at how they grow. When herbs that need full sun are planted in too-shady sites, they tend to grow taller than normal, with weak straggly stems and large thin leaves that are spaced farther apart than usual. They may flower sparsely or not at all. Perennials may survive for a few years, but gradually they weaken and die. Plants on a winter windowsill often show these same symptoms, because insufficient light is a major problem with trying to grow herbs indoors.

"Part sun" or "part shade" generally refers to a site that gets full sun for a few hours a day and is shaded the rest of the time. For example, a garden bed on the east side of a building or hedge gets sun for several hours in the morning but is shaded in the afternoon. "Part shade" can also refer to the dappled pattern of light and shade cast by trees with open branching and not-too-dense foliage. Either way, the condition of part sun/part shade is fine for many herbs. Those that need more light will show the symptoms described above.

"Shade" means little or no direct exposure to the sun, because the garden site is shaded by trees, buildings, or other barriers. Usually we talk about plants that tolerate shade, since only a minority of plants actually require or prefer full shade. Those that do need shady conditions are damaged by too much sun. Their growth can be stunted, and their leaves may be small and distorted. The leaves may also turn a pale yellow-green color, or they may get bleached-looking white blotches, called sunburn. (Patches of sunburn may appear on any plant that is suddenly exposed to more light; for example, when a houseplant is moved outdoors, or when seedlings that were started indoors are transplanted into the garden without a period of gradual acclimation.) Plants exposed to too much bright sun may struggle along, or they may suffer briefly and soon die. Prevent sudden damage by moving plants outdoors on cloudy days, then shading or screening them for a few days with an inverted box or basket, a teepee of leafy twigs, a lath trellis, or a thin sheet of fabric.

Some sites that are shaded by adjacent buildings are actually quite bright, because sunlight is reflected down from the open sky. Sites shaded by trees are more problematic, for three reasons: (1) The shade is darker, because the foliage overhangs the garden and blocks the sky; (2) the situation keeps getting worse from year to year (unless you keep pruning the trees), as the growing limbs project farther over the garden; and (3) underground, the tree roots are competing with anything else you plant and taking water and nutrients from the soil. If you have to plant under trees, remove several of their lower limbs to let more light come through to the ground, and be prepared to supply extra water during dry spells to meet the needs of both the trees and the plants below.

Some herbal plants grow well in part or full shade, but few of these are culinary herbs. Many are woodland wildflowers native to the eastern United States, used as medicinal herbs by Native Americans. Others are medicinal or fragrant plants from other parts of the world. Check the encyclopedia entries for more information about the herbs listed below.

Herbs That Can Take Part or Full Shade

Sweet flag (*Acorus calamus*)
Lady's-mantle (*Alchemilla mollis*)
Angelica (*Angelica archangelica*)
Wild ginger (*Asarum canadense*)
Tea (*Camellia sinensis*)
Blue cohosh (*Caulophyllum thalictrioides*)
Black cohosh (*Cimicifuga racemosa*)
Foxglove (*Digitalis purpurea*)
Sweet woodruff (*Galium odoratum*)
Wintergreen (*Gaultheria procumbens*)
Alumroot (*Heuchera americana*)
Goldenseal (*Hydrastis canadensis*)
Gotu kola (*Hydrocotyle asiatica*)
Blue lobelia (*Lobelia siphilitica*)
Corsican mint (*Mentha requienii*)
Bee balm, wild bergamot (*Monarda didyma, M. fistulosa*)
Bayberry, wax myrtle (*Myrica cerifera, M. pensylvanica*)
Sweet cicely (*Myrrhis odorata*)
Ginseng (*Panax quinquefolius*)
Solomon's-seal (*Polygonatum biflorum*)
Cowslip (*Primula veris*)
Heal-all (*Prunella vulgaris*)
Bloodroot (*Sanguinaria canadensis*)
False Solomon's-seal (*Smilacina racemosa*)
Hemlock (*Tsuga canadensis*)
Sweet violet (*Viola odorata*)
Yellowroot (*Xanthorhiza simplicissima*)

Soil Conditions

Gardeners sometimes recite old wives' tales without stopping to think about what they're saying. For example, it's often said that herbs thrive in poor soil or even that herbs *need* poor soil. What nonsense! That generalization is too simple to be true, and it has led many beginning herb gardeners down the path to disappointment.

There are two problems with saying that herbs thrive in poor soil. The first is that many kinds of plants are called herbs, and they each have different requirements and tolerances. For example, rosemary and lavender grow best in dry soil that drains quickly after a rain, but mints and sweet flag flourish in soil that stays wet all the time. Parsley and dill respond to loose, deeply tilled soil that has been amended with plenty of nutrient-rich manure or compost, but horehound and lady's bedstraw can glean all the nutrients they need from dense, mineral-based soil that has virtually no organic matter.

Just as "herb" has many meanings, so does the term "poor soil." Soil can be judged "poor" because it's too shallow, too compacted, too rocky, too acidic, too alkaline, too sandy, too clayey, too dry, too wet, and so forth. In each case, the "poor" soil would be acceptable for some particular kinds of herbs, but there's no basis for the idea that poor soils in general are good for growing herbs.

Any discussion of soil returns to the two approaches to gardening mentioned at the beginning of this chapter. You can evaluate the soil you have and choose plants that are suited to it, or you can change the soil to make it suitable for different kinds of plants. Whether you're filling a large area or just a problem spot (such as the wet area around a downspout), the easiest way to establish a healthy garden is to rely on plants that are well adapted to the existing soil conditions. On the other hand, if you want to grow herbs that aren't adapted to your conditions, it's often possible to modify the soil to accommodate them.

Loosen compacted soil

The most basic improvement is simply to loosen the soil by digging or tilling it to a depth of at least 8 inches (dig deeper if you have the time and energy). Soil gets compacted by foot traffic (even the repeated passes of someone pushing a lawn mower), by vehicle traffic or parking, by heavy snow or rain, or simply by the force of gravity and weather acting over time. Not many herbs can cope with compacted soil. Loosening it makes a big difference. When soil is loosened, water soaks in quickly instead of running off or standing on the surface. Roots penetrate deeper and explore a larger volume of soil, all the better for absorbing water and nutrients. Air flows through loose soil, bringing oxygen to plant roots. Whenever you're making or replanting a garden bed, start by loosening the soil. Then designate specific pathways or stepping points where you will walk, stand, or kneel, and try to keep your weight off the rest of the bed, to avoid recompacting the soil you just loosened.

Check the drainage

Many herbs are described as needing good drainage, or fast drainage, or sharp drainage, or well-drained soil—all different ways of saying the same thing: that water drains through the soil within hours of a rainfall or irrigation. When water drains out, air flows back into the soil, and when we say that an herb needs good drainage, what we really mean is that it needs air around its roots and the base of its stems. Not all herbs need good drainage, but for those that do, it's a matter of life or death. Herbs growing in well-drained soil have vigorous top growth and firm roots, the latter usually bright white, with no odor. Herbs damaged by poor drainage have weak shoots that tend to wilt or die back at the tips and mushy roots, which are usually dark brown or black, with a rotten smell. (Those symptoms occur on herbs grown in a flowerpot or container with no drainage holes, as well as on herbs in a soggy garden bed.)

To check the drainage of your soil, observe what happens after a rain. Does the water disappear quickly? Better yet, dig a hole several inches deep and fill it with water. How soon does the water soak away? If all the water soaks away within a few hours, that's fast drainage. If water is still standing in the bottom of the hole after a day, that's poor drainage. In between a few hours and a day is the range of average drainage.

Building raised beds is a good way to improve soil drainage. You can simply mound up the existing soil or bring in enough additional topsoil or soil amendments to raise the surface of the bed above the surrounding grade. Even a few inches makes a difference, and you can mound soil that high without needing an edge or frame to support it. For higher raised beds, you'll need to make a sturdy frame of boards, landscape timbers, blocks, or stones to keep the soil from slumping down around the edge.

You can make small raised beds for individual shrubs or trees, or you can try "planting high," a one-plant-at-a-time approach for providing better drainage. Planting high means setting plants with their crown—that region where roots and stems come together—a few inches higher than the surrounding soil. Dig a shallow hole, position the plant with as much as one-third of the root ball above grade, then heap a mound of soil up, around, and over the root ball. Add a layer of mulch to cover the soil and keep it from washing away and exposing the roots. Be sure to water regularly for the first season, until the plant's roots have penetrated down into the soil.

Sometimes you can improve a soil's drainage by incorporating gravel, coarse sand, volcanic pumice, horticultural vermiculite, composted bark, or other amendments, but you'll have to do some experimenting to decide how much material to add—there's no rule of thumb, because it all depends on your particular soil and climate. You might need as little as a 1-inch layer spread over the bed and worked into the soil, or as much as several inches. Try amending the soil in a small bed first, then watch to see what happens and how plants respond before investing the time and money into amending the soil over a larger area. The same amendments that can be worked into the soil to improve drainage can be used as surface mulches for herbs that need well-drained soil. As mulches, they help to protect roots from the sun and wind, to reduce soil compaction and soil erosion, to moderate soil temperatures, and to control weeds.

Herbs That Need Well-Drained Soil

Bearberry (*Arctostaphylos uva-ursi*)
Wormwood, southernwood, etc. (*Artemisia* spp.)
New Jersey tea (*Ceanothus americanus*)
Pyrethrum daisy (*Chrysanthemum pyrethrum*)
Cuban oregano (*Coleus amboinicus*)
Purple coneflower (*Echinacea purpurea*)
Ephedras (*Ephedra* spp.)
Curry plant (*Helichrysum angustifolium*)
St.-John's-wort (*Hypericum perforatum*)
Hyssop (*Hyssopus officinalis*)
Yaupon holly (*Ilex vomitoria*)
Orrisroot (*Iris germanica* var. *florentina*)
Common juniper (*Juniperus communis*)
Lavenders (*Lavandula* spp.)
Mexican oregano (*Lippia graveolens*)
Horehound (*Marrubium vulgare*)
Wild bergamot (*Monarda fistulosa*)
Myrtle (*Myrtus communis*)
Catnip (*Nepeta cataria*)
Opium poppy (*Papaver somniferum*)
Mexican oregano (*Poliomintha longiflora*)
Rosemary (*Rosmarinus officinalis*)
Rue (*Ruta graveolens*)
Cleveland sage (*Salvia clevelandii*)
Garden sage (*Salvia officinalis*)
Santolinas (*Santolina* spp.)
Soapwort (*Saponaria officinalis*)
Winter savory (*Satureja montana*)
Jojoba (*Simmondsia chinensis*)
Sweet goldenrod (*Solidago odora*)

Germander (*Teucrium chamaedrys*)
Thymes (*Thymus* spp.)
Chaste tree (*Vitex agnus-castus*)
Yuccas (*Yucca* spp.)

Add organic matter

Some herbs need soil that retains moisture and stays evenly
damp without drying out. That's not quite the same thing as
soil with poor drainage, although a few herbs do tolerate
poor drainage. The best way to increase water retention while
still providing adequate drainage is to incorporate some organic matter into the soil. Organic matter in the soil acts like
millions of tiny squeezed-out sponges that hold plenty of
water but aren't sopping wet. To add it to your garden, use
garden compost, composted tree leaves or lawn clippings, rot-
ted sawdust, aged cow manure, peat moss, or whatever else
is available in your area. Spread a layer 2 to 3 inches deep
over the surface of the garden, then mix the organic matter
thoroughly into the soil with a fork or tiller. Herbs that need
moist, organic soil usually benefit from a layer of organic
mulch, too. The mulch helps keep the soil cool and moist,
and as it gradually decomposes it enriches the soil below.
Cocoa hulls, peanut hulls, rice hulls, chipped bark, composted tree leaves, and chopped straw are all organic materials that make good mulch.

Herbs That Prefer Moist, Organic Soil
(* indicates herbs that tolerate poor drainage)

Balsam fir (*Abies balsamea*)
*Sweet flag (*Acorus calamus*)
Angelica (*Angelica archangelica*)
Sweet vernal grass (*Anthoxanthum odoratum*)
Wild ginger (*Asarum canadense*)
Tea (*Camellia sinensis*)
Blue cohosh (*Caulophyllum thalictrioides*)
Black cohosh (*Cimicifuga racemosa*)
*Joe-Pye weed (*Eupatorium purpureum*)
Queen-of-the-prairie (*Filipendula rubra*)
*Meadowsweet (*Filipendula ulmaria*)
Wintergreen (*Gaultheria procumbens*)
Alumroot (*Heuchera americana*)
Goldenseal (*Hydrastis canadensis*)
*Gotu kola (*Hydrocotyle asiatica*)
Lovage (*Levisticum officinale*)
*Spicebush (*Lindera benzoin*)
*Blue lobelia (*Lobelia siphilitica*)

*Sweet bay magnolia (*Magnolia virginiana*)
*Mints (*Mentha* spp.)
*Bee balm (*Monarda didyma*)
 Sweet cicely (*Myrrhis odorata*)
*Watercress (*Nasturtium officinale*)
 Ginseng (*Panax quinquefolius*)
 Solomon's-seal (*Polygonatum biflorum*)
*Vietnamese coriander (*Polygonum odoratum*)
 Cowslip (*Primula veris*)
 Heal-all (*Prunella vulgaris*)
*Willows (*Salix elaeagnos* and other spp.)
*Elderberry (*Sambucus canadensis*)
 Bloodroot (*Sanguinaria canadensis*)
*False Solomon's-seal (*Smilacina racemosa*)
 Arborvitae (*Thuja occidentalis*)
 Hemlock (*Tsuga canadensis*)
*European cranberry bush (*Viburnum opulus*)
 Sweet violet (*Viola odorata*)
*Yellowroot (*Xanthorhiza simplicissima*)

Improve soil fertility

Another version of the notion that herbs need poor soil is the advice that herbs don't need to be fertilized. Again, this is an oversimplification. Herbs differ and soils vary. Some herbs thrive in soil of low fertility, but others need high nutrient levels in order to produce normal foliage and flowers. Some gardeners are planting in rich native topsoil or garden plots that have been developed and amended over a period of years to bring the soil to maximum fertility, but other gardeners are starting with virtually sterile subsoil or soil that's been neglected for years.

If you'd like an objective analysis, you can have a sample of your soil tested through your state extension service or agricultural college or by a private testing lab. Often it's sufficient to judge the fertility of a plot of land by looking at the plants that are growing there. If other plants such as turfgrass, vegetables, flowers, or even weeds have been flourishing in a place where you want to make an herb garden, you can go ahead and plant the herbs without worrying about a soil test. Most likely the herbs will grow fine, too. (If a site is barren, think twice before planning an herb garden there. The soil might simply be infertile, but there could be other problems—the soil might be very shallow, underlain with rocks or debris, extremely compacted, subject to periodic flooding, or otherwise unsuitable for gardening.)

In many gardens, the native soil contains enough nutrients to keep herbs alive but not enough to stimulate maximum growth and yield. In this common situation, adding small doses of nutrients from time to time can greatly improve the appearance and vigor of herb plants, giving them taller stems, larger leaves, more flowers, bigger root systems, more resistance to heat and cold, and faster recovery from harvest or pruning. An often-heard argument against fertilizing herbs is that it produces large plants with little flavor or fragrance. That's not necessarily true—sometimes fertilizing produces large plants with all the more flavor and fragrance. If you're curious, try comparison plantings of the same herb. Fertilize one but not the other, see what difference it makes, and decide for yourself whether to fertilize or not. Try the same experiment with different kinds of fertilizers, and compare the results.

There are dozens of good fertilizer products available—farm manures and processed manure products; animal by-products such as blood meal and bone meal; agricultural commodities such as alfalfa meal and cottonseed meal; fish emulsion and seaweed extracts; worm castings; mineral dusts such as rock phosphate and greensand; and synthetic fertilizers in granulated, soluble, and timed-release forms. They supply different nutrients, in different ratios, but they all work. Follow package directions for measuring and applying commercial products. There's little risk of overfertilizing herbs if you use natural fertilizers, which are usually quite dilute, and apply them with restraint. Water well after applying any kind of fertilizer, and continue to water regularly throughout the season, since nutrients must be dissolved in water before a plant can absorb them.

Pests and Diseases

It's sometimes claimed that herbs don't suffer from pest and disease problems. Wouldn't it be nice if that were true! But it isn't. Many herbs are generally trouble-free, just as many other plants are, especially if they're well established in favorable growing conditions. But some herbs have a particular susceptibility to one problem or another, and a few are prone to multiple ailments. These characteristics are noted in the individual entries in the encyclopedia section of this book.

Common pest problems

Indoors, tender herbs grown as houseplants are often infested with aphids, whiteflies, and/or spider mites. All are tiny pests that suck the juices from tender leaves and stems. They move from plant to plant, and they can be found on a very wide variety of herbs indoors and also in the garden. They can fly into your garden from around the neighborhood, or they may arrive on plants that you buy at a nursery or bring home from a friend's garden. You don't need strong chemicals to control them, but you need strong discipline. You usually have to spray at least three times at weekly intervals to eliminate an infestation, because when you spray, you almost inevitably miss a few insects or their eggs, and at the rate insects multiply, these survivors soon rebuild the population. Also, you have to repeat the process whenever a new crop of pests finds your plants.

Insecticidal soap and lightweight horticultural oil, both available at garden centers, are safe and effective controls for aphids, whiteflies, and spider mites, or you can use a simple homemade spray developed and recommended by the USDA. Prepare a concentrate by mixing one tablespoon of liquid dishwashing detergent with one cup of salad or cooking oil. To use, mix one to two teaspoons of the concentrate with a cup of water and spray on the infested plant. Be sure to spray both the tops and bottoms of the leaves, wetting them thoroughly.

Mealybugs and scale insects also attack herbs indoors and sometimes outdoors, usually clinging to woody stems or hiding near the bases of leaves. These pests typically are centered on a specific plant, not scattered through a garden, but they can spread from plant to plant if you ignore them. Watch for them, and treat at the first sign of an infestation by dabbing the individual insects with a cotton swab dipped in rubbing alcohol. This dehydrates the pests, and they dry and shrivel. Check again in a week to see if any escaped the first treatment, re-treat if needed, and keep an eye on that plant in the future.

Herbs in the garden are subject to a variety of insect pests that rarely kill plants but can seriously weaken them, and insect damage makes a plant look ugly and unappetizing. Unfortunately, two of the worst outdoor pests are virtually impossible to defeat. In the eastern United States, Japanese beetles cause serious damage to rose flowers and foliage. They swarm to basil plants, and they also attack many other herbs. In the Midwest, and sometimes in other regions, grasshoppers can ravage a garden. They are especially destructive during dry spells, when plants are suffering anyway, and can fully defoliate a garden. There are various chemical and biological control measures for Japanese beetles and grasshoppers, but these pests are so abundant over such large areas that they inevitably return. One strategy is to stop growing the kinds of herbs that suffer most from these pests. Another approach is to grow extra plants and to keep them as healthy as possible by providing excellent soil and plenty of water so that they'll keep growing despite predation and you'll end up with something to harvest.

A few kinds of caterpillars—the larvae of butterflies and moths—attack herbs in the garden, but they are usually big enough, and few enough, that you can find them and pick them off one at a time. For more serious infestations, you can control most caterpillars with a spray or dusting of *Bacillus thuringiensis*, or Bt, a biological control sold under various trade names and available at any garden center. Apply according to label directions. If you're lucky enough to find a black, green, and yellow caterpillar on parsley, dill, caraway, fennel, or related plants, leave it alone. It won't eat much, and it grows up into the beautiful black swallowtail butterfly.

Common disease problems

Most plant diseases are aggravated by moisture. Root rots commonly happen when soil stays too wet because of poor drainage, overwatering, or too much organic matter. The best cure is prevention. Once a plant's roots have been damaged, it rarely recovers full vigor and health, even if you dig it up and replant it in a more suitable site or repot it into a different pot with looser soil.

Verticillium, fusarium, rhizoctonia, and Texas root rot are fungal organisms that linger in the soil for decades, sometimes as dormant spores, sometimes as low-grade infections that mildly inhibit the growth of tough or adapted plants. Under certain conditions, these diseases flare up and infect susceptible plants, causing root damage, wilted foliage, reduced yield, and sometimes death. You probably won't recognize what is happening if one of these diseases afflicts one of your plants. It may seem like a mysterious plague. Cut off a branch and take it to a county extension agent, a Master Gardener's clinic, or a local nursery, and ask for help. If any of these soil problems are common in your area, an experienced horticulturist should recognize the symptoms. There isn't a ready cure or solution for any of these diseases, but if the problem is there, it's good to know about it, and local authorities can tell you which plants are most susceptible or most resistant to the problem.

Various bacteria and fungi that attack leaves and stems are fairly common and widespread, but they don't necessarily cause much damage. Much of the time, their presence is invisible. However, blights, molds, mildews, rots, rusts, scabs, and leaf spots can show up suddenly and acutely when temperature and moisture conditions are just right. Herbs with leaves that are densely covered with hairs, such as yarrow, lamb's-ears, woolly thyme, several artemisias, and pearly everlasting, are especially subject to foliar fungal infections during hot, humid weather. In a matter of days, these plants can "melt" into a smelly mound of mushy dark debris.

Again, the best plan is to take preventive steps. Where summers are rainy or humid, space plants far enough apart to allow air to circulate between them and dry the foliage. Prune out a few inner shoots or limbs to open up a dense shrub or perennial. Avoid organic mulch, which stays damp and hosts fungal spores, and use coarse sand or gravel instead. There are fungicide sprays you can use, but most work better for prevention than cure, and to use them effectively, you have to know what particular disease you're trying to prevent and when it is likely to strike. It takes years of careful observation to know that much about how plants grow in your garden.

In the meantime, when disease strikes, remove all the infected leaves and discard them. (Don't add them to the compost pile unless you make hot compost, where the temperature in the pile reaches about 160° F. Disease organisms aren't killed in compost made at cooler temperatures, and spreading the compost would spread the disease.) Depending on how severely the plant is afflicted and how many leaves are lost, an herb may recover from a fungus, blight, or mildew attack, or it may not. Some herbs just aren't meant to grow in some climates. But remember, if one herb keeps dying out, you can always try something else.

Growing Herbs in Containers

Growing herbs in containers is a popular alternative to planting them in the ground because it offers several advantages. Most suppliers grow herbs in pots because it's so much easier to produce, pack, ship, and sell plants grown in pots than plants grown in nursery beds. Customers like potted plants because, unlike plants dug from a nursery bed, they're easy to carry home in the car and you don't have to hurry to get them back in the ground.

Growing herbs in pots allows you to try plants that aren't adapted to your regular garden soil or growing conditions. You can fill a pot with a custom soil mix and water and fertilize exactly as required. Keeping tender plants in pots means you can carry them indoors for the winter and keep them from year to year.

Potted plants add color and fragrance to patios, balconies, entryways, and other outdoor living areas, and it's easy to move them around, rearranging the display to highlight the specimens that look best at any particular season. Featuring special herbs in pots, especially specimens that have been carefully trained or shaped over a period of time, calls attention to their value and transforms them from mere plants into objects of sculpture. Big old potted myrtles, bay laurels, citrus trees, lemon verbenas, or rosemaries are cherished elements in many herb gardens, stored each winter in a cool greenhouse, sunporch, or sunny room and brought outdoors every summer to a place of honor.

Basic Principles of Container Growing

Gardeners often develop a very personal approach to growing plants in containers, and they express their style through the plants and containers they choose, their ideas for combining and arranging different herbs, and their standards— ranging from casual to formal—for grooming, shaping, staking, and training individual plants. There are many options for expressing your creativity and personal style when you grow potted plants, as long as you pay heed to some basic principles of horticulture.

Light

Plants growing in containers have the same light requirements as plants growing in the garden. Herbs that need full sun in the ground still need full sun when planted in a container. This point sounds obvious, but it's often overlooked. Inadequate light is the major limitation to growing many herbs in containers. Patios or balconies adjacent to a building may be shaded for several hours a day by the building itself or by overhanging roofs or nearby trees. In that case, there may not be enough light for herbs that need full sun.

Indoors, light levels are rarely sufficient for lavender, thyme, dill, parsley, and many other popular herbs. Even a south-facing window doesn't get full sun, compared with full sun outdoors in a garden, and during the winter months when days are short, the amount of daylight on a windowsill is brief and weak. Only a few herbs can grow year-round on a windowsill without getting weak and leggy. If you want to grow herbs indoors, consider using fluorescent lights as a supplemental light source. Use adjustable shelving or supports so you can position the light bulbs just a few inches above the herbs' leaves and keep moving them as the plants grow, and install an automatic timer to turn the lights on for about 16 hours a day.

Soil

Basically, there are two kinds of potting soil: soil-based mixes that contain some real earth, and soilless mixes composed mostly of shredded peat moss or finely ground pine bark and perlite, vermiculite, or sand, with no real soil at all. Both types of soil mixes have pros and cons. Soil-based mixes are usually less expensive and heavier. The added weight is good for plants outdoors, because it helps keep the pots from blowing over in the wind, but it's burdensome when you are moving large potted plants from place to place. Lightweight soilless mixes cost more, but they are popular in nurseries for ease and economy in transporting the plants, and prepackaged soilless mixes are very consistent from batch to batch, so a nursery can grow uniform crops without having to make adjustments for different lots of soil.

At home, including some real soil makes a more stable mix for long-term plantings such as potted shrubs or trees, and it helps buffer against problems of excess or inadequate fertilization. Soilless mixes tend to break down into smaller particles over time, becoming so dense and compact that they don't drain well, and sometimes the soil pH and nutrient balance go awry. It can be difficult to diagnose and correct those conditions. You can make your own potting soil by mixing equal parts of good garden loam, perlite or coarse sand, and peat moss or compost. Add about a cupful of ground limestone and two cupfuls of composted steer manure per bushel of soil mix.

Good potting soil contains no weed seeds, insects or related pests, or disease organisms. Most commercial potting soils are sterile, but if you start with compost or garden loam and mix your own soil, it's a good idea to sterilize it by heating it in an oven or over a barbecue grill to about 160° F for 30 minutes (use a meat thermometer to check the temperature), to kill any undesirable elements.

Watering and fertilizing

Deciding when and how much to water is one of the most difficult, yet most important, aspects of growing plants in pots. Some herbs are very forgiving of neglect or error. They recover, look normal, and keep growing even if you occasionally let the soil get completely dry before rewatering or if you let water stand for days in a saucer at the base of the pot before pouring it out. These herbs are the exceptions. Most herbs need to be watered regularly before they wilt; if you let them wilt, their leaves may get brown tips or edges or turn yellow and fall off. And most herbs need soil that's porous enough for any excess water to soak right down and run out the drainage holes in the bottom of the pot. If you leave water standing at the bottom of a container, most herbs suffer root damage, which shows up, ironically, when the leaves wilt because the damaged roots can't supply enough water.

How often you have to water depends on the herb, the pot, the soil, the weather, and the time of year. In winter or during cloudy or rainy weather, a plant may go a week or more between waterings. In summer or sunny weather, it's not uncommon to have to water potted plants every day. In general, it's better for the plant if you have to water it frequently, with the soil starting to dry out in between waterings, than if the soil stays wet for days on end. If your schedule doesn't allow for frequent watering, you might want to experiment with the new polymer gels — products that greatly increase the water-holding capacity of soil.

Plants in containers need to be fertilized. The limited amount of soil in a pot is never sufficient to supply, or even to retain, enough nutrients for sustained growth, especially when regular watering keeps washing the nutrients away. Use whatever fertilizer you prefer, organic or synthetic, or alternate between two or more products to provide a more balanced diet of nutrients. Soluble fertilizers, which you mix with water, are particularly convenient. Figure the capacity of your watering can, and set aside a special measuring spoon to use for measuring the amount of fertilizer to dissolve in a canful of water.

It's a good idea to mark the date on the calender each time you fertilize and to maintain a regular schedule. Frequent dilute applications promote steadier growth than occasional heavy doses do. During spring and summer, when most plants are growing the fastest, it's not too much to apply dilute fertilizer once a week. Herbs that keep growing through fall and winter need to be fertilized only once or twice a month, because growth slows down when the days are short. Herbs that go dormant in winter shouldn't be fertilized at all from late summer until spring. During the season of active growth, you can tell if you aren't using enough fertilizer, or applying it often enough, by observing the plants. If underfertilized, most herbs stop growing and fail to flower, and gradually their leaves turn yellow and fall off. Overfertilizing isn't usually a problem unless the soil dries out. Then it often causes root damage and scorched (brown and brittle) leaf edges.

Container Material and Size

Terra cotta, glazed ceramic, plastic, wood, fiberglass, concrete, metal — many different materials make acceptable containers for growing plants. Suit yourself, considering cost, weight, durability, resistance to weather damage, and appearance. From the plant's point of view, the container itself is not as important as the soil you fill it with and the judgment you apply to watering and fertilizing.

Many herbs grow best if their roots are confined to a relatively small pot — one that's about one-third the height of an upright-growing plant or about one-third the width of a spreading plant. In a smaller pot, the soil dries out more quickly, letting air get to the roots. In too large a pot, the wet soil can suffocate roots. This is especially true for herbs that grow slowly in general or for any herbs in containers during the winter months.

Annual and perennial herbs planted in containers outdoors for the summer grow quickly enough to fill large containers, and it's okay to start the season by putting one small plant into a 6-inch or larger pot or hanging basket. The plant will look adrift at first, and you should be careful not to overwater it, but within a few weeks it will grow into scale with the pot. Some robust herbs, such as pineapple sage and peppermint-scented geranium, may need replanting into a 10-inch or 12-inch pot by midsummer.

An older specimen of an herbal tree or shrub such as rosemary or bay laurel can be kept in a 10-inch or 12-inch pot for years. Every spring, you can renew it by carefully lifting the plant out of the pot, scraping a thin layer of soil off the top, bottom, and sides of the root ball, and replacing that with fresh soil as you repot the plant. At this time, it's a good idea to give the pot a thorough scrubbing, inside and out, to remove any salt deposits or algal growth.

Long-Term Plantings

Like bonsai specimens, some potted herbs outlive their owners. These old-timers are usually tender shrubs or trees, such as dwarf lemon, bay laurel, or myrtle. Keeping a potted herb alive for decades is a real horticultural achievement that represents dedication, patience, and skill. When you see one of these older herbs, with its thick trunk and limbs, think of all the times that someone has carefully watered, fertilized, pruned, and repotted it, treated it for insect attacks, and carried it back and forth with the changing seasons.

Tender perennials, shrubs, and trees are the best candidates for long-term container plantings, although their lives normally are measured in years, not decades. If you start with a small plant that you purchase in a 3-inch pot or propagate yourself, you can step it up one pot size at a time as it grows, ending up in a 10-inch, 12-inch, or larger pot after a few to several years. You may choose to train and shape the plant into a sphere, cone, ball-topped standard, or other formal shape; or you may prefer to let it grow naturally, simply pruning out weak, damaged, crossing, or unruly limbs.

Herbs That Can Live in a Pot for Years

Aloe vera (*Aloe vera*)
Lemon verbena (*Aloysia triphylla*)
Tea (*Camellia sinensis*)

Chat (*Catha edulis*)
Carob (*Ceratonia siliqua*)
Camphor tree (*Cinnamomum camphora*)
Crimson-spot rock rose (*Cistus ladanifer*)
Lemon (*Citrus limon*)
Coffee (*Coffea arabica*)
Cardamom (*Elettaria cardamomum*)
Eucalyptus (*Eucalyptus* spp.)
Yerba maté (*Ilex paraguariensis*)
Jasmine (*Jasminum sambac*)
Bay laurel (*Laurus nobilis*)
Henna (*Lawsonia inermis*)
New Zealand tea tree (*Leptospermum scoparium*)
Myrtle (*Myrtus communis*)
Moujean tea (*Nashia inaguensis*)
Mexican oregano (*Poliomintha longiflora*)
Rosemary (*Rosmarinus officinalis*)
Costa Rican mint bush (*Satureja viminea*)

Short-Term Plantings

Many container plantings look attractive for a single grow-ing season or perhaps a year or two but need to be renewed or replaced after that time. These short-term plantings can be designed for indoor or outdoor enjoyment.

For one season's enjoyment, fill half-barrels, window boxes, strawberry jars, large pots, or any other containers with fast-growing herbs such as dill, basil, parsley, cilantro, calendula, nasturtium, chili peppers, shoo-fly plant, German chamomile, and sweet marjoram. Most of these are annuals, and the others are usually treated as annuals.

Many hardy perennials grow well for a year or two in a large pot. When their roots get too confined, they need to be lifted, divided, and replanted. Chives, southernwood, calamint, hyssop, lemon balm, oregano, hardy lavender, gar-den sage, lemon thyme, and various mints can be treated this way. Put a starter plant in a 6-inch or larger pot in spring, and keep it growing with regular watering and fertilizing all summer. When growth slows in fall, keep watering but hold back on fertilizing. Where winters are mild, you can leave the pot in the same place all year. Where winters are severe, sink the pot into the soil for the winter and spread mulch around the top to insulate the roots from cold damage. The next spring, put the same plant into a larger pot to have a larger specimen for the second year, or divide and replant it in the same size pot. Most hardy perennials can be kept in pots for only two to three years before needing division, unless they are in a very large (12-inch or wider) container.

A number of tender perennials grow very well in containers, especially outdoors in the summer, but they, too, fill a pot quickly and need to be replaced from year to year. Herbs in this group include the new hybrid agastaches, curry plant, menthol plant, Cuban oregano, patchouli, fringed lavender and other tender lavenders, dittany of Crete and other tender oreganos, pineapple sage and other tender salvias, lemon grass, vetiver grass, gotu kola, Vietnamese coriander, and most of the scented geraniums. The easiest way to enjoy these plants is to treat them as annuals, buying new starts every spring. Unless you have a big greenhouse or several south-facing picture windows, you won't have enough space to bring large plants indoors when the weather turns cold and keep them healthy until spring. Even if you do have enough well-lit space, it's a good idea to start again with small plants the next spring—they usually look better and have more vigor. If you particularly want to save your own plants, for sentimental or financial reasons, plan ahead and root cuttings or make divisions in late summer, bringing the new small plants indoors for the winter. Harvest and preserve the fragrant leaves or other useful parts of the big plants outdoors before frost damages them.

One final approach to short-term container plantings is to bring herbs indoors in fall, even though they won't survive, or certainly won't thrive, at low indoor light levels until spring. This strategy is worth a try in northern or mountain gardens, where it's a way to extend the fresh-herb season from frost until Thanksgiving or Christmastime. If you have space on a sunny windowsill, it's worth bringing in pots of chives, parsley, basil, dill, Mexican mint marigold, mint, lemon balm, sorrel, or other culinary herbs that you enjoy using fresh for flavor or garnish. None of these will put out much new growth after you bring them indoors, but you can continue to harvest leaves until you use them up, then discard the stems and roots. Be sure to plan ahead and pot up divisions or start new seedlings in mid- to late summer, so they'll be well developed when it's time to bring them indoors.

Propagating Herbs

With so many nurseries selling all kinds of herbs at very reasonable prices, there's really no need to propagate your own plants, especially if you want only one of each kind. You can buy almost any herb in a pot, ready to pop into your garden. On the other hand, propagating your own herbs can be a lot of fun, and the savings can be significant if you want enough of the same plants to use as a ground cover or edging, to repeat throughout a large garden, to harvest as a crop, to share with friends, or to sell at a plant sale or fund-raiser. Whether by seed, cutting, or division, some plants are much easier to propagate than others—they develop quickly, and they need only routine attention and care. The encyclopedia entries note herbs that can be easily propagated by home gardeners with no special skills or equipment. For more advanced information about propagation, refer to *Taylor's Guide to Gardening Techniques* (Boston: Houghton Mifflin, 1991).

Raising Herbs from Seeds

All annual and biennial herbs are grown from seeds, and many perennial and woody herbs can be raised from seeds, too. You can buy herb seeds from herb nurseries and general garden seed catalogs, or you can save seeds from your own plants.

If the seeds are rare, expensive, or tiny, it's a good idea to sow them indoors, where you can keep an eye on them and provide ideal conditions for germination and growth. Starting seeds indoors is also a good way to get a head start on the growing season. Some perennials will bloom the first year if started early indoors, and if you don't start tender annuals such as basil indoors, you won't be able to start using them until late summer. You can sow herb seeds in small pots of sterile potting soil or screened compost and grow them under fluorescent lights or on a sunny windowsill, as you would start tomatoes, peppers, petunias, or other seedlings. Thin or transplant the seedlings as they grow. When they are a few inches tall and have several leaves, gradually prepare them for outdoor conditions. Set them outdoors in a place sheltered from direct sun and wind for a few days (bring them in at night or during severe storms), then expose them to the full range of weather for a few more days before planting them in the ground.

Sowing seeds directly in the garden has advantages and disadvantages. It can be wasteful, as you can lose tiny seeds or fragile seedlings owing to hot or cold weather, wet or dry weather, high winds, bird or rodent activity, running dogs or digging cats, or your own forgetfulness or carelessness. When successful, though, direct-sown seedlings often grow into particularly healthy plants. Direct sowing is especially recommended for annual herbs that grow very quickly, such as cilantro and borage, and for herbs that develop a single deep taproot, such as caraway and opium poppy, but you can try it with other annuals and perennials, such as basil, parsley, Roman chamomile, purple coneflower, and butterfly weed. For individual specimens, sow a few seeds in each spot where you want a plant to grow, mark the spot, and check daily to make sure the soil doesn't dry out until the seedlings have emerged. Remove extra plants, leaving just the strongest seedling at each spot. To grow a patch or row of plants, scatter or sow at least two to three times as many seeds as you want plants, and thin the seedlings to a suitable spacing after they emerge.

You can count on some herbs to self-sow (that is, sow their own seeds) and come back from year to year as "volunteers." Once you start these herbs, you'll always have them. Just watch for seedlings every spring. You'll be surprised at where they show up, sometimes at some distance from the parent plant. Herbs that volunteer too readily can become weeds in your garden, producing many more seedlings than you want, so you have to keep pulling them out. To prevent that, cut off their flowers as soon as the petals fade, before the seeds have a chance to ripen and scatter.

Herbs That Often Self-Sow

Anise hyssop (*Agastache foeniculum*)
Garlic chives (*Allium tuberosum*)
Dill (*Anethum graveolens*)
Sweet Annie (*Artemisia annua*)
Borage (*Borago officinalis*)
Mustards (*Brassica juncea* and other spp.)
Calamint (*Calamintha grandiflora*)
Epazote, ambrosia (*Chenopodium ambrosioides, C. botrys*)
Feverfew (*Chrysanthemum parthenium*)
Dyer's coreopsis (*Coreopsis tinctoria*)
Foxglove (*Digitalis purpurea*)
Mole plant (*Euphorbia lathyris*)
Fennel (*Foeniculum vulgare*)
Woad (*Isatis tinctoria*)
Motherwort (*Leonurus cardiaca*)
Horehound (*Marrubium vulgare*)
Lemon balm (*Melissa officinalis*)
Catnip (*Nepeta cataria*)
Shoo-fly plant (*Nicandra physaloides*)
Black cumin (*Nigella sativa*)
Evening primrose (*Oenothera biennis*)
Opium poppy (*Papaver somniferum*)
Perilla (*Perilla frutescens*)
Salad burnet (*Poterium sanguisorba*)
Weld (*Reseda luteola*)
Sorrels (*Rumex acetosa, R. scutatus*)
Clary sage (*Salvia sclarea*)
Soapwort (*Saponaria officinalis*)
Mother-of-thyme (*Thymus pulegioides*)
Nasturtium (*Tropaeolum majus*)
Sweet violet (*Viola odorata*)

Propagating Herbs by Division

Many of the most popular and desirable perennial and shrubby herbs cannot be propagated by seed. Either they don't bear seeds or the seedlings grow too slowly to bother with, or the seedlings would not match the desirable characteristics of the parent plant. These herbs are usually propagated by making divisions or cuttings.

Propagation by division is an ideal technique for home herb gardeners—it's fast and easy, and nearly always successful. You can divide almost any perennial that spreads sideways, whether it extends itself by distinct horizontal runners, as mints and passionflower do; knits a dense tangled patch of rooted stems and shoots, as thyme, sweet woodruff, and costmary do; forms an upright clump of separate shoots that can be pulled apart, as lemon grass, chives, and purple coneflower do; or produces little plantlets around the base of a parent plant, as aloe vera and yucca do. Many herbs can be divided in either spring or early fall. Just allow enough time for the divisions to send out new roots and get well established before being stressed by the heat of summer or cold of winter.

If you just want a new start of a plant to put in another part of the garden, or a piece to give to a friend, you can often cut and lift a division with a sharp trowel, like taking a slice of pie, without disturbing the parent plant. If you want to divide a large plant into several pieces, or if you have an old, overgrown plant that needs to be renewed, it's better to fork up the whole mass and pull or cut it apart, replanting the healthy new sections and discarding any weak or aged material.

If you can't replant the divisions immediately, you can store them for a few days. Wrap them in damp newspaper, then seal them loosely in a plastic bag, and put it in a cool, shady place. As soon as possible, replant the divisions into freshly prepared soil. Water them in well, and continue to water as often as needed to prevent wilting. A new division sometimes looks limp and has a pale gray-green color at first, and some of its leaves may wither and turn yellow or brown. In a matter of days or weeks, depending on the herb and the season, the new plant will perk up noticeably, as its roots recover from the shock of division and start growing again. After a few months, or within a year at most, it should be well established.

Propagating Herbs by Rooting Cuttings

Propagation by cutting is very important in the nursery business, because it's an economical way to make dozens of new starts from one parent plant. Home gardeners, however, have mixed results with making cuttings. Some people seem to have a knack for it, but others, alas, rarely see success. The challenge is keeping cuttings alive until they form roots, and the problems are that cuttings are very vulnerable to desiccation if conditions are too dry or to rotting if conditions are too wet. It can take anywhere from a few days to several months for a cutting to form roots. The faster the better, because a cutting with roots is on its way to independence. The longer a cutting is rootless, the more likely it is to wither or rot. It takes patience, skill, perseverance, and luck to keep slow-starting cuttings alive until they form roots.

If you want to give cuttings a try, here's a method for herbs that form roots fairly quickly and easily in a glass of water. These include the mints, bee balm, tender salvias, perennial basils, Vietnamese coriander, and willows. Remove the lower leaves from healthy sections of actively growing stems, cut to about 6 inches long, and stick them in a jar of water in a bright place out of direct sun. Change the water every day or two, to keep it fresh, and watch for any sign of emerging roots. As soon as the roots are about $1/4$ inch long, pot the cuttings in individual small pots filled with loose-textured, sterile potting soil or with a half-and-half mix of potting soil and perlite. Water gently to settle the soil around the base of the cutting. Set the potted cuttings inside a cardboard box or plastic tub that's just deep enough to hold them, and cover the top of the container with a sheet of clear plastic sheeting to keep the air inside moist. Set the box or tub in a bright place—right next to a north window, on the north side of a building, or under artificial light. Avoid direct sun, which would overheat it and burn the new plants. Check the cuttings every day. As soon as a potted cutting has started making new top growth, take it out of the container, but keep it in a shady and sheltered place for another few days before moving it to full sun and open air.

More challenging, because they take longer to root, are cuttings of various kinds of lavender, rosemary, roses, scented geraniums, and many other herbs. For these, it's usually best to make cuttings 3 to 4 inches long, choosing the tips of new shoots that are firm and mature but not too hard or woody. Remove the lower leaves, dip the bottom end of the cutting in a commercial rooting preparation such as Rootone™ powder, and stick the cutting in a pot or flat of moist perlite, vermiculite, or coarse sand. To keep the cuttings from drying out, you'll need to mist them frequently—as often as several times a day, or cover them somehow. You can invert a glass jar over a single cutting, or place several little pots or trays inside a clear plastic storage container, such as the boxes designed for storing sweaters. Put the cuttings in a warm, bright location but out of direct sun. Check for progress periodically by gently tugging on a cutting. Unrooted cuttings pull up easily. You'll know that roots have formed when a cutting resists your pull. Gently transplant rooted cuttings from the rooting mix to individual containers filled with potting soil, and gradually acclimate them to full sun and open air.

Controlling Invasive Plants

Some herbs go beyond being easy to propagate. They multiply like weeds, spreading through your garden, overwhelming less aggressive plants, and filling valuable space with too much of a not-so-good thing. It isn't necessary to avoid these plants altogether; in the right place and the right quantity, they're attractive, useful, and desirable. The wise strategy is to acknowledge an herb's potential invasiveness and take appropriate steps to accommodate or to limit it.

Herbs that spread by self-seeding, as described and listed earlier in this chapter, are good choices for filling large open areas such as roadside verges, fields, or meadows or for casual, country-style gardens. In small gardens, where you don't want them to produce excess seedlings that you'd have to pull out, the thing to do is prevent seed formation by cutting off the faded flowers. That's an easy task, and it helps keep the garden looking tidy, too, but you have to keep up with it throughout late summer and fall.

Herbs that spread by runners, rhizomes, or roots are also good candidates for filling large open areas, and they can make useful ground covers or mass plantings on steep banks, on rough ground where it's difficult to maintain a lawn, along stream banks and pond shores, at the edge of a woods, in highway medians or parking islands, or between buildings. Rather than cursing herbs that spread to make dense patches, a smart gardener puts them to use and takes advantage of this tendency.

In a small garden, though, an herb that spreads vigorously soon grabs more than its share of space. One solution is to dig up the entire plant every year or two, normally in spring; break off a small division to replant; and discard or give away the rest. Another technique is to confine the plant with a buried barrier, such as a large plastic nursery pot or similar container with the bottom cut off. Watch out, though—some plants will jump over the rim of such a container, and others will sneak under the bottom. Also, vigorous plants soon fill a container with roots and need extra water and nutrients to keep from looking stunted. It's a good idea to dig up a confined plant and its buried container every few years, divide the plant, reinstall the container, and refill it with fresh soil.

It's not uncommon to buy a house and find patches of tenacious herbs or other perennials already established on the property, or to start such a patch yourself and regret it years later. If you have a patch of horseradish, comfrey, soapwort, or another perennial herb that you don't want anymore, you can eradicate it without using herbicides. In late spring, after new growth has fully emerged, use a lawn mower or string trimmer to cut the leaves and stems close to the ground. Don't disturb the roots. Cover the whole area with sections of newspaper, several pages thick, overlapped like shingles. Then spread a 6-inch-thick layer of hay, straw, leaves, or other mulch over the paper. By blocking off the light, this covering of paper and mulch will eliminate a weedy perennial, but the process takes at least one growing season. If you don't want to look at a big patch of bare mulch in the meantime, plant a hill of pumpkins or gourds at one side, and let the vines scramble over the mulch. Pick the pumpkins or gourds in fall and pull up the vine after frost, but leave the mulch on the ground all winter. By the next spring, both the mulch and the newspaper underneath will have decomposed so much that you can till it all into the soil as you reclaim the land for the plants of your choice.

Herbs That Can Spread Invasively by Runners or Roots

Horseradish (*Armoracia rusticana*)
Artemisia 'Silver King' and 'Silver Queen' (*Artemisia ludoviciana*)
Mugwort (*Artemisia vulgaris*)
Costmary (*Chrysanthemum balsamita*)
Horsetail, scouring rush (*Equisetum hyemale, E. arvense*)
Goat's rue (*Galega officinalis*)
Sweet woodruff (*Galium odoratum*)
Lady's bedstraw (*Galium verum*)
Licorice (*Glycyrrhiza glabra*)
Sweet grass (*Hierochloe odorata*)
Gotu kola (*Hydrocotyle asiatica*)
Mints (*Mentha* spp.)
Bee balm, bergamot (*Monarda* spp.)
Oregano (*Origanum vulgare*)
Passionflower (*Passiflora incarnata*)
Vietnamese coriander (*Polygonum odoratum*)
Heal-all (*Prunella vulgaris*)
Mountain mints (*Pycnanthemum* spp.)
Sorrels (*Rumex acetosa, R. scutatus*)
Soapwort (*Saponaria officinalis*)
Comfrey (*Symphytum officinale*)
Tansy (*Tanacetum vulgare*)
Creeping germander (*Teucrium chamaedrys* 'Prostratum')
Coltsfoot (*Tussilago farfara*)
Valerian (*Valeriana officinalis*)
Sweet violet (*Viola odorata*)

Designing a Traditional, Formal Herb Garden

Traditionally, herb gardens have been designed as formal gardens. The term "formal" implies several things about these gardens. They have a simple geometric form. The design is precise and clear, with well-defined lines that relate to the existing site and architecture. The beds and paths are usually edged with bricks, stones, wood, or low clipped plants. The garden as a whole is often enclosed by a neatly trimmed hedge, fence, or wall.

A formal herb garden is furnished with an abundance of hardscape elements—paths, edgings, fences, walls, arbors, trellises, and benches—that are chosen to complement the plants, provide year-round interest, and coordinate with nearby buildings. Ornaments such as a sundial, fountain, pool, urn, sculpture, birdbath, or potted topiary are used to mark important positions in the geometry of the design.

The plant palette is usually limited and features perennials and shrubs with a neat growth habit and attractive foliage. Compared with the showy splashes of color in most flower beds, this creates a subtle, quiet, and elegant effect. Foliage alone can provide a wide range of colors and textures, and several herbs are evergreen or nearly so, keeping the garden appealing over a long season.

A highly ordered, geometrical garden portrays a classical beauty and balance, blending quiet simplicity with rich visual interest. Whether you create a freestanding formal herb garden in an open area of your property or integrate your garden design into the architectural fabric of spaces next to your home, the geometry underlying the design will ensure that your herb garden will be a work of garden art rather than a mere random grouping of plants.

This chapter gives you many ideas to ponder and practical information to put to use in the process of designing your own formal herb garden, one that is personally tailored to your site, your sense of beauty, and your style of gardening. Incorporating formal design principles in your garden isn't an all-or-nothing decision; it's a matter of degree. The term "formal" and the appearance of a formal garden generate different reactions in different people. Some people reject formality as too rigid and controlled. To many people, however, formality is seen and felt in the positive sense of an orderly garden with a calm, simple, elegant ambience. For most of us, the solution is to blend elements of formality and informality. Determining the degree of formality you're comfortable with is something to think about while visiting other gardens, looking at pictures in books and magazines, and planning the design for your own herb garden.

Site Selection and Analysis

The first steps in designing any garden are selecting and analyzing the site. Light is a primary consideration, since the most popular Mediterranean herbs such as lavender, thyme, sage, and rosemary all require 6 hours or more of sunlight daily. However, there are also many herbs that grow well in part shade, such as sweet woodruff, sweet cicely, wild ginger, bloodroot, wintergreen, sweet violet, wood germander, and red or blue lobelias.

When analyzing the light at a potential garden site, be sure to take into account the shade cast from nearby buildings, trees, fences, and other obstructions. Study the shadow patterns throughout the seasons, since shadows are much longer in winter than in summer. Note whether nearby trees cast a heavy shade or allow speckles of sun to pass through. In the city, where buildings surround a garden, indirect or reflected light may supplement limited hours of direct sun.

Observe the pattern and level of wind at the site. Good air circulation is important for healthy plants, but too much wind causes problems. It can tip over tall plants, unless they are staked. In the winter, wind aggravates cold damage to marginally hardy plants. During the growing season, wind-blown plants dry out dramatically faster than those located in a protected area near a building or behind a shelter-giving hedge or garden wall.

Look at the topography or natural slope of the terrain. Does rainfall and snowmelt water drain away from the site, or does it collect there? Good drainage is critical for most herbs; although some thrive in moist soil, few survive in boggy sites where water accumulates. If well drained, a flat site is easy to work with, and you can get started with the staking, measuring, and layout. If the site is not well drained, building raised beds will make it possible to grow a much wider variety of herbs, and it will also give you the opportunity to create interesting changes of level. A sloping site is usually well drained but difficult to work on. Carving the slope into a series of low terraces can give you flat beds for planting and interesting walls that add character and definition to the garden.

Integrating House and Garden

Integrating an herb garden with the existing architecture can create a sense of pleasing visual and physical continuity between the house and the garden. Establishing a grid is a helpful design tool for connecting the garden to the house. Start with a drawing that shows your house and property, and draw lines to project a grid outward from the house. The grid is useful for aligning the house and garden and for dividing the garden into room-sized spaces that relate to the proportions of the house.

Another integrating technique is to repeat and incorporate the type, color, texture, and other qualities of the building materials of your house into the garden. For example, if you have a brick house, you might plan to use brick paving in the garden or to use strips of brick to accent common concrete paving. With a stone house, you could use stone to edge the garden's beds or paths, or you might include a stone bench or birdbath. Even if you don't repeat the materials, selecting complementary styles of garden structures, furniture, and ornaments will help you achieve house and garden continuity.

Consider the view out to the garden from key vantage positions inside your house. If possible, locate the garden where you can see it from indoors. A geometric herb garden outside your favorite window will reward you with pleasure every day of the year. Because of the hardscape and evergreen plants, the form or "bones" of the garden will be satisfying even in winter.

Design the Garden on Paper First

Before you start buying plants or digging beds, spend time thinking about the garden and planning it on paper. Ask yourself several questions: Who will use the garden? Will more than one person visit it at the same time? Do you want a feeling of privacy? How much time are you willing to spend on maintenance? What is your budget?

Try drawing the garden design on paper, and keep reworking and refining the design until you're satisfied with the arrangement of lines and shapes. Unlike with common flower beds that depend primarily on the flowers and foliage of the plants, the success of a formal garden depends on its underlying geometry. Within a geometric system, you can easily create clear, harmonious relationships among the garden components—the plants and the hardscape—and compose a design that is unified, balanced, and pleasing.

The design basics of a formal garden

A formal herb garden is basically geometric. Its overall form is a simple regular shape, such as a circle, oval, rectangle, or square, which is divided into equal or proportionately related sections. Formal herb gardens frequently display bilateral symmetry; that is, one side of the garden is the mirror image of the other side.

The quadripartite or four-quarter motif is the most traditional design for a formal garden. It has four bilaterally symmetrical compartments, formed by bisecting a square or rectangle. The quadripartite motif is beautiful, functional, and elegant in its simplicity, and it has rich historical, religious, and literary significance. It was used in the ancient Roman and Greek kitchen gardens, the medieval cloister and physic gardens, and the colonial American kitchen garden, and it is still the most popular design for an herb garden.

Drawing your own design

To design your own garden, start by drawing a simple circle, oval, square, or rectangle. Next, subdivide that shape. The resulting subdivisions do not have to be equal, but they should balance each other proportionately. The lines you use to subdivide the overall form are referred to as axes (one line is called an axis). When you move from paper to the garden, the subdivisions become the planting beds, and the axes become the paths.

The point where the primary and cross axes intersect is an important position in the design. In traditional herb gardens, this point typically is marked with a special feature such as a sundial, birdbath, fountain, sculpture, specimen plant, or topiary. The termination of an axis—the end of a path—is another design point to punctuate with a garden bench, wall fountain, potted plant, or other feature.

The quadripartite motif is only one of several options. You might prefer another geometric configuration, such as a circle or oval divided into wedges, or a ladderlike row of square or rectangular beds. You could borrow a design from a pieced quilt or copy a pattern from a handwoven basket. Instead of a bilateral design, you could choose an asymmetric pattern, or you might simply arrange a row of beds in front of a straight or curved wall or hedge. Whatever design you decide on, take time to draw and redraw it until the overall effect is a simple and clear arrangement of beds and paths. Bear in mind that designs that look strong on paper tend to weaken when they're installed in the outdoor environment. Also, garden ornaments and hardscape features must be designed on a bold, oversize scale, as they always seem to shrink in size when placed outdoors.

From the Drawing Board to the Garden

When you're pleased with the design you have drafted on paper, use a tape measure, stakes, and string to transfer it to the ground. Be sure to mark out the entire garden before starting any construction. This gives you a chance to confirm that the design is practical as well as attractive.

Garden paths

Walk down the paths and notice if they feel too narrow or too wide. A path 18 inches wide is fine for one person to move through and tend the garden, but allow 4 feet for two people to walk side by side. Try out your wheelbarrow or garden cart to be sure the path is wide enough to accommodate it. Live with the staked-out design for a few days and adjust it as needed.

Paved paths are attractive and make the garden more accessible during wet weather. Many paving materials and patterns are appropriate for a traditional herb garden. Ever-popular bricks can be laid in basketweave, herringbone, running-bond, or other patterns. Cut stone and flagstone pavers come in many beautiful earthen colors and in regular or irregular shapes. Granite sets, cobblestones, riverstones, and Belgian blocks are other paving choices. These can be laid in either a sand or a concrete base. Concrete pavers and poured concrete are available in many colors today, including rose, warm browns, and gray tones that complement many herbs. In any case, be sure that any bricks, stones, pavers, or tiles that you use for paths are designed for outdoor use. They should resist moisture and frost damage and have a surface texture that is not slippery when wet.

Making paved paths requires little preparation in warm climates. In cold climates, however, the soil under a path must be excavated and replaced with at least 4 inches of gravel. This gravel foundation must be placed under any concrete slab or any sand base that is then topped with brick, stone, or concrete pavers. The gravel keeps soil water from climbing up into the concrete or sand by capillary action, and it is needed to prevent the heaving, cracking, and breakage caused by alternate freezing and thawing.

Soft-surface paths are less expensive and easier to make than paved paths. Again, there are several materials to choose from. In most cases, you'll need to install a slightly raised edging of landscape timbers, brick, or stone to keep the path material from spilling over into the adjacent beds. Stone dust or crushed stone is inexpensive and available in a variety of earth-tone colors, depending on the type of stone quarried in your area. It packs down into a firm surface, but low spots may hold puddles after a rain. Gravel dries quickly and allows surface water to drain down into the subsoil; however, loose gravel is difficult to walk on. Mulch materials such as pine straw and chipped bark are comfortable to walk on but can be soggy, and they have to be replaced every year or two when they decompose.

Garden beds

The garden beds must be big enough to accommodate the mature spread and size of the plants you wish to grow in them, but not so big that you can't reach in to care for the plants. Four feet is the maximum width for reaching comfortably into a bed to plant, cultivate, or harvest your herbs. If a bed is wider than that, you'll need stepping-stones to make it accessible. Install a few flat stones or rounds of wood so that you'll always step in the same places and limit soil compaction to those designated spots. Of course, the soil in the beds will need to be prepared for planting, as described on pp. 22–25 in the essay "Growing Herbs in the Garden." Usually it's easier to make the paths first and prepare the soil later, but you can reverse that order if you choose.

There's an interesting and often overlooked psychological benefit to subdividing a garden into smaller compartments.

Such a garden is easier to approach when care is required, and you'll experience a rewarding sense of achievement when you finish planting, pruning, weeding, or mulching each section. This benefit is important—it can make the difference between gardening as pleasure or gardening as chore. Even the most passionate gardening enthusiast wants a garden that is easy, accessible, and enjoyable to tend.

Defining edges

Herb gardens typically contain both hard edges and planted edges. The hard edges can be made of wood, brick, stone, or concrete and are often slightly raised. These edgings mark the separation between path and planting bed and help contain gravel or other loose path coverings. Hard and planted bed edges also prevent people and critters from entering the beds and injuring the plants.

Planted edges can be uniform or varied, soft or stiff. The herbs you choose and the way you arrange them along the edges of the beds greatly influences the character of your garden. Using an assortment of creeping, mounding, sprawling, flopping, and spirited plant forms gives a casual, natural effect. By contrast, a single clipped herb repeated entirely around the beds and paths gives a very formal effect, as seen in the gardens at Colonial Williamsburg. Even if they have the same geometric design, two gardens have very different characters if their edge treatments are different.

The regularity of planted and/or hard edges helps unify the different plants growing in a bed. In fact, the edge benefits the whole design so effectively that even if the beds are not perfectly manicured and weeded, the garden holds together in a visually pleasing way.

Enclosing the Herb Garden

There are several benefits to the traditional practice of enclosing a formal herb garden with a hedge, fence, or wall. The enclosure defines the scale and space of the garden. It creates the often illusive and very desirable qualities of privacy and intimacy. An enclosed herb garden is an exceptionally lovely haven, a serene refuge from the hurried pace of modern life. Even the air is special, perfumed by the fragrant plants. Visiting an outdoor room of herbs is one of the most pleasurable and memorable garden experiences.

There are practical advantages, too. An enclosed garden is a protected garden, safe from pesty animals or inconsiderate neighbors. The enclosure creates a favorable microclimate for growing herbs, protected from dry winds, severe cold, and violent storms. Many trees, shrubs, and vines can be grown a full hardiness zone north of their usual limit if they are trained against a wall (east-facing walls are best for this purpose). An espaliered fruit tree or grapevine is an excellent and appropriate companion to an herb garden. In summer, its foliage is a leafy backdrop for the herbs. In winter, the bare branches make an intriguing piece of sculpture.

Walls and fences

A wall of your house, garage, or other building may provide one edge of an enclosed herb garden. The other edges may be freestanding walls, fences, or hedges.

Brick, stone, or stucco walls are beautiful, but they are usually expensive to build. They are permanent structures that require careful planning and construction. By comparison, wooden fences are versatile and relatively inexpensive. Redwood has long been popular for its beauty and durability, but it's a limited resource now. Cedar and cypress are alternatives that weather to a nice gray color and hold up well outdoors. Pressure-treated pine lumber has excellent rot resistance and can be stained, painted, or left to weather from a greenish tan to a gray color. Untreated softwood fences are used only in dry, sunny climates. They are the least expensive to install, but they have to be replaced after several years outdoors.

A picket fence is a good choice for a garden associated with a wooden house, and it can be painted white, off-white, or the same color as the house. The historical wattle fence is an appropriate enclosure for a more rustic herb garden. Wattle fences were pictured in medieval woodblocks and are still used in rural England. They are simple to make: simply install wooden posts at regular intervals, then weave pliable shoots of willow or hazel back and forth between the posts. A carefully woven wattle fence is as neat as a willow basket.

For any wooden fence, the posts must be set deep enough to support the weight of the fence against the forces of wind and gravity. Normally one-third of the post should be underground; for example, a 6-foot post should be set 2 feet deep. To reduce moisture contact with the soil, place several inches of aggregate at the bottom of the posthole. Better yet, pour concrete piers and set the posts on metal post anchors to keep the wood above ground and away from moisture.

Hedges

Hedges, particularly closely clipped ones, are a prototypical enclosure for the traditional herb garden. Yews, boxwoods, myrtle, bay laurel, small-leaved hollies, arborvitae, hemlock, and many other evergreens are excellent plants for formal hedges.

When choosing a plant for a hedge, consider how much clipping it will need. A robust, fast-growing hedge demands frequent attention. Slower-growing plants take longer to fill in and make a visual screen, but they require much less of your time and energy. For example, boxwoods are excellent hedges for herb gardens because they have a naturally rounded, mounding form and can be maintained by an annual once-over with hand pruners in all but the most formal gardens.

Think also about how tall you want the hedge to grow. A hedge 6 to 8 feet tall is high enough to screen most views and provide privacy but not so tall that it shades a garden of sun-loving plants. Choosing a hedge plant that doesn't grow too tall can save you countless hours of difficult pruning. Compact cultivars are available in many of the species commonly used for hedging. Planting selected cultivars might cost a little more at first, but that investment is quickly repaid by the savings in maintenance.

Unless you want a dense evergreen hedge for complete enclosure and privacy, even in winter, a more transparent, deciduous hedge may suit your needs. Hedges made from deciduous shrubs can offer flowers, fruits, and fall color as well as enclosure. Bayberry, spicebush, elderberry, viburnums, and roses are among the many deciduous shrubs that make excellent hedge plants, and they all have herbal uses as well. Deciduous shrubs are especially popular for gardens in cold climates, where the choice of evergreen plants is limited.

In planting a hedge, be sure to space the plants close enough together so that within a reasonable number of years they read like a line instead of a series of dots. The enclosing hedge is an important component of your traditional herb garden design, so if your budget allows, start with plants a few feet tall and space them just 2 to 3 feet apart. Be sure to water the hedge plants regularly for the first two years after planting. Water well before the ground freezes in cold climates to protect from winter injury, and keep watering all year where winters are mild.

To make a passageway, you can leave a simple opening in the hedge or span the space with a wooden or wrought-iron gate mounted on wooden posts or brick or stone piers. A wooden arbor is another way to bridge an opening in a hedge, and it's an ideal place to grow a climbing rose, jasmine, passionflower, or other vine.

Garden Ornaments and Furnishings

As much as the plants you grow, the ornaments and furnishings you choose establish the character of your herb garden.

The subdued colors of weathered wood, stone, brick, wrought iron, bronze, and other traditional materials blend beautifully with the rich silver, gray, green, and blue tones of herb foliage and complement the flower colors as well.

Using materials such as stone and brick creates a sense of permanence appropriate for these historically rich garden plants, but the hand-carved stonework prevalent in Old World gardens is out of reach of most contemporary Americans. Fortunately, precast concrete is a practical and affordable substitute. Concrete can be molded to form beautiful replicas of the exquisite marble carvings or garden statuary of the past. Although plain concrete is basically gray, it can be lightened to a whiter color by adding marble dust or be tinted various shades of brown, gray, beige, rose, or gold. Spraying concrete with buttermilk encourages the growth of moss, which gives a soft, natural, aged appearance even to new statues or garden features. Concrete planters are especially practical in cold climates because they can be left outside all winter, unlike terra-cotta pots, which must be protected from freezing and thawing.

You'll want to select a special ornament to mark the center of a geometric herb garden. This can be a traditional sundial, pool, fountain, or potted topiary, or you might pick something more personal or contemporary, such as a modern sundial or outdoor sculpture. You might use a family heirloom such as an iron farm bell or a copper wash kettle. A birdwatcher might choose a birdhouse or feeder. Art festivals, craft fairs, antique shops, and flea markets are great places to shop for garden ornaments.

Potted plants in handsome containers are important ornaments for a formal herb garden. Place single or grouped specimens in locations that correspond to the garden's geometry. This is a traditional way to display standards or topiaries of plants that are not hardy in cold climates. Potted specimens of bay, myrtle, lavender, rosemary, scented geraniums, and other herbs benefit from a summer outdoors and can be carried back indoors for winter protection.

Be sure to include a bench or seat, or perhaps a set of chairs and a table for outdoor dining. Comfortable furniture encourages you to linger in the garden. Position the seating to take advantage of a beautiful view, a shady spot, or a fragrant plant.

Just remember to practice restraint in the choice and placement of garden ornaments, furnishings, and focal points. Stick with a selected palette of materials and colors. Limit the placement to key design positions in your garden. Use the features to mark the garden's center, terminate a path, or signal a change in grade, not just for decoration.

Our eye wants to be led in a rhythmic manner and occasionally rest upon a focal point. Too many focal points will fight for our eye's attention and cause a cluttered and chaotic garden composition. Using too many different materials or simply too many objects disrupts the unity and elegant simplicity of a traditional herb garden. Finally, note that vertical elements in the outdoor environment strongly demand the eye's attention; thus vertical ornaments are primary focal points in any garden design. Use them thoughtfully and with restraint.

Using Plants as Focal Points in the Garden

Individual plant specimens make natural focal points in the garden. Select plants with particularly striking characteristics such as a sculptural branching pattern, a columnar growth form, or lovely flower or foliage color. A pair of small upright trees such as arborvitae, eastern red cedar, or the columnar form of ginkgo can be used to frame an entryway or a view. Flowering dogwood, hawthorn, common hoptree, or other small trees with rounded crowns are good choices for the end of a path, and you can put a bench or seat in the shade under their limbs. Sweet bay magnolia, highbush cranberry, chaste tree, variegated elderberry, and smoke tree deserve a prominent location in the center of a garden, where their flowers and foliage can be admired from all sides.

On a smaller scale, annuals and perennials make excellent focal points for marking a turn or step in the path, carpeting the ground under a birdbath or sundial, flanking a bench, or adding a burst of color. Golden oregano, 'Tricolor' sage, variegated pineapple mint, or variegated lemon thyme will draw your attention to ground level, as they are colorful low-growing plants. Showy mid-height herbs are too numerous to list, but for a stunning display of flowers at eye level, try angelica, queen-of-the-prairie, Joe-Pye weed, black cohosh, pineapple sage, or other tall herbs.

Knot Gardens

A knot garden is another way of using plants to create a focal point. Knot gardens are composed of low-growing, neatly trimmed herbs planted close together to form continuous bands that are interwoven in knotlike patterns. The bands consist of just a few herbs that have distinctively contrasting foliage colors and textures, so you can easily perceive and follow the interlocking patterns that make up the knot. Upright common thyme, gray and green santolina, hyssop, germander, winter savory, dwarf yaupon holly, and other compact, bushy herbs with dense evergreen foliage are traditional choices for knot gardens. The spaces between the bands of clipped herbs can be carpeted with creeping thyme, pennyroyal, moss, or other low plants or be filled with decorative mulch or colorful stones.

A small knot garden makes a beautiful and appropriate centerpiece for a larger geometrical herb garden, but it can also stand on its own. The design of a knot garden fits easily into the geometric spaces around a house or the architectural streetscape of a city or town. Knot gardens are ideal for courtyards or terraces, where they can be viewed from indoors and from windows and balconies above. Rooftops are wonderful places for knot gardens because people can enjoy them from different angles. (Such gardens are also perfect for roofs where weight limitations could restrict the use of larger plants.) However, it takes frequent and careful pruning to keep a knot garden looking tidy, and you will need a backup supply of replacement plants to fill holes caused by the inevitable fungal disease, winterkill, or accidental damage.

Thematic Plantings

There are countless ways to fill the planting beds in an herb garden, but one of the most interesting approaches is to plant with a theme in mind. The arrangement of beds in a geometric garden is an ideal basis for organizing and displaying thematic plant collections.

One kind of theme is a collection of related plants, such as thymes, basils, or lavenders. Another is a collection of plants with similar fragrance, such as lemon verbena, lemon grass, lemon geranium, lemon balm, lemon eucalyptus, and lemon thyme. An avid cook might plant herbs for a particular cuisine, such as Mexican herbs or Thai herbs, or a variety of favorite culinary herbs for everyday meals. Anyone who enjoys herb teas could have fun planning and planting a special tea garden. Other ideas are a potpourri garden, a dye garden, or a garden of medicinal plants.

Some gardens are based on a color scheme. A moonlight garden of herbs with silver or gray foliage or white flowers is a most enchanting theme garden. The light foliage and pale flowers gleam in the dark even without moonlight. Plants for this garden would include the silvery-leaved wormwoods and artemisias, lavender, horehound, curry plant, gray santolina, lamb's-ears, and woolly thyme. A dark-colored fence or wall or an evergreen hedge would provide a contrasting background for this garden.

Following a few basic design guidelines is the key to creating an attractive bed of herbs. First, make sure there's enough of each kind of plant to make it show in the overall garden. For example, one clump of angelica is enough to be dramatic, but individual plants of coriander or summer savory are too small to notice. Plant small or delicate herbs in groups or blocks of three or more, or cluster several to make a natural-looking drift.

Another effective technique is to plant the same herb, or herbs with similar characteristics, in different parts of the garden. This repetition has a unifying effect. You might repeat herbs with gray or silver foliage or herbs with a particular growth habit. For example, planting clumps of orrisroot iris at various intervals throughout the garden is quite effective because the vertical foliage of the iris contrasts well with the rounded forms of many other herbs.

The Value of Design

We all appreciate the pleasures of a well-designed garden when we see it and move through it, but we often don't know why it affects us in this positive way or how to create such positive feelings in our own gardens. Although serendipity and intuition play a role, good garden design is mostly a matter of thoughtful preparation and planning. There's no secret to creating a formal herb garden; it's simply a matter of following the time-tested principles and techniques discussed in this chapter.

Your reward for spending time on the design process will be a garden of quiet elegance and beautiful simplicity. Herbs are a special group of plants with a rich historical legacy, and modern herb gardens that exhibit traditional design elements have an allure and mystical quality of unparalleled appeal.

Integrating Herbs into the Landscape

If you don't have the space, time, or inclination for a traditional herb garden, there are many other ways to grow herbs. You can include herbs in seasonal flower beds and borders, vegetable gardens, rose gardens, foundation plantings, and patio borders. Herbal shrubs and trees make hedges or specimens with year-round ornamental value. Many herbal plants are native or naturalized species, ideal for meadow gardens and natural landscapes. Some herbs thrive in window boxes, hanging baskets, raised planters, or other containers and are appropriate for gracing entryways, condominium and townhouse courtyards, balconies, decks, terraces, or rooftop gardens. Wherever you grow them, herbs add color, texture, fragrance, and interest.

The key to using herbs creatively is remembering that the term "herbs" encompasses a wide variety of plants. Gardeners often generalize about herbs, thinking only of the smaller culinary herbs such as sage or thyme, or believing that herbs are suitable only for formal herb gardens receiving full sun. In fact, herbs can be small or large, tender or hardy, annual or perennial, herbaceous or woody; and there are herbs adapted to sunny or shady sites, dry or wet soil, and hot or cold climates. Once you put aside limiting perceptions, you'll find many beautiful ways to integrate herbs into your landscape, and ultimately into your life.

An Herbal Entryway

The yard in front of a house, townhouse, or apartment is often wasted space, with a boring foundation planting and an unadorned lawn. Why not transform it into an herb garden? One approach is to replace or supplement the traditional foundation evergreens with a selection of herbs. Instead of the typical euonymus and holly, choose from artemisias, lavenders, santolinas, sages, rosemary, germander, bearberry, wax myrtle, and other shrubby herbs. (These and other plants named in this chapter are described in the plant encyclopedia at the back of this book.) To avoid spottiness and make a unified composition, repeat the same plant or those with similar visual characteristics, such as silver foliage or small rounded leaves, throughout the foundation planting, and use enough of each kind of plant to make an effect that's visible from the street.

Another idea is to replace the foundation planting with an evergreen hedge at the property line, to separate your front yard from the sidewalk or street. Visitors can pass through a wooden or metal gate to enter a secluded haven that welcomes them to your home. The hedge will offer privacy by marking a separation between the public and private domains, and you can plant a garden at the base of the hedge to view from inside the home. That garden can include annual and perennial herbs and other favorite plants.

An entrance planting that blends herbs with other plants has historical precedence. In colonial times, herbs were blended with other useful plants and flowers in combination plantings called dooryard gardens. The herbs selected for these gardens typically were those that could be used for flavoring and fragrance or as pest deterrents. Herbs suitable for colonial-style gardens include anise hyssop, bee balm, calendula, catnip, chives, fennel, feverfew, foxglove, germander, horehound, lamb's-ears, lavender, lovage, orrisroot, parsley, peppermint, rue, sage, southernwood, spearmint, sweet cicely, sweet marjoram, sweet woodruff, tansy, thyme, valerian, yarrow, and many more.

Front yards are sometimes the only suitable locations for gardens in urban sites surrounded by sun-blocking buildings. Fortunately, some of the most popular herbs originate from hot, dry, gravelly slopes in the Mediterranean region and grow well in the similar conditions typical of urban front yards. Rosemary, thyme, sage, lavender, oregano, hyssop, winter savory, horehound, and catnip all thrive in hot sun and appreciate the heat reflected from pavement and walls. City plots often have terrible soil, but you can bypass that by building raised beds with lumber or masonry walls and filling them with good topsoil. Raising the beds provides the good drainage that herbs love and brings them up closer for you to enjoy. Design the raised bed with a cap or top wide enough that you can sit there to tend and enjoy the plants.

Another solution for small front yards is a colorful pavement of brick, stone, or concrete. A knot garden (see pp. 55–56) makes an intriguing centerpiece for a paved entrance court, and the combination of hardscape and evergreen plants provides year-round interest. Fill wooden, terra-cotta, concrete, or fiberglass containers with a variety of herbs to add more color, texture, and fragrance. Use single specimens or arrange groups of containers to mark a gate, frame a doorway, or soften a corner. Many annual and perennial herbs grow quickly to fill an outdoor container in summer. Tender perennials and shrubs such as sweet bay, myrtle, lemon verbena, and scented geraniums thrive outdoors in summer but need protection in winter.

Make an Outdoor Room

An outdoor room is a small private garden enclosed by a hedge, fence, or wall. The sense of enclosure makes an outdoor room a comfortable, intimate place to relax and get away from the world. If you already have a patio or terrace, you may want to install a hedge around it to form the major "walls" of the space. Be sure to leave enough room between the hedge and the paving for the planting beds. These beds can vary in width depending on the plants you want to grow in them.

One idea for planting the beds is to integrate herbs with vegetable plants. You could make a salad garden with lettuce, endive, and other greens; chives, garlic chives, parsley, dill, basil, tarragon, sorrel, and other herbs; nasturtiums, calendulas, and other edible flowers; and one or two plants of cherry tomatoes. If you like Mexican food, you could plant cilantro, Mexico oregano, Mexican mint marigold, and other herbs, along with plenty of garlic and an assortment of chili peppers, which are beautiful plants with glossy foliage and colorful pods.

Yet another idea is to fill the garden room with herbs that have fragrant foliage or flowers, creating a perfumed oasis. Scented geraniums, pineapple sage, lemon balm, various thymes, rosemary, lavender, shrub roses, and passionflower are all good choices for a scented garden room.

Herbs in the Vegetable Garden

Herbs are natural companions to vegetables, both in the garden and in the kitchen. If you already have or are planning a vegetable plot, you'll be delighted to see the colorful foliage and flowers of herbs intermingled with your favorite vegetable crops. Of course, you'll also enjoy sniffing and nibbling the herbs as you tend your garden.

Dill, borage, mustard, epazote, cilantro, black cumin, fennel, summer savory, and nasturtium are all annual herbs that you can sow directly in the vegetable garden, wherever you want them to grow. Basil, sweet marjoram, chili peppers, and Mexican mint marigold benefit from a head start—you can sow the seeds indoors 8 weeks before last frost, or purchase started plants at a local nursery. Plant garlic cloves in the fall, like bulbs; they will mature the next summer. Any of these herbs can be interspersed among the rows or beds of vegetables, as they all benefit from fertile, well-drained soil and regular watering. It's easy to replace and replant annual herbs each year, just as you plant new tomatoes and beans.

You might want to choose a special place for perennial culinary herbs such as chives, garlic chives, oregano, sage, and thyme. One idea is to design a geometric herb garden in the center or to the side of your rows of crops. This precise herb garden need not be expansive in size or expensive to install. Mark out a simple square, rectangle, or circle, and divide it into quarters with two paths that cross in the center. Edge the perimeter of the beds and outline the paths to define the geometric design. Use stepping-stones to provide easy access to the plants in the beds for planting, tending, and harvesting. The satisfaction you'll reap from having this garden will be well worth the effort required to make it.

Adding Herbs to Flower Beds and Borders

Herbs are a refreshing alternative to common annual bedding plants. Many of the perennial, annual, and biennial herbs have a softer, subtler flowering effect than the showy flowering annuals and perennials typically used in border plantings.

Other herbs do, however, offer a showy splash of color when in bloom. For example, bee balm's vivid red, pink, or magenta blooms are attention grabbers in any flower bed. Balloon flower displays beautiful periwinkle blue, pink, or white bell-shaped flowers. Creeping thymes offer a colorful carpet of red, pink, and white. Foxglove creates a colorful, stately sculptural presence in the flower garden. The bright daisylike blossoms of calendula, pyrethrum, and purple cone-flower are flower-garden favorites, as are the new hybrid yarrows. The sages or salvias produce countless spikes of flowers in exquisite shades of blue, purple, red, pink, white, and bicolor.

If you like rose, pink, lilac, blue, or white flowers, try combining them with herbs that have purple, blue-gray, or silvery foliage. Opal basil, purple perilla, and purple sage have rich dark purple leaves. Bronze fennel has elegant, feathery, purple-bronze foliage. Several artemisias, gray santolina, woolly thyme, curry plant, lavender, and garden sage all have gray or silvery foliage. Use a low edging of parsley, lamb's-ears, thyme, or dianthus to unify and complete the design.

Perennial Herbs with Attractive Flowers

Yarrows (*Achillea millefolium* hybrids)
Agastaches (*Agastache* hybrids)
Lady's-mantle (*Alchemilla mollis*)
Chives, garlic chives (*Allium schoenoprasum, A. tuberosum*)
Angelica (*Angelica archangelica*)
Dyer's chamomile (*Anthemis tinctoria*)
Butterfly weed (*Asclepias tuberosa*)
Calamint (*Calamintha grandiflora*)
Feverfew, pyrethrum daisy (*Chrysanthemum* spp.)
Bugbane (*Cimicifuga racemosa*)
Clove pink (*Dianthus caryophyllus*)
Gas plant (*Dictamnus albus*)
Foxglove (*Digitalis purpurea*)
Purple coneflower (*Echinacea purpurea*)
Joe-Pye weed (*Eupatorium purpureum*)
Queen-of-the-prairie (*Filipenula rubra*)
Meadowsweet (*Filipenula ulmaria*)
Lady's bedstraw (*Galium verum*)
Hyssop (*Hyssopus officinalis*)
Orrisroot (*Iris germanica* var. *florentina*)
Lavenders (*Lavandula* spp.)
Blue lobelia (*Lobelia siphilitica*)
Bee balms (*Monarda* spp.)
Catmint (*Nepeta* × *faassenii*)
Passionflower (*Passiflora incarnata*)
Balloon flower (*Platycodon grandiflorus*)
Garden sage, other sages (*Salvia* spp.)
Soapwort (*Saponaria officinalis*)
Winter savory (*Satureja montana*)
Sweet goldenrod (*Solidago odora*)
Betony (*Stachys officinalis*)

Tansy (*Tanacetum vulgare*)
Germanders (*Teucrium* spp.)
Thymes (*Thymus* spp.)
Society garlic (*Tulbaghia violacea*)
Sweet violet (*Viola odorata*)
Yucca (*Yucca filamentosa*)

Combine Herbs with Roses

A garden devoted exclusively to roses (especially hybrid tea roses) often resembles an orchard with rows or blocks of neatly spaced bushes that are carefully pruned to bear maximum crops of flowers. The flowers are indeed lovely, but the overall effect is rather stark. By contrast, there's nothing more romantic than a garden of old-fashioned shrub roses combined with billowing mounds of lavender, catmint, calamint, dianthus, and other herbs. There are thousands of roses to choose from, but in general the old-fashioned shrub roses, modern landscape roses, and new English roses are the easiest to care for. They require less pruning and winter protection than hybrid tea roses, tolerate a wider range of soil and water conditions, and are much more resistant to diseases and pest problems. Most are upright or spreading shrubs, 3 to 6 feet tall, with lovely fragrant flowers. Old-fashioned shrub roses usually bloom profusely in late spring or early summer, with just a few scattered blossoms later in the season. Modern landscape roses and new English roses keep blooming over a long season from late spring through late fall.

Among herbs, lavenders are favorites for combining with roses. The hardy English lavender forms a mound of lovely silver-gray, fine-textured foliage and holds its flower spikes on long stems that sway gracefully in the breeze. Different cultivars have dark blue-purple, lavender, pink, or white flowers. Spanish lavender, French lavender, and other tender lavenders are equally lovely. Treat them as annuals in cold regions, or enjoy them all year where winters are frost-free.

Herbs as Ground Covers

Using ground covers is a practical solution for difficult areas next to buildings or pavements, under and around trees and shrubs, on steep or rough slopes, or in places too shady for turfgrass. Several herbs make attractive, easy-to-maintain ground covers. Some are deciduous, but others provide an evergreen carpet in all seasons.

Herbal ground covers can fill those hard-to-enhance, hard-to-maintain landscaping areas around your home, such as the dry, narrow, planting strip between a sidewalk and a building wall, or a wet spot by the rainspout. Peppermint, spearmint, pennyroyal, or other mints will thrive in that wet spot, in either sun or shade. Yarrow, 'Silver King' and other artemisias, costmary, most of the sages, creeping thymes, oregano, hyssop, tansy, and gray or green santolina are all good choices for difficult dry spots. They tolerate heat, drought, and neglect.

Ground covers are a useful substitute for grass under trees and shrubs. Unlike trees in the lawn, trees in ground-cover beds are safe from bark-damaging lawn mowers and weed eaters. Choosing a single ground cover helps unify a planting of different trees and shrubs, with patches of spring bulbs for added color. The lines and form of a ground-cover bed should complement the size and style of your house and surrounding grounds. In general, large strokes work best. You can use flowing, curvilinear, organic lines or set up a more structured shape based on an underlying design grid.

Several herbs make good ground covers for shady sites under and around trees, and they also grow well on the north side of buildings, hedges, or walls. Bloodroot, sweet cicely, and wild ginger all prefer moist soil and die down to the ground in winter. Creeping germander, sweet violet, and wintergreen also do best in moist soil and are evergreen. Lady's-mantle and sweet woodruff are the most adaptable herbs to grow under trees—they don't require moist soil, and they tolerate moderate dry spells. Both are evergreen where winters are mild but die down to the ground in cold regions.

Bearberry is one of the best herbal ground covers for sunny sites or lightly shaded ones. This hardy shrub stays under 1 foot tall but spreads 4 to 8 feet wide. It has beautiful scarlet berries in fall and glossy round leaves that turn purple-bronze in cold weather but hang on all winter. Other sun-loving ground-cover herbs include lady's-mantle, yarrow, pearly everlasting, chamomile, all mints (with regular watering), creeping rosemary (hardy only to zone 8), and santolinas. For a stunning low ground cover in sun, combine different kinds of creeping thymes. Flowering thymes make a carpet of red, white, pink, and rose, and the various shades of green, gold, gray, and purplish thyme foliage are handsome before and after bloom.

Growing ground covers

Ground-cover beds require good soil preparation prior to installation as well as regular watering and weeding for the first few years after planting. Once established, however, most ground covers are relatively carefree. They benefit from an annual shearing or mowing to trim off dead shoots in early spring, and from an occasional deep soaking during dry spells in the summer.

Installing large areas of ground cover can be expensive. You can keep the cost down by using starter plants sold as rooted cuttings, typically in flats of 20 to 50 plants. Sometimes a friendly local nursery will propagate these for you on request. Plants in separate small pots cost more, but sometimes that's all you can get. Yarrow, mother-of-thyme, pearly everlasting, and chamomile are among the few herbal ground covers that can be raised from seed; all develop quickly in the first season and are hardy perennials that last from year to year.

Some ground-cover plants are better than others at excluding weeds. Herbs with dense foliage or aggressive runners, such as lady's-mantle and creeping germander, are more effective than those with airier foliage or a clumping habit. It is the sunlight reaching the weed seeds in the ground that initiates their growth. When the ground cover is mature and filled in, typically within 3 years after installation, weeding maintenance is greatly reduced, often limited to pulling a few stray weeds every now and then during the growing season.

Ground covers may or may not tolerate foot traffic. For large beds consider designing a stepping-stone path through the bed, and limit your movement to this designated route. Be sure to provide access to drifts of herbal perennials, shrubs, and trees you may have incorporated in the bed.

Herbal lawns

Many gardeners, especially those wanting to avoid excess use of fertilizers and herbicides, are starting to reconsider their lawns. Rather than continuing to fight for a perfectly pristine monoculture of turfgrass, they welcome the blend of species that nature intended. Their lawns aren't immaculate, but they are healthy, easy to care for, fun to explore, and pleasant to mow.

Several low-growing herbs can be naturalized in your lawn, where they add color, texture, and fragrance. These herbs all tolerate light foot traffic and regular mowing (set the mower blade 2 to 2½ in. high). Sweet vernal grass and sweet grass are two grasses that release a vanilla-like fragrance when mown. Yarrow and Roman chamomile both have finely divided, fernlike leaves and a sweetly pungent aroma. Mother-of-thyme forms a low carpet of tiny leaves with a spicy or lemony aroma and is covered with rosy pink flowers in summer. Sweet violet makes drifts of heart-shaped leaves and violet, blue, or white flowers. Its sweet fragrance is a nostalgic symbol of spring.

Herbal Shrubs for Hedges

Hedges are important elements in most home landscapes. They define the lines of the design, particularly when used as a living wall to enclose an outdoor space. They provide privacy and give a comforting sense of enclosure. Hedges are often used as statements of ownership to mark property boundaries and separate adjacent homes. They can screen undesirable views and reduce the noise and disturbance of passing traffic, nearby businesses or schools, or other neighborhood activities. Evergreen hedges can be located to divert cold winter winds away from the house and outdoor living areas and to protect the more tender plants in your landscape. Also, a hedge makes a great backdrop for a border of mixed perennial and annual flowers and herbs.

If you're thinking of planting a hedge, consider choosing an herbal shrub. There are several candidates, evergreen or deciduous, for different growing conditions. Evergreen conifers are especially popular, and the following examples are available from any garden center in areas where they grow well. Junipers and arborvitae require average soil and full sun. There are several cultivars with prickly or scaly foliage in different colors of green, blue-green, and gold; some turn bronzy or purplish in winter. White pine and hemlock both prefer moist soil and summers that aren't too hot. Although these two make towering trees in the forest, they can be shaped into lovely dense hedges if given an annual shearing in late spring, just after the new shoots expand.

Where winters aren't too cold, several broad-leaved evergreen shrubs do well. Tea is a hardy camellia with glossy leaves and small white or pink flowers in fall. Yaupon holly has tiny leaves and thousands of juicy red berries that last all winter. Wax myrtle has slender leaves with a wonderful aroma and silvery blue berries. Sweet bay has dark green, leathery leaves crowded on stiff branches. These four shrubs can all be clipped or allowed to develop their natural shape. They grow 8 to 12 feet tall over several years' time.

Several deciduous shrubs also make good hedges and can be used alone or in combination with each other or with evergreens. Spicebush is a popular native shrub that prefers rich, moist soil and part shade. All parts of it are fragrant, and it bears cheerful yellow flowers in early spring and shiny red berries in fall. Bayberry has glossy aromatic leaves that turn purple and hang on until late fall, finally dropping to expose clusters of waxy gray berries. European cranberry bush has lacy white flowers in spring and red berries that dangle from the bare limbs all winter. Rugosa roses have fragrant blossoms, handsome crinkly-textured foliage, and plump red fruits. These and other deciduous shrubs usually look best if they're trimmed with hand clippers, rather than sheared.

Herbal Trees

Trees grace the landscape with beauty and majesty as they provide shade, shelter, and food for people, birds, and other wildlife. Herbal trees do even more—their bark, leaves, and fruits provide flavorings, fragrances, and medicines. Planting any tree is an important and satisfying task, but deciding to plant an herbal tree adds another layer of significance.

There are several herbal trees to choose from and many ways to use them in the landscape. Individual trees make focal specimens for a lawn or planting bed. A pair of trees can frame a beautiful view. A double row of trees symmetrically arranged and regularly spaced along a drive or pathway creates an outdoor corridor or colonnade. Several trees can be spaced closer than normal and set in an irregular pattern to make a natural-looking grove, or aligned with a grid to make a formal, orchardlike setting.

Evergreen trees

Evergreen trees have a strong presence in the landscape in every season, especially winter. In cold regions, most evergreens are conifers. Juniper, arborvitae, white pine, and hemlock—the same conifers used for hedges in those regions— can also become herbal trees if left unpruned. Balsam fir, another hardy conifer, is shaped like a Christmas tree (and often used for one) and has wonderfully fragrant, shiny needles.

Sweet bay magnolia drops its leaves by early winter in zones 5 and 6, but in warmer zones it keeps its glossy, smooth foliage year-round. It is a small but graceful tree with lemon-scented white flowers in early summer and prefers part shade and rich, moist soil.

Tender evergreen herbal trees can be grown in zones 9 and 10, where winters are very mild. Lemons and other citrus are beautiful trees with shiny green leaves, sweetly fragrant flowers, and colorful tasty fruits. The dwarf and semidwarf forms in particular make excellent specimens, topiary, and espaliers for small gardens. Camphor tree is another herbal tree for mild climates. Its smooth bark and glossy leaves have a spicy fragrance. Carob trees have handsome compound leaves and interesting pods. Silver-dollar eucalyptus is wonderfully aromatic, with coin-sized round leaves in an unusual shade of silver-blue. Lemon eucalyptus is a slender tree with pale bark, drooping limbs, and oblong leaves with a rich lemony aroma.

Deciduous trees

Deciduous herbal trees are adapted to a wide variety of climatic conditions and renew their beauty as they change with the seasons. These trees are lovely sculptural elements in any landscape. Their branches trace interesting shapes against the sky and cast intriguing shadows on the ground. Their tender new leaves delight us in spring, rustle and shimmer in the summer breeze, and make a blaze of color in fall.

Trees with colorful or textured bark are good candidates for winter gardens. For example, sweet birch is an interesting herbal native tree to consider for winter interest. It has a tall straight trunk whose dark brown bark is textured with thin horizontal marks. Scratching the bark off a twig releases a spicy wintergreen aroma. Sweet birch grows best on moist or average sites in the northern and eastern United States, where it develops beautiful gold fall color.

Sweet gum is an herbal tree with shiny, dark green, star-shaped leaves that turn yellow, orange, scarlet, or purple in fall. It has a conical, upright habit and grows fairly quickly. Although native to the Southeast, it is widely planted in other parts of the United States. It is not fussy about soil and has few pests or diseases, but it drops gallons of prickly fruit balls in fall and winter. Some gardeners consider these a messy nuisance; others find them easy to rake up with the leaves and enjoy using them in holiday decorations.

Littleleaf linden is a handsome herbal shade tree that tolerates the urban environment and is often used as a street tree. It has a neat, dense, pyramidal crown; small heart-shaped leaves; and tiny, white, sweetly fragrant blossoms in early summer. Ginkgo is another popular street tree for towns and cities because it can tolerate compacted soil and polluted air. Regular ginkgos are large spreading trees, but the narrow-growing forms are tall and slender, good for small gardens. Be sure to plant a male tree, as the females bear messy, smelly fruits. Gingkos have graceful, dangling, fan-shaped leaves that turn a brilliant yellow in fall. In winter the distinct branching pattern and stubby twigs make a sculptural silhouette.

Flowering dogwood is a beautiful small herbal tree native to deciduous woodlands throughout the eastern United States. Attractive all year, it's an excellent choice for planting near an entryway or patio. It has large white or pink blossoms in spring, bright red berries in fall, and pretty dark green leaves during the summer. Dogwood's red, orange, and burgundy fall foliage is stunning in the autumn landscape. The horizontal branches with turban-shaped buds on upturned twigs are eye-catching in winter.

Another tree with four seasons of ornamental interest is Washington hawthorn. This is a versatile small native herbal tree that adapts easily to a wide variety of soil conditions. Masses of pretty white flowers in spring are followed by substantial clusters of red fruits that hang from the thorny twigs until birds eat them in late winter. The small toothed leaves are glossy green in summer, with brilliant hues of orange and red in the fall.

Witch hazel is also native to woodlands in the eastern United States. It has large rounded leaves with scalloped edges. About the time the leaves turn golden yellow and drop in October, the unique ribbonlike yellow flowers appear. This tree prefers rich, moist soil and grows well in shade or sun. It tends to sucker and spreads to make a thicket, especially on shady sites. By planting it in sun and removing the suckers, you can train it into a vase-shaped specimen tree.

Sassafras is another native that spreads by suckers. It's often seen as a broad, dome-shaped colony in old fields or open land, but if thinned to one or several shoots, it makes a single specimen with spreading limbs or a quiet grove of tall trunks. All parts of sassafras are fragrant—its roots, wood, and bark; the yellow flowers in early spring; the dark blue berries; and the mitten-shaped leaves that turn red and purple in fall.

Aspen or quaking aspen is a great native herbal tree found across the United States and famous for the brilliant yellow-gold fall color that brightens whole mountainsides in autumn. It has an upright trunk and a narrow crown and looks most inviting when planted in irregular clumps or open groves, as it grows in nature. In winter the bark has an unusual gray-green color that contrasts beautifully with dark conifers. In summer the small rounded leaves quiver in the slightest breeze and rustle entrancingly in the wind.

All of these and several other herbal trees such as smoke tree, common hoptree, and wild cherry are described in the encyclopedia section of this book. Give them careful consideration when you're thinking of planting a tree, because they offer something more than ordinary trees. Beyond shade, shelter, and beauty, herbal trees provide useful products, and they have interesting histories, too.

Cooking with Herbs

Unless you grew up in an ethnic family, chances are that salt and pepper and an occasional parsley leaf garnishing a restaurant plate were the only "herbs" you encountered as a child. As you got older, you probably became aware of other herbs, such as dill in a jar of pickles, oregano in spaghetti sauce or on pizza, or the mysterious blend called poultry seasoning that your mother rubbed on the Thanksgiving Day turkey.

But these common herbs are just the tip of the iceberg of what's available to today's cooks. Thanks to the growing interest in eating healthful foods made from natural ingredients and the increasing popularity of ethnic restaurants, we are welcoming more and more kinds of herbs into our everyday meals. Herbs are no longer just for garnishing a plate or flavoring pizza. The possibilities for adding flavor with herbs are endless, limited only by your personal taste and imagination. Salads, appetizers, soups, breads, beverages, and even desserts can all be enhanced by the addition of a well-chosen herb or spice.

While the supermarket will continue to be the source for exotic spices such as vanilla beans and cinnamon, there are many advantages to growing your own herbs. Homegrown herbs offer freshness, quality, purity, variety, and economy—values you can't take for granted in purchased herbs. Herbs produced in developing countries may have been sprayed with pesticides that are restricted here. Then, to top it off, most imported herbs are fumigated or irradiated prior to sale. Herb products may be contaminated with weeds or other plants, the plants may be misidentified, or they may be surrogates. For example, the oregano you buy in a commercial spice jar may not be true oregano at all but another plant that smells (but not necessarily tastes) similar.

By contrast, when you grow your own herbs, you have almost complete control over the whole process from beginning to end. You decide which varieties to grow, whether or not to spray, when and what to pick, and how to use or preserve what you harvest. Once you discover the flavor and quality of homegrown herbs, you'll find more and more ways to include them in your meals.

Guidelines for Using Herbs

Growing and harvesting fresh herbs is one of the pleasantest jobs in the garden, but first you have to know your plants. Most important is the need to distinguish between edible plants and inedible look-alikes. Just as you wouldn't eat a wild mushroom without knowing what kind it was, don't even think about tasting a plant unless you can name it with confidence. Learn to use botanical names, as the same common name is sometimes applied to several different plants. Most reputable herb nurseries provide botanical names on the plants they sell.

Although allergic reactions to herbs are rare, they do occur. Certain herbs, such as chamomile, are likelier than others to trigger an allergic response, but any plant has the potential for producing allergies in sensitive individuals.

When expanding your use of herbs and spices in cooking, it's best to begin with small amounts. If you and your family like the flavor, you can add more the next time. Gradually you'll develop more confidence in deciding which herbs to include and how much of each to use.

Remember that herbs are used for flavor, not for texture. Be sure to remove woody stems or twigs before you add herbs to a dish. Chop tough leaves such as rosemary into tiny bits, and crumble dried herbs into fine flakes. Extract leathery leaves such as bay leaves before serving the food.

Preserving Fresh Herbs

Fresh leaves from most herbs can be harvested throughout the growing season. This continuous pruning often makes the plants bushier and improves their appearance. Prime time for picking is in the morning, after the dew has evaporated and before the hot sun has begun to dissipate the volatile oils that give herbs their flavor.

Some herbs, such as chives and oregano, can be harvested over a very long season, especially in regions where winters are mild, but many other herbs flourish only during the summer months. Fortunately, it's easy to preserve homegrown herbs for year-round use. Several methods are described below, with their advantages and disadvantages. Try experimenting with different methods to see what works best in your situation and for your favorite herbs.

Fresh bouquet method

Many fresh herbs from the garden can be stored for up to a week or more, just as you would store fresh flowers. Gather little snippets, leaving stems long enough to place in a vase of warmish water. Strip the leaves that would be submerged under water, as you would with flowers, to prevent mold. Use these trimmings immediately, or dry them on a clean paper towel for storage. Change the water in the vase regularly to eliminate bacteria.

A majority of fresh herbs will stay perky when stored this way. A few, such as dill, will flop over no matter how soon you get them into water, but they keep their flavor anyway. Parsley and basil are two herbs that do better in a vase than if stored in the refrigerator's vegetable drawer. The cool, dry environment of the refrigerator tends to wilt parsley and discolor basil.

Advantages: The bouquet method keeps fresh herbs in sight, reminding you to use them, and it adds a decorative and fragrant touch to the kitchen counter. Disadvantages: This method is limited to short-term storage. Stems will rot if the water is not changed or if leaves are submerged. Some herbs may look wilted and untidy.

Air drying

For many centuries, herbs have been preserved by air drying. Traditionally, small bundles of fresh herbs would be tied and hung in front of the kitchen fireplace or in a special room called a stillroom, dried until crisp, then placed in airtight containers until a recipe called for their use. Today, air drying is still the primary technique for preserving most fresh herbs harvested from the garden.

Some gardeners start by washing the herbs to remove any dust or insects. The easiest way to do this is to spray the plants with a hose early in the morning, then harvest after the sun has evaporated the extra moisture. Gather small bunches of stems and secure them with rubberbands. (Rubberbands are better than string because they contract as the stems dry and shrink, holding the bundles together.) Make the bundles small, so air can circulate around the stems and reduce the chance of mildew formation or uneven drying. If you have stalks of herb seeds such as dill, fennel, or mustard, put them inside a paper bag to catch the seeds as they dry.

Put the bundled herbs in a dry, well-ventilated, not-too-hot place, away from direct sun. You can hang them up or spread them out flat on screens, racks, or slatted trays. Don't crowd them close together—leave plenty of space between and around them. If there's a cabinet above the refrigerator in your kitchen, you can convert it into an ideal, dust-free, out-of-the-way place for drying herbs. Replace the solid shelves with customized screen trays, and drill some holes in the cabinet base and top so air warmed by the refrigerator coils can flow up through the herbs.

Check frequently and turn or adjust the bundles to make sure they dry evenly and no mold forms. When the herbs feel crisp and brittle, transfer them to lidded glass jars. Try not to crumble the leaves when you do this, as every break in a dried leaf or stem releases some of the herb's oils and causes flavor loss. Store the containers out of direct sunlight and away from heat sources.

Advantages: Air drying is quick and inexpensive, and most herbs retain good flavor this way. Disadvantages: Herbs can mildew if the humidity is high. If left too long, they can get too dry and dusty and lose flavor.

Slow oven drying

If you don't have a good place for air-drying herbs, or if your climate is simply too rainy or humid for air-drying, you can dry herbs in the oven of your stove. A gas stove with a pilot light is ideal. To use an electric oven or gas oven with electric ignition, preheat the oven at the lowest setting, then turn it off. Spread herbs in a single layer on a cookie sheet and put it in the oven. Leave the oven door slightly ajar to allow air to circulate. The herbs may need to be stirred or re-arranged occasionally to ensure even drying. They should be crispy dry within a few days. Of course, don't forget to remove them before preheating the oven for dinner!

Advantages: Oven drying is faster than air drying. Disadvantages: Only limited amounts can be dried at one time, and the herbs must be watched carefully to avoid overdrying. This method can be a nuisance if you use the oven a lot.

Microwave drying

The possibility of drying herbs in a matter of minutes is appealing to today's busy people, but this method is tricky. It requires some experimentation with your particular microwave oven, a watchful eye, and a finger that's quick at the "stop" button.

Depending on the succulence of the herb being dried, processing time will vary. Begin by spreading about a cup of fresh herbs between two paper towels and cook on the high setting for one minute. Check for dryness, repeating the process for smaller increments of time until the herbs are completely dry. Replace the bottom paper towel if it becomes too moist. Some herbs may need to be stirred, rearranged, or removed as they dry.

Because of the high temperatures and internal cooking involved, microwave drying may result in more flavor loss than other methods. You be the judge. In any case, microwaves are wonderful for drying herbal flowers such as nasturtiums and violets to be used as garnishes, where color rather than flavor is the important factor.

Advantages: Microwave drying is very fast, and the herbs retain good color. It's convenient when you want to dry small amounts of herbs in a hurry. Disadvantages: Only small batches can be dried at one time. The herbs may scorch or overcook if not timed carefully, and they may lose flavor. Be careful; paper towels can catch on fire if they get too hot and dry.

Dehydrator drying

Using an electric food dehydrator is a terrific way to dry herbs while retaining their fresh green color. Most dehydrators come with manufacturer's instructions for drying herbs, so guesswork is mostly eliminated. Dehydrators are designed to dry food by the combination of constant air circulation and relatively low heat (105° to 115° F). Although low, this temperature is still higher than usual for air drying, and some herbs, such as basil, may lose flavor in a dehydrator. Experiment, and taste the results to see what you think.

Advantages: Most herbs retain good flavor and color. Manufacturers supply instructions and recommended timing. This method doesn't require constant watching. Disadvantages: Batches are limited to the size of the dehydrator. Some flavor loss may occur.

Cold drying

This relatively new method of preservation is especially good for drying herbs such as parsley, dill, and chives that lose most of their flavor when air-dried or heat-dried. It takes more time but uses no heat; in fact, the drying is done in a frost-free refrigerator. To dry fresh herbs in the refrigerator, spread them in a thin layer on a tray, plate, or wire rack such as the type used for cooling cakes and pies. A small square of wire-mesh hardware cloth works well, too. If the tray or rack would be a nuisance, you can hang small bundles or net bags of herbs on magnetic hooks or clips on the inside of the refrigerator door or walls. Check for dryness daily. This method can take up to a week or more depending on outside humidity.

Advantages: Flavor and color are retained. Herbs are kept in sight where you'll check them frequently. Disadvantages: The herbs dry slowly, and extra trays or racks get in the way of regular refrigerator use.

Freezing

Many herbs can be frozen dry or in water. This is the best way to preserve chives, in particular, and also works very well for parsley and dill. Chop clean, dry leaves into small pieces with scissors or a knife or in a food processor, and seal them in a plastic freezer bag or container. This method will keep them flavorful and green. Other herbs may discolor or get mushy when frozen dry but will keep well if frozen in water. Put chopped herbs in plastic ice cube trays and add just enough water to cover. When completely frozen, remove the cubes from the trays and store in freezer bags or containers. If you freeze different herbs, be sure to label which is which, since they all look the same in ice.

Advantages: Large quantities can be preserved in this way, and individual cubes are convenient to use. Disadvantages: Some herbs don't freeze well. Unless you have a separate freezer unit, space may be limited.

Preserving in oil as pastes

Preserving chopped fresh herbs in an oil base is an excellent way of adding fresh flavor when dried herbs just won't do. The best example of this process is pesto, traditionally made from a combination of fresh basil, pine nuts, olive oil, parsley, garlic, and Parmesan cheese. Herb pastes don't, however, have to be as complex as pesto to give a fresh-from-the-garden flavor.

To preserve herbs in oil, you need to chop the fresh herbs in a food processor or blender, using a ratio of 2 cups packed herb leaves to ½ cup vegetable oil. While olive oil is the traditional choice for herb pestos, you may want to use a lighter-flavored oil such as canola or safflower to avoid an overpowering oily taste in the final recipe. Different herbs can be processed this way, and you can also add parsley or chives to a mixture. Remember to cut chives into short pieces before adding them to the blender, to keep them from becoming hopelessly entwined around the blades.

Herb pastes can be used fresh or can be stored in the refrigerator for a maximum of 2 weeks. Herbs packed in oil can develop botulism, so freezing is required for long-term storage. Small frozen portions are especially convenient. Try filling a plastic ice cube tray with the paste; when frozen, the cubes can be popped out and stored in a freezer bag or resealable container. If properly sealed, herb pastes will keep in the freezer for 1 to 2 years.

Advantages: Fresh herb flavor and color are preserved. Disadvantages: Herb pastes may become dangerously rancid if not used promptly or frozen. Oil adds extra fat to recipes.

Preserving in vinegar

Herbs can be used to flavor vinegar for special salad dressings, and they can also be preserved in vinegar as a method of storage. Unlike herbs packed in oil, vinegar solutions contain enough acid to prohibit the growth of botulism. To preserve herbs in vinegar, wash the herbs and pat dry with a paper towel. Pack in enough herbs to fill a clean wide-mouth jar, and add vinegar until they are completely submerged. Cap the jar and store in the pantry or refrigerator. To flavor the vinegar itself, heat it before pouring it over the herbs, and put the jar in a sunny place to steep for about 2 weeks.

Advantages: The acid base makes for a long, safe shelf life. Flavored vinegars make attractive gifts. Disadvantages: The vinegar flavor limits uses for herbs preserved this way, and some herbs become mushy and discolored.

Herbs for Tea

Many herbs slip easily into a cup or pot of hot water to become a delicious tea. Taken hot or cold, for health or pleasure, herb teas are increasingly popular beverages.

To make herb tea, bring a pot of water to a boil, then pour it over the tea herbs and steep for 5 to 10 minutes. Strain and serve. As a rule of thumb, use 1 heaping teaspoon of herb for each cup of water. Remember that dried herbs are usually, but not always, stronger flavored than fresh herbs, and adjust the amounts accordingly.

To make tea for a crowd, try preparing a concentrate ahead of time. Pour a quart of boiling water over $2/3$ cup or more of loose dried herbs. Cover and let stand for 10 minutes, then stir and strain into a clean teapot or pitcher. To serve, pour about 2 teaspoons of concentrate into each serving cup, and fill with hot water. This concentrate is also good for making iced tea. You can prepare a batch and keep it in the refrigerator for several days. To use, add a few tablespoons of concentrate to a glass and fill with water and ice.

Popular Tea Herbs to Grow

Common name (Latin name)	Part used
Anise hyssop (*Agastache foeniculum*)	Leaves, flowers
Basil (*Ocimum basilicum*)	Leaves
Bee balm (*Monarda didyma*)	Leaves
Catnip (*Nepeta cataria*)	Leaves
Chamomile, German (*Matricaria recutita*)	Flowers
Chamomile, Roman (*Chamaemelum nobile*)	Flowers
Goldenrod, sweet (*Solidago odora*)	Leaves
Lemon balm (*Melissa officinalis*)	Leaves
Lemon grass (*Cymbopogon citratus*)	Leaves
Lemon verbena (*Aloysia triphylla*)	Leaves
Mexican mint marigold (*Tagetes lucida*)	Leaves
Mints (*Mentha* spp.)	Leaves
Raspberry, blackberry (*Rubus* spp.)	Leaves
Roselle (*Hibiscus sabdariffa*)	Flower calyxes
Rugosa rose (*Rosa rugosa*)	Hips (fruits)
Sage, garden (*Salvia officinalis*)	Leaves
Sage, pineapple (*Salvia elegans*)	Leaves

Ideas for Cooking with Herbs

Pasta and rice
• Use a pinch of safflower petals for a saffronlike color.
• Add poppy seeds and chopped parsley to buttered noodles.

Poultry and meat
• Make a marinade for pork or chicken with $1/2$ cup soy sauce, 1 tbsp. lemon juice, and 1 tbsp. grated fresh ginger root.
• Place sprigs of fresh sage, rosemary, tarragon, and/or thyme under the skin of a chicken or turkey before roasting.
• Sprinkle a beef roast or pot roast with finely chopped rosemary.
• After thickening veal pan drippings, add $1/2$ tsp. dill and sour cream to form a creamy gravy.

Fish and seafood
• Use fresh sorrel leaves in tuna sandwiches or salad, instead of lettuce, to give a lemony tang.
• Add lemon thyme to clam chowder.
• Grill fresh fish over fresh sprigs of fennel or thyme.
• Use a bundle of fresh herbs as a basting brush for grilled seafood.

Eggs
• Fold fresh tarragon leaves into a cream cheese omelet filling for a breakfast or dinner entrée.
• In a lunch box, include a packet of chopped chives, dill, or tarragon to sprinkle on hard cooked eggs.

Cheese
• Add flavor to grilled cheese sandwiches by dusting the inner sides of the bread with ground cumin before grilling.
• Use a pinch of cayenne pepper to add zip to sharp cheddar cheese dishes.
• Add chopped chives to cream cheese or cottage cheese.

Vegetables
• Toss steamed vegetables with chopped fresh dill and sour cream.
• Sauté squash slices in butter with a few whorls of sweet woodruff.
• Use chopped fresh mint leaves to add a cool flavor to steamed peas.
• Sprinkle fresh rosemary over potato slices before roasting.
• Coat boiled new potatoes with butter and fresh parsley or dill.
• Add coriander seeds to the water used for steaming artichokes.

Fruit
• Mince cinnamon basil or pineapple sage and mix with yogurt or sour cream as a dip or topping for fresh berries and fruit.
• Use sprigs of mint or lemon balm to garnish sherbets.
• Dust homemade applesauce with freshly ground coriander.

Breads, cakes, and cookies
• Make a quick hors d'oeuvre by topping thick slices of Italian bread with homemade or store-bought hummus, crumbled feta cheese, a drizzle of olive oil, and fresh chopped oregano.
• Add orange juice and fresh chopped rosemary to muffin batter.
• Add lavender flowers to a sugar cookie recipe.
• Use chives to give an onion flavor to old-fashioned soda biscuits.
• Line a cake pan with scented geranium leaves before baking to impart a subtle flavor to pound cake or yellow cake.

Fragrant Herbs

After years of neglect, gardeners have rediscovered fragrance, and "fragrant" is now a much-used word in plant catalogs, garden magazines, and books. To most people, a fragrant plant means a plant with fragrant flowers, so the current trend features roses, lilies, daphnes, viburnums, jasmines, stocks, daturas, narcissus, freesias, and other delightful blossoms. Fragrance adds an extra dimension of pleasure to any garden, and herb gardeners welcome today's wider choice and increased supply of plants with fragrant flowers. But to herb gardeners, fragrance isn't a new discovery. These gardeners have always treasured fragrant plants, and they realize that fragrance can emanate from leaves and stems, seeds and fruits, bark and wood, and even roots, as well as from flowers. Further, although the fragrance of flowers is usually fleeting, the fragrant compounds produced in these other plant parts can sometimes be preserved for years by the simple technique of drying.

Botanists believe that the fragrance of flowers serves a definite purpose: to attract pollinators. For example, some of the most fragrant flowers, such as flowering tobacco or evening stocks, release their fragrance only after dusk, when the moths that pollinate them are active. Moths are very sensitive to fragrance; in the dark, it's one of the best ways to locate a flower. By contrast, flowers that have evolved to attract hummingbirds are rarely fragrant, since hummingbirds have virtually no sense of smell and instead use their excellent vision to look for flowers.

Surprisingly, scientists have few explanations for the other fragrant compounds that plants produce. There's no simple answer to the question of why some plants have intensely aromatic leaves or roots when most others don't. Only recently have some botanists proposed that fragrant compounds produced by a plant may help protect it from infection by fungi or bacteria or may deter herbivores, and so far there have been only a few detailed studies of these interactions. These initial reports reveal a wonderfully balanced give-and-take between plants and other organisms and pose a fascinating challenge to the traditional view of plants as passive fodder.

But we don't have to understand why plants make fragrant compounds in order to appreciate the results. Fragrances from plants touch many aspects of our lives, as they are used commercially to perfume soaps, lotions, powders, cleansers, polishes, inks, stationery, air fresheners, candles, and countless other products. Easy as it is to buy these products off the shelf, there's real fulfillment in growing your own fragrant herbs and preserving them for future enjoyment.

Fragrant Herbs to Grow

There are dozens of fragrant herbs to choose from, and many herbs that are used primarily as culinary herbs or medicinal herbs are also notable for their fragrance. For example, rosemary, basil, and sweet marjoram are as desirable for their perfumes as for their flavors. Passionflower and meadowsweet have very fragrant blossoms, but they're used chiefly as medicinal herbs. No matter where you live, if you have a sunny spot for an herb garden, you can fill it entirely with fragrant herbs and still not grow all that are available. Growing fragrant herbs can be a lifelong pursuit, because the choices are so numerous and so diverse.

One way to review the options is to think of how fragrance is produced in different parts of plants. Roses, lavenders, pinks, jasmines, and violets are outstanding for their fragrant flowers. Fennel, coriander, cardamom, sweet cicely, spicebush, bayberry, and lemon all have fragrant fruits or seeds. Sweet birch, wild cherry, and cinnamon have fragrant bark. Pine and red cedar have fragrant wood. Vetiver, sweet flag, orrisroot, lovage, and wild sarsaparilla have fragrant roots or rhizomes. Scented geraniums, artemisias, eucalyptus, and countless herbs in the mint family—mints, mountain mints, calamints, catmints, thymes, salvias, basils, agastaches, lemon balm, rosemary, lavenders, savories, hyssop, and many more—all have fragrant leaves. Unlike the fragrance of flowers, which wafts on the air and typically can be detected at great distance, the aromas produced by other plant parts usually don't float on the breeze. You may have to rub, scratch, or cut an herb to detect its fragrance. Then, breathe deep! First-time visitors to an herb garden are often amazed at the intense aromas hidden in plain green leaves.

Usually the fragrance is concentrated in one part of an herb plant, but it's not uncommon for an herb to produce different fragrances in different parts of the plant. Sometimes all parts of the plant are fragrant, each with slightly—or significantly—different aromas. Lovage, sweet cicely, sassafras, sweet bay magnolia, white pine, eastern red cedar, and lemon are examples of these herbal overachievers. They're all pretty to look at, too, and deserve a place of honor in any herb garden where conditions are suitable.

If you like to focus or specialize on a particular group, it's interesting to collect herbs that share a fragrance, such as lemon-scented herbs. A lemon theme garden could include lemon grass, lemon verbena, lemon balm, lemon thyme, lemon-scented geraniums, lemon-scented eucalyptus, a lemon tree, 'Lemon Gem' marigold, and lemon lilies (*Hemerocallis lilio-asphodelus,* not really an herb, but a lovely old-fashioned daylily with fragrant clear yellow blossoms in early summer). Another popular group for a theme planting would feature plants that produce coumarin, a compound with a vanilla-like fragrance that gives the aroma to new-mown hay. This group includes sweet woodruff, sweet grass, sweet vernal grass, sweet clovers (*Melilotus officinalis* and *M. alba*), deer's tongue (*Trilisa odoratissima*), vanilla-leaf (*Achlys triphylla*), and several other perennials. Other fragrances that show up in various plants are the aromas we call mint, oregano, caraway, pine, and balsam.

Essential Oils

Commercially, fragrant herbs are usually not used in bulk. Instead, the fragrance of an herb is extracted, normally by distillation, into a very concentrated liquid form called an essential oil—"essential" because it captures the very essence of the herb, and "oil" because the liquid is oily and doesn't mix with water. It takes truckloads of herb material to produce a small bottle of essential oil, and the product is so concentrated that a single drop can perfume a whole room.

It's impractical to extract essential oils at home—the process takes specialized equipment and agricultural-scale quantities of herbs. You can buy essential oils from mail-order suppliers or in local stores that sell herbs, health foods, and other natural products. Essential oil typically is packaged in ½-ounce glass bottles and costs $3 to $7 per bottle. Be aware that quality varies, depending on the source and quality of the herb that was used, the extraction process, and whether or not the product was diluted or extended with any synthetic oils or solvents.

Try putting a few drops of essential oil on a cotton ball and touching it to a light bulb or radiator; the heat will cause the oil to evaporate quickly and perfume a room. Most people enjoy the fragrance of cinnamon, jasmine, pine, or lavender. In the summer, put a drop of lemon, orange blossom, or vetiver oil on the air-conditioner grill. Use a cotton ball oiled with peppermint, eucalyptus, lemon verbena, or lavender oil to freshen the air in a musty closet or basement, a stale-smelling car, or a house or apartment that's been vacant. Try adding a few drops of your favorite essential oil to a tub of bathwater, or mix a few drops into a jar of almond or jojoba oil to use as skin lotion. But be careful: don't use these oils to flavor food or tea, and avoid handling essential oils during pregancy. Because essential oils are so concentrated, it's important to treat them with restraint and caution. Used in excess, their powerful aromas can be unpleasant or disturbing. What you perceive as a delightful perfume presence may seem overbearing to someone else. Experiment with small amounts of different oils to see how their aromas affect you and your family and friends.

Potpourri

Potpourri is a mixture of dried herbal flowers and leaves that are chosen and treated in a way that maximizes both the intensity and the longevity of their fragrance. Traditionally, making potpourri was both an art and a science. Choosing a combination of herbal fragrances that coordinate into a pleasing blend is an art that takes judgment and experience. Treating the herbs to make a long-lasting product is a science that requires a knowledge of suitable fixatives and how to use them. The purpose of a fixative is to enhance and stabilize the fragrance of the potpourri and to fix or capture it so that it won't evaporate too fast. Salt is a mineral fixative. Orris-root, sweet flag root, lemon and orange peels, and the resins from sweet gum, balsam fir, and other trees are herbal products used as fixatives. Cinnamon, cloves, and other spices are sometimes added to potpourri for their fragrance, and they may have a fixative function as well.

Except in the workrooms of a few devoted herbalists, potpourri making is not an art or a science now. It's a big business. Factories make tons of the stuff, and you can buy it in cellophane packets at any gift shop, drugstore, grocery store, or discount center. Much of what is sold as potpourri today is an insult to the tradition. It generally consists of wood chips or ground corncobs, dyed in fashion colors, dosed with essential oil (or more often with synthetic fragrance), and decorated with a few dried flowers, miniature pinecones, or seedpods that look cute but are irrelevant to the fragrance. In this guise, potpourri has become as common as sliced bread, but, unfortunately, the difference between dyed, dosed wood-chip potpourri and all-natural potpourri made from homegrown herbs is like the difference between an air-filled loaf of white bread and a solid loaf of sourdough or whole-grain bread.

Actually, making potpourri is a lot like baking bread. It helps to start with a recipe, but as you gain experience, you learn how to adjust or make your own recipes. You need a bread-bowl-sized container (plastic pails or tubs are good) and a wooden spoon for stirring. After you first measure and combine the ingredients, the work is intermittent. You let potpourri age, stirring it at regular intervals, just as you let bread rise. Either project, baking bread or mixing potpourri, makes the house smell good. There isn't space in this book to give recipes and detailed instructions, but there are several books about potpourri listed in the appendices on pp. 433–434.

Fragrant Dried Products

The easiest way to preserve fragrant herbs at home is to dry them. Many herbs keep their fragrance for months or years when dried carefully and quickly and stored in a dry environment. To dry fragrant herbs, follow the same methods described on pp. 72–75 in the essay "Cooking with Herbs." There are many ways to use dried fragrant herbs in your home. Here are a few ideas to get you started.

• Fill small cloth bags with dried herbs to make sachets for your closets and drawers. Use lavenders, roses, carnations, vetiver, rosemary, sweet marjoram, balsam fir, lemon verbena, various scented geraniums, patchouli, sweet grass, or other herbs of your choice, singly or in blends.

• Use camphor basil, pennyroyal, eucalyptus, southernwood, or rosemary to make moth-repellent sachets for protecting wool sweaters and blankets. For full protection, close the woolens and sachets inside a tight-fitting chest, box, or drawer—don't leave them out in the open air. Replace the sachets at least once a year.

• Fill a small pillow with lavender, sweet woodruff, or hops and keep it in your bed. Squeeze the pillow and breathe deeply to induce calm, restful sleep. If you like, add mint, lemon verbena, and/or sweet marjoram.

• Put a few spoonfuls of dried (or fresh) lemon thyme, lemon verbena, rose-scented geranium, sweet cicely seeds, sweet flag rhizomes, vetiver roots, fir or pine needles, or other fragrant herbs into a small porous bag made of loosely woven cotton or cheesecloth. Put the bag in a mixing bowl and cover with boiling water. Let steep for 5 minutes, then add the bag of herbs and the fragrant water to a tub of hot water, and enjoy a fragrant bath.

• When you have a cold, use eucalyptus, camphor basil, peppermint, spearmint, sage, rosemary, common thyme, or yarrow to make a perfumed bath. The sharp, penetrating aromas of these herbs help clear a stuffy nose and relieve congestion.

• Save the woody stems and twigs when you prune rosemary, basil, lavender, spicebush, sassafras, juniper, and other fragrant herbs, and toss them in the fireplace, wood stove, or barbecue grill. The smoke is as fragrant as burning incense.

• Attach long, pliable shoots of sweet Annie, wormwood, 'Silver King' and other artemisias, ambrosia, rosemary, eucalyptus, bay, Cleveland sage, garden sage, and other herbs to a straw or grapevine base to make a decorative wreath. (Use fresh herbs to make the wreath, then hang it to dry.) Brush or shake the wreath occasionally to release more fragrance.

An Introduction to Medicinal Herbs

Some gardeners might consider the medicinal uses of herbs as nothing more than history, a throwback to medieval times, something perhaps our grandmothers used, but certainly not a subject of current relevance. The facts tell a different story. Medicinal and aromatic plants play an exceedingly important role in human affairs today, as they have from the beginning of time.

Historical Underpinnings

Herbal medicine has thrived since antiquity. *Shen-Nong Ben Cao Jing,* the earliest Chinese herbal, survives as a list of 366 drugs, attributed to the divine plowman emperor Shen-Nong, believed to have lived about 2800 B.C. Shen-Nong's list names most of the herbs still used in China's system of traditional medicine. Among the drugs included by Shen-Nong was ephedra, source of the alkaloids ephedrine and pseudo-ephedrine, ingredients in many decongestant products now available at any pharmacy. The famous *Ebers Papyrus* of Egypt dates to 1550 B.C. and mentions many plant drugs used today, including opium and aloes. The *De Materia Medica* of

Dioscorides, the classic medical work of the Greek physician who served as a surgeon in the Roman army, was written in A.D. 78. It served as the basic source of information for drugs used in Western medicine for more than 14 centuries.

Then, in the 1500s, a Swiss physician known as Paracelsus advocated the development of chemical medicines from mineral salts, acids, and other substances. This began a process of change that continued over several centuries in Western medicine, culminating in the United States in the 20th century. Herbs were gradually replaced by mineral drugs and later by synthetic drugs. Now chemical medicines reign, but herbs still play a greater role than many people realize.

Medicinal Plants in the Modern World

Botanists conservatively estimate that there are a quarter million flowering (higher) plant species on Earth. An economic botanist with the United States Department of Agriculture, Dr. James A. Duke, has created a database of folk remedies worldwide, which includes up to 80,000 species. From these figures it can be estimated that at least one-third of the world's flowering plants have been used for medicinal purposes at one time or another.

Dr. Norman Farnsworth, of the Program for Collaborative Research in the Pharmaceutical Sciences, University of Illinois, Chicago, has often stated that as much as 25 percent of the prescription drugs sold in the United States contain at least one plant-derived ingredient. Seven of the 20 best-selling drugs in the United States are based on or modeled after compounds derived from plants.

For example, bark from willows (*Salix* spp.) traditionally was used in teas to relieve the pain and inflammation of rheumatism. Its effectiveness can be explained by the presence of salicin, a compound with anti-inflammatory and analgesic properties similar to its chemical cousin, acetylsalicylic acid, better known as aspirin. The anti-anxiety agent reserpine, which was developed in the early 1950s, is an alkaloid from the Indian snakeroot (*Rauwolfia serpentina*). Traditional Indian herbalists used snakeroot as a treatment for lunacy.

Other important examples include the alkaloids vincristine and vinblastine from the Madagascar periwinkle (*Catharanthus roseus*), familiar as a bedding plant that blooms all summer, even in hot weather. These alkaloids, first isolated in the mid-1960s, are important agents in chemotherapy for various forms of cancer, especially leukemia and Hodgkin's disease. Glycosides of the foxglove (*Digitalis purpurea*) are regularly prescribed for various conditions associated with heart disease treatment.

The plant kingdom has been the primary source of raw material for the biosynthesis of steroidal hormones, a group of drugs with unequaled social, economic, and political impact. Consider, for example, the birth control pill. Its progesterone precursors were derived from compounds in Mexican yams (*Dioscorea* spp.).

With all the advances of modern medicine, there is still nothing to replace morphine, derived from the opium poppy (*Papaver somniferum*), as a pain reliever for major trauma. Taxol, derived from various species of yew, such as the Pacific yew (*Taxus brevifolia*), was approved by the Food and Drug Administration (FDA) in early 1993 for the treatment of ovarian cancer. In the next few years, it will probably be approved for use against a number of other difficult-to-treat cancers. The impact of medicinal plants is not only undeniable, it is dramatic.

The Example of Traditional Chinese Medicine

Even today, a larger percentage of the world's population relies on traditional forms of medicine, such as herbal medicine, than on orthodox Western medicine for primary health care. The World Health Organization (WHO) has estimated that as much as 80 percent of the world's population relies on traditional medicine. The WHO's Traditional Medicine Programme has helped governments, primarily in developing countries, to integrate traditional medicine systems into national primary health care delivery systems.

The most famous example is traditional Chinese medicine, which relies on herbal combination prescriptions along with acupuncture and specialized diagnostic techniques such as pulse diagnosis. It serves as much as 60 percent of China's rural population and 40 percent of urban residents—not as folk medicine but as primary health care. More than 500 different plants are cited as "official drugs" in the 1985 *Pharmacopoeia of the People's Republic of China*.

Nearly 7,000 medicinal plants are recognized in China, either as official drugs or as folk medicines. American gardeners are familiar with many of these plants, such as daylily, forsythia, blackberry lily, and gingko. Unaware of their medicinal properties, we think of them simply as ornamentals. The Chinese know them as herbs.

Medicinal Herb Products in the United States

Given the abundance of medicinal plants, why are so few herb products actually labeled with therapeutic claims in the United States? Because of government regulations. Before any new drug can be put on the market, it has to be proven safe and effective. The intent of these regulations, of course, is to protect consumers from dangerous products and spurious claims. But the regulations themselves have had an unintended side effect, which is to direct drug research away from simple herb products.

It's estimated that the cost of developing and testing a new drug now exceeds $350 million. It takes years to recoup an investment like that, even with the guarantee of exclusive rights to market the product for up to 22 years. Therefore, plant drug research in the United States is limited largely to isolating or synthesizing complex molecules that can be patented. Plenty of herbs are indeed safe and effective, but anyone can grow them at home. No pharmaceutical company is going to spend millions of dollars testing a plant product that's common and inexpensive.

Thousands of herb products are available in the United States, but they are sold as "dietary supplements"—as foods, not drugs. The primary outlets for these products are health and natural food stores. A growing number of pharmacies carry them also. Since these products are technically and legally foods, rather than drugs, the product labels cannot include any information on medicinal uses. Garlic is a good example. Everyone is familiar with the culinary uses of garlic, but many people are unaware of medical research that shows that garlic can benefit the circulatory system and may help prevent major cardiovascular disease, if used at appropriate doses over a specified period of time. Under present laws, however, a consumer cannot learn about these health benefits of garlic from the product label or from the seller.

Herb Products in Germany

The situation in some European countries is quite different. In Germany, for instance, medicinal herb products such teas, capsules, and liquids—often the same products sold as dietary supplements in the United States—are allowed to carry therapeutic claims. These products include the whole plant or plant part in the formulation, rather than just a single isolated chemical compound. Such products are known in Europe as "phytomedicines."

The German BGA, the equivalent of our FDA, has a separate committee known as the "Commission E" that develops regulations for herb products. They define phytomedicines as therapeutic agents derived from plants or parts of plants, or preparations made from them, but not isolated chemically defined substances. A phytomedicine must therefore represent the totality of the medicinal plant, or one of its parts (for example, root, leaf, flower, or fruit), rather than a single isolated compound. By contrast, only isolated, purified compounds derived from plants, rather than whole plant extracts, would be considered drugs in the United States.

The Commission E has produced nearly 300 "Therapeutic Monographs on Medicinal Products for Human Use." Each monograph, published in the German *Federal Gazette* (*Bundesanzeiger*), describes the constituents of an herb product, its general properties or therapeutic value, indications, contraindications (if any), side effects (if known), interactions with other drugs or agents (if known), details on dosage, and the method of administration. This set of monographs provides the best information available today on the proper use of many phytomedicines. German medical students are required to take courses in the clinical use of herbal medicines and must pass a section on phytomedicines in the license exams.

The combination of rational regulation and professional education means that German consumers can choose from a wide array of well-defined, quality-assured, properly labeled, and safe medicinal herb products, many of which are prescribed or recommended by doctors and pharmacists. About three-fourths of the German women interviewed in a recent survey said they use herbal teas for health benefits, and more than half of the women said they take herbal remedies, at least in the beginning stages of a disease.

What medicinal herb products used in European households might be familiar to Americans? Consider parsley, sage, rosemary, and thyme. Preparations of fresh or dried parsley are used for ailments of the lower urinary tract and the prevention of renal gravel. Sage preparations are used as a gargle for sore throats and as tea for upset stomachs. Rosemary preparations can relieve digestive complaints, and external applications provide therapy for rheumatic diseases and circulatory problems. Small doses of thyme leaves or extract are used for bronchitis and catarrh in the upper respiratory tract. These four and several other common culinary herbs are included in the German monographs and labeled for therapeutic use in a number of European countries.

Native American Medicinal Plants

In recent years, many American gardeners have taken an interest in growing native trees, shrubs, grasses, and wildflowers. More and more native plants are being propagated by nurseries and distributed through local garden centers and specialty mail-order catalogs. Magazine articles and books such as *Taylor's Guide to Natural Gardening* (Boston:

Houghton Mifflin, 1993) describe outstanding natives and tell how to use them in your garden.

Many gardeners recognize Joe-Pye weed (*Eupatorium purpureum*), queen-of-the-prairie (*Filipendula rubra*), black cohosh (*Cimicifuga racemosa*), flowering dogwood (*Cornus florida*), and arborvitae (*Thuja occidentalis*) as common ornamentals that are native to North America. But how many gardeners realize that these plants have medicinal value? Like the Chinese plants cited earlier, these popular plants are more than just ornamentals. They all have a long history of herbal use by Native Americans, and many were important to the early settlers and pioneers.

Some American medicinal plants are significant today. One of the most outstanding groups is the genus *Echinacea*, or purple coneflowers. Nine species of echinacea are found exclusively in North America. In Europe, preparations of several species are used to help stimulate the immune system. Taken at the first sign of symptoms, they help prevent colds and flus. Other echinacea products are used externally for hard-to-heal wounds and sores. More than 280 different echinacea products, offered by dozens of manufacturers, are registered and available in Germany.

Several native American medicinal plants are included in this guide, along with many medicinal herbs that grow wild here but are not native. The early settlers brought along their favorite European herbs, and a number of these plants are now common as weeds and wildflowers along roadsides, in pastures and clearings, and on vacant lots. Yarrow (*Achillea millefolium*), coltsfoot (*Tussilago farfara*), ground ivy (*Glechoma hederacea*), heal-all (*Prunella vulgaris*), plantain (*Plantago major*), mullein (*Verbascum thapsus*), and St.-John's-wort (*Hypericum perforatum*) are just a few of the many examples of common American wildflowers that were introduced as European herbs. Nearly all are tough, adaptable plants (though not necessarily attractive) that provide home remedies for common ailments. For more information on the medicinal properties of 500 species of native and introduced plants found in eastern and central North America, see the *Peterson Field Guide to Medicinal Plants* (Boston: Houghton Mifflin, 1992).

When Is It Appropriate to Use Herbal Remedies at Home?

There are times when relying on herbs is appropriate and times when it is not. One guideline is to use herbal remedies for self-limiting diseases or conditions that will heal on their own, whether treated or not. The common cold is a good example. If you have a cold, it's going to go away whether or not you use garlic or echinacea to lessen its severity, gargle sage tea to soothe a sore throat, or drink thyme tea to relieve congestion. In this case, the herbs relieve the symptoms while the illness runs its course.

Herbs can also provide relief for minor wounds that would soon heal anyway, such as cuts, scrapes, and burns. A tincture of calendula flowers is useful for the minor cuts and scrapes that all gardeners encounter. A poultice of fresh yarrow flowers, plucked from the edge of the garden, can be used to stop bleeding from a minor injury. Aloe vera soothes minor burns or sunburn.

Home herbal remedies should be used only when needed and only in appropriate amounts. Some people tend to think that more is better. This is not true. And herbs are not a cure-all. When using them for self-limiting conditions in your household, it's always good to follow those warnings that appear on the side panel of all over-the-counter drugs: "If symptoms persist, discontinue use and consult your physician. Continued symptoms could be a sign of a serious disease."

Another critical guideline is to use only gentle herbs that are generally recognized as safe. Don't even think about treating yourself with an herb described as powerful or poisonous. Such herbs are definitely not in the category of home remedies. Traditionally, they were always administered by a medicine man, wise woman, or healer with years of training and experience.

Preparations

Generally a specific plant part is used for medicinal purposes. This might be the inner bark of a tree, the root or root bark, leaves, flowers, seeds, or the whole herb—that is, the above-ground parts of the plant harvested prior to flowering. Herbs are administered in specific delivery forms, usually using water or alcohol as the carrier for the plant's medicinal constituents, some of which may be soluble only in water, others only in alcohol.

The most familiar form for using herbs as medicine is as a tea or infusion. A tea is made by soaking the herb in hot water for 10 to 15 minutes. A decoction is also a form of water extraction, typically used for tough roots or bark. A decoction is made by simmering the plant material for an extended period of time, sometimes several hours. Multi-herb prescriptions in traditional Chinese medicine are frequently taken in the form of a decoction. The prescription may be simmered in two quarts of water, until it has evaporated down to one-half or one-quarter of its original volume, making a type of simple crude extract. The process is quite similar to that of making maple syrup or maple sugar—the longer you simmer the liquid, the more water evaporates, and the more concentrated the preparation becomes.

Another common form of herb preparation is a tincture, or alcohol extraction, made simply by soaking the herb in ethyl alcohol or ethanol (not rubbing alcohol, which is toxic). Depending on the herb material used, a tincture may be intended for external or internal use. Most tinctures are made with dilute alcohol—100 proof, or a mixture of 50 percent ethanol and 50 percent water. Add the herb to the liquid at about a 1:5 ratio (one part herb to five parts liquid) by weight. Seal in a glass jar or other container. Shake daily. After about two weeks, strain off the liquid. Store it in a cool, dark place until needed. Tinctures can often be stored for several years without losing strength.

Herbs are prepared in various forms for external application. A wash is simply a cooled tea or decoction applied externally. A poultice is a layer of crushed herb, fresh or dried (in which case it has been reconstituted in water), applied to the affected area of the body. Normally a layer of cotton cloth is placed between the herb and the skin. Ointments and salves are preparations with herbal ingredients in an oil, grease, or wax base.

Cautions

Remember that just because herbs are "natural" they are not necessarily safe. What makes herbs effective, in fact, is their complex chemistry. Sometimes those chemical components are very powerful.

Often different parts of a plant produce different compounds, some safe, some toxic. For example, castor bean (*Ricinis communis*), commonly grown in herb gardens for its dramatic foliage and height, produces oil-rich seeds, which are, of course, the source of castor oil. That oil has therapeutic effects known to all, primarily as a laxative. But the seeds themselves (or the pulp left from pressing the oil) are highly toxic. One seed may contain enough of the toxic protein ricin to make an adult extremely ill and perhaps even be fatal to a child.

Sometimes a plant is innocuous in the short run but can be dangerous in the long run because it contains toxic compounds that accumulate in the body. For instance, comfrey leaf tea was a popular folk remedy for many ailments. Taken occasionally, it won't produce an acute reaction. If used over a period of time, however, comfrey leaf tea may cause serious liver damage, because of toxic alkaloids found in small amounts in the leaves. (Comfrey root tea, although used in the past, is not recommended at all now, because the toxins are 10 times more concentrated in the root than in the leaves.)

Toxicity is always related to dosage. Many herbs that are generally considered safe if taken in small amounts can have unpleasant or dangerous side effects if taken in quantity. Often the threshhold of tolerance varies among individuals. And for any plant or plant part, there is the possibility that someone, somewhere, may have an allergic or toxic reaction to ingesting it or even to coming into contact with it. Again, this varies among individuals, and it changes over a lifetime. You can develop sensitivity to a plant that previously you were immune to. Use common sense and avoid any plant that gives you irritation or discomfort.

The Color Plates

The first group of color plates shows several examples of herbs growing in gardens around the United States. These pictures will give you ideas for how to combine herbs and arrange them in pleasing ways, and will illustrate traditional and contemporary approaches to herb garden design.

The rest of the color plates feature a variety of herb plants. The plates are grouped into five categories: hardy trees and shrubs, tender trees and shrubs, hardy herbaceous perennials, tender herbaceous perennials, and annuals and biennials. The distinction between hardy and tender is drawn at 0° F. Plants called hardy in this book are hardy at least to USDA zone 6, where average winter low temperatures range between 0° and −10° F. Many are hardier in colder zones, as noted in the individual entries. Plants called tender in this book cannot tolerate temperatures below 0° F and survive outdoors only in USDA zone 7, where average winter low temperatures range between 10° and 0° F, or warmer zones, as noted. Some tender plants cannot tolerate any frost at all and must be brought indoors for winter protection in almost all parts of the United States. However, many of the plants that are grouped into the categories of tender trees and shrubs or tender herbaceous perennials grow quickly enough to make an impressive display in one season and can be treated as annuals in the garden.

Each plant photo is accompanied by a short description that gives the plant's botanical and common names, its height, notes about its appearance or growth, its hardiness zone, a brief summary of its herbal use, and the page on which you will find the encyclopedia entry.

Garden Scenes

This small knot garden in North Carolina has interwoven bands of gray and green santolina, accented with upright specimens of rosemary and two flowering rues. A knot is a classic centerpiece for this formal garden. Beds around the edge of the garden hold basil, perilla, nasturtiums, sage, and other culinary herbs.

Red brick paths and brick edging outline geometric beds in the formal herb garden at the Huntington Botanical Gardens in southern California. Starting with a strong design makes a garden attractive in all seasons and provides a versatile backdrop for an ever-changing display of flowers and foliage.

Flowering lavender, tansy, and yarrow add bright color that complements the lovely range of silver, gray, and green foliage in this demonstration garden at Catnip Acres herb nursery in Connecticut. A white archway separates the billowing perennials in this part of the garden from a closely trimmed knot planting beyond.

Lavender, rosemary, Jerusalem sage, and scented geraniums spill over a stone retaining wall on this hillside herb garden at the Wild Animal Park in southern California. Herbs that would freeze back in most parts of the United States are evergreen in California, and some even flower through the winter there.

An herb garden doesn't have to be large to be special. An edging of short round posts, a willow trellis, and hand-lettered ceramic name tags add plenty of charm to this doorside planting of catmint, garden sage, southernwood, and other herbs at Heard's Country Garden in southern California.

A large wooden planter box filled with fragrant herbs could edge a patio or greet visitors at the front door. This planter at the Cornell Plantations in Ithaca, New York, combines peppermint- and lemon-scented geraniums, dusty-miller, and Helichrysum petiolare *to illustrate a variety of leaf shapes, textures, colors, and fragrances.*

Hardy Trees
and Shrubs

Abies balsamea

Balsam fir
Height: 40–60 ft.
Needs moist soil
Prefers cool
summers
Zone 3

Dried needles make
fragrant sachets
p. 258

Arctostaphylos
uva-ursi

Bearberry,
kinnikinnick
Height: under 1 ft.
A fine ground cover
Leaves are
evergreen
Zone 3

Used medicinally
p. 269

Betula lenta

Sweet birch
Height: 50 ft.
Attractive bark has
a wintergreen
flavor
Zone 4

Used in medicine
and for flavoring
and tea
p. 277

Camellia sinensis

Tea
Height: 6 ft.
Leaves are
evergreen
Flowers in fall
Zone 6

Leaves are used to
make tea
p. 281

Ceanothus americanus

New Jersey tea
Height: 3–4 ft.
Thrives in dry, rocky soil
Blooms in early summer
Zone 4

Dried leaves have been used as a tea substitute
p. 285

Cornus florida

Flowering dogwood
Height: 30 ft.
Flowers are white or pink
Fall color is red
Zone 5

Bark has been used to treat malaria
p. 297

Cotinus obovatus

American smoke
tree
Height: 30 ft.
Vivid fall color
Tolerates poor soil
Zone 4

Twigs and wood
give a yellow dye
p. 298

**Crataegus
phaenopyrum**

Washington
hawthorn
Height: 25 ft.
Red berries all
winter
Tolerates poor soil
Zone 3

Fruits and flowers
are used as a heart
medicine
p. 299

Ephedra sinica   *Chinese ephedra*   *Used in China to*
                      Height: 2 ft.   *treat colds, coughs,*
                      Twigs are evergreen *flu, etc.*
                      Easy to grow   *p. 306*
                      Zone 6

Ginkgo biloba

Gingko
Height: 50–80 ft.
Leaves turn gold in
fall
Tolerates city
conditions
Zone 4

Leaves are used in
Chinese medicine
p. 315

Hamamelis virginiana

Common witch hazel
Height: 20 ft.
Blooms in fall
Prefers rich, moist soil
Zone 4

Extract from twigs is a common home remedy
p. 318

Juniperus communis

Common juniper
Height: 10 ft.
Low-growing cultivars make good ground covers
Zone 2

Dark blue berries are used to flavor gin
p. 330

***Juniperus
virginiana***

*Eastern red cedar
Height: 30 ft. or
more
Easy to grow
Makes a good
hedge
Zone 2*

*Fragrant wood is
used to make cedar
chests
p. 330*

***Lavandula
angustifolia***
'Hidcote'

*Hidcote lavender
Height: 2 ft.
Dark purple
flowers in early
summer
Zone 5*

*Flowers are used in
sachets and
potpourris
p. 332*

Lavandula angustifolia 'Jean Davis'

Jean Davis lavender
Height: 2 ft.
Pale pink flowers in early summer
Zone 5

Flowers are used in sachets and potpourris
p. 332

Lavandula angustifolia 'Nana Alba'

Dwarf white lavender
Height: 1 ft.
Needs a warm, sunny spot with well-drained soil
Zone 5

Flowers are used in sachets and potpourris
p. 332

Lavandula × intermedia

*Lavandin
Height: 3–4 ft.
Flowers are
especially fragrant
Zone 5*

*Essential oil is used
in perfumes
p. 333*

Lindera benzoin

*Spicebush
Height: 8–10 ft.
Blooms in early
spring
Red berries in fall
Zone 5*

*All parts are
fragrant
Used in folk
remedies
p. 337*

Liquidambar styraciflua

*Sweet gum
Height: 60 ft.
Excellent fall color
Easy to grow
Zone 6*

*Sticky sap is used in
home remedies
p. 340*

Magnolia virginiana

*Sweet bay
magnolia
Height: 20–60 ft.
Foliage can be
evergreen or
deciduous
Zone 5*

*Leaves can
substitute for bay
laurel in cooking
p. 342*

**Myrica
pensylvanica**

*Bayberry
Height: to 8 ft.
Leaves are very
fragrant
Berries ripen in fall
Zone 4*

*Waxy berries are
used to make
bayberry candles
p. 350*

Pinus strobus

*Eastern white pine
Height: to 75 ft.
Needles are soft
Prefers rich, moist
soil
Zone 3*

*Inner bark was
used in cough
remedies
p. 369*

**Populus
tremuloides**

*Aspen
Height: 25–30 ft.
Yellow-gold fall
color
Smooth pale bark
Zone 2*

*Buds were used in
traditional home
remedies
p. 375*

Premna japonica

*No common name
Height: 3–4 ft.
White flowers in
summer
Leaves are fragrant
Zone 5*

*Leaves are used as
a moth repellent
p. 376*

Prunus virginiana

Wild cherry
Height: to 20 ft.
Shrub or small tree
Fruit is very sour
Zone 3

Bark has been used
to treat wounds
p. 379

Ptelea trifoliata

Common hoptree
Height: 15–20 ft.
Flowers are very
fragrant
Good for small
gardens
Zone 4

Historically, the
roots were used as
a tonic
p. 379

Rhus typhina   Staghorn sumac
Height: 15–25 ft.
Red fall foliage
Fruits last all
winter
Zone 4

Berries were used
in cough syrup and
beverages
p. 381

Rosa canina   Dog rose
Height: 10 ft.
Canes are thorny
Good for
hedgerows
Zone 5

Orange-red hips
are used in tea and
preserves
p. 382

| *Rosa × centifolia* | Cabbage rose
Height: 6 ft.
Flowers are very
fragrant
Canes need support
Zone 6 | Petals are used in
potpourri, rose
water, and rose oil
p. 383 |

| *Rosa ×*
damascena | Damask rose
Height: 6 ft.
Excellent fragrance
Blooms in late
spring
Zone 5 | Petals are used in
perfumery
Important
historically
p. 383 |

Rosa eglanteria

*Sweet briar rose
Height: 10 ft.
Canes are very
thorny
Shiny leaves are
fragrant
Zone 5*

*Flowers are used in
confections and
medicine
p. 384*

***Rosa gallica
'Officinalis'***

*Apothecary rose
Height: 3 ft.
Flowers are very
fragrant
Stems need support
Zone 5*

*Dried petals are
used medicinally
p. 384*

Rosa rugosa

Rugosa rose
Height: 4–6 ft.
Flowers are very
fragrant
Makes an excellent
hedge
Zone 4

Hips make good
tea or jam
Use petals in
potpourri
p. 385

Rubus idaeus

Raspberry
Height: 3–5 ft.
Stems are prickly
Berries ripen in
summer
Zone 4

Leaves and dried
berries make a tasty
tea
p. 387

| *Salix elaeagnos* | Rosemary willow
Height: 8–12 ft.
Prune hard to keep
it compact and
bushy
Zone 5 | Bark tea was a
traditional remedy
p. 389 |

| *Sambucus*
canadensis | Elderberry
Height: 6–12 ft.
Flowers in early
summer
Berries attract birds
Zone 4 | Flower tea has been
used medicinally
p. 394 |

Sassafras albidum   *Sassafras*
Height: 40–60 ft.
Often makes a
thicket
Bright fall color
Zone 5

All parts are
fragrant
A popular folk
remedy
p. 397

Thuja occidentalis

American
arborvitae
Height: varies
Compact cultivars
make excellent
hedges
Zone 3

Leaf tea was used
in traditional cures
p. 409

Tilia cordata

Littleleaf linden
Height: 50 ft.
Very fragrant
flowers dangle in
clusters
Zone 3

Flowers make a
soothing, fragrant
tea
p. 414

Tsuga canadensis

Canada hemlock
Height: 50–100 ft.
A very graceful tree
Prefers cool, moist
sites
Zone 4

Bark and leaf tea
have been used
medicinally
p. 416

**Umbellularia
californica**

California bay
Height: 60–75 ft.
Glossy evergreen
leaves have a strong
fragrance
Zone 7

Leaves are used in
potpourri and as
seasoning
p. 418

Viburnum opulus   European
                        cranberry bush
                        Height: 8–12 ft.
                        White flowers in
                        May
                        Red berries all
                        winter
                        Zone 3

Bark preparations
were used to relieve
cramps
p. 420

Viburnum setigerum

Tea-leaf viburnum
Height: 8–10 ft.
Abundant red
berries last for
several months
Zone 5

Dried leaves make
a mild tea beverage
p. 421

Zanthoxylum americanum

Prickly ash
Height: 15–25 ft.
Easy to grow
Trunk is very
thorny
Zone 4

Bark is a popular
folk remedy and
painkiller
p. 426

Tender Trees
and Shrubs

Aloysia triphylla

*Lemon verbena
Height: to 10 ft.
Whorled leaves
have a strong
lemony aroma
Zone 8*

*Leaves are used for
flavor and
fragrance
p. 264*

Catha edulis

*Chat, khat
Height: to 20 ft. or
more
Grows well in
containers
Can be shaped or
trained
Zone 8*

*Fresh leaves are
used as a stimulant
p. 284*

Ceratonia siliqua   *Carob*
Height: to 40 ft.
Female trees bear
beanlike pods
Zone 9

Pulp from pods is a
substitute for
chocolate
p. 287

Cinnamomum   *Camphor tree*
camphora   *Height: to 50 ft.*
Grows well in a
pot
All parts are
fragrant
Zone 9

Processed in Africa
as a source of
camphor
p. 292

Cistus ladanifer

*Crimson-spot rock
rose
Height: 3–5 ft.
Leaves are resinous
Thrives on hot, dry
sites
Zone 8*

*Fragrant resin is
used in perfumes
and medicinally
p. 292*

Citrus limon   *Lemon
Height: 20–25 ft.
Dwarf forms grow
well in pots and
bear good fruit
Zone 9*

*Widely used as
flavoring and
fragrance
p. 293*

Coffea arabica

*Coffee
Height: to 20 ft.
An excellent
houseplant
Flowers are very
fragrant
Zone 10*

*Roasted seeds make
a popular beverage
p. 294*

**Eucalyptus
cinerea**

*Silver-dollar
eucalyptus
Height: 25–40 ft.
Seedlings grow very
fast
Grows well in
containers
Zone 9*

*Dried leaves are
used for bouquets
and in dyeing
p. 307*

Eucalyptus citriodora

Lemon-scented gum
Height: to 60 ft. or more
A slender, graceful tree
Grows well in containers
Zone 9

Lemon-scented leaves are good for potpourri
p. 308

Eucalyptus globulus

Blue gum eucalyptus
Height: to 200 ft.
Very common in California
Leaves have a strong aroma
Zone 9

Essential oil is used in cough drops and antiseptics
p. 308

Ilex paraguariensis

Yerba maté
Height: 4–5 ft.
Makes a good hedge
Red berries in fall
Zone 7

Dried leaves make tea, high in caffeine
p. 325

Ilex vomitoria

Yaupon holly
Height: 15–20 ft.
Leaves are very small
Responds well to pruning
Zone 7

Leaves were used medicinally by Native Americans
p. 325

Jasminum officinale

Jasmine
Height: to 15 ft.
White flowers are
very fragrant all
summer
Zone 9

Essential oil is used
in perfumes and
flavorings
p. 329

Laurus nobilis

Bay laurel, sweet
bay
Height: to 30 ft.
Stiff, leathery leaves
are very aromatic
Zone 8

Leaves are a
popular seasoning
p. 331

Lavandula latifolia

Spike lavender
Height: 3 ft.
Blooms in late summer
Aroma is slightly camphorous
Zone 7

Oil is used in perfumes, paints, and varnishes
p. 333

Lavandula stoechas

Spanish lavender
Height: 18–24 in.
Thrives in dry soil
Very pleasant aroma
Zone 7

Flowers were used medicinally and in perfumes
p. 334

Lawsonia inermis   *Henna*
Height: to 25 ft.   *Dried leaves are*
White flowers are   *used to dye hair*
very fragrant in   *and skin*
midwinter   *p. 335*
Zone 10

Leptospermum   *New Zealand tea*   *Leaves make a*
scoparium   *tree*   *pleasant beverage*
                                  Height: 6–10 ft.   *tea*
                                  Easily pruned to   *p. 336*
                                  shape
                                  Grows well in
                                  containers
                                  Zone 9

Myrtus communis

Myrtle
Height: 15–20 ft.
Leaves are very
aromatic
Flowers are sweet-
scented
Zone 7

Used in perfume,
medicine, and
seasoning
p. 351

**Rosmarinus
officinalis**

Rosemary
Height: 4–6 ft.
Makes a good
standard
Grows well in
containers
Zone 8

Fragrant leaves are
used for seasoning
and sachets
p. 385

Rosmarinus officinalis

Rosemary
Height: 4–6 ft.
Flowers from fall to spring
Very drought-tolerant
Zone 8

Fragrant leaves are used for seasoning and sachets
p. 385

Rosmarinus officinalis 'Prostratus'	*Creeping rosemary* *Height: under 1 ft.* *An excellent ground cover for dry climates* *Zone 8*	*Fragrant leaves are used for seasoning and sachets* *p. 385*

Simmondsia chinensis

Jojoba
Height: 6 ft.
Very drought-
tolerant
Makes a good
hedge
Zone 9

Oil from the seeds
is used in shampoos
and cosmetics
p. 400

Vitex agnus-castus

Chaste tree
Height: 10–20 ft.
Leaves have a spicy
aroma
Thrives in hot
weather
Zone 7

Seeds are used
medicinally
Leaves are used as
seasoning
p. 423

Hardy
Perennials

Achillea
millefolium

Common yarrow
Height: 2–3 ft.
Blooms for a long
season
Carefree and easy
to grow
Zone 3

Leaves are used to
stop the bleeding of
minor wounds
p. 258

Acorus calamus

Sweet flag
Height: 4 ft.
Prefers rich, moist
soil
Leaves have a spicy
aroma
Zone 3

Leaves are used for
fragrance
Rhizome is used as
a remedy
p. 259

***Agastache
foeniculum***

*Anise hyssop
Height: 4 ft.
Leaves smell like
licorice
Attracts many
butterflies
Zone 4*

*Fresh or dried
leaves make a tasty
tea
p. 260*

***Agastache
'Firebird'***

*'Firebird' agastache
Height: 2 ft.
Attracts
hummingbirds
Leaves are
aromatic
Hardiness
uncertain*

*Leaves make a
pleasant hot or iced
tea
p. 260*

Agastache rugosa

*Korean mint
Height: 5 ft.
Blooms for a long
season
Smells like mint
and anise
Zone 5*

*Leaves and roots
are used in Chinese
medicine
p. 261*

Alchemilla mollis   *Lady's-mantle
Height: 1 ft.
Flowers last for
weeks
Good ground cover
or edging
Zone 3*

*Historically used as
an astringent and
styptic
p. 261*

Allium sativum

Garlic
Height: 18 in.
Needs full sun and
good soil
Harvest in late
summer
Zone 4

A versatile
seasoning and a
popular home
remedy
p. 262

**Allium
schoenoprasum**

Chives
Height: 12–18 in.
Blooms in late
spring
Harvest leaves
anytime
Zone 3

Use fresh or frozen
leaves for seasoning
or garnish
p. 262

Allium tuberosum

*Garlic chives
Height: 2–3 ft.
Blooms in late
summer
Makes a slender,
erect clump
Zone 3*

*Fresh leaves have a
mild garlic flavor
p. 263*

Anaphalis margaritacea

*Pearly everlasting
Height: 12 in.
Tolerates poor soil
Flowers dry easily
Zone 4*

*Leaf tea is a
traditional folk
remedy
p. 266*

Angelica
archangelica

Angelica
Height: 6 ft.
Prefers rich, moist
soil
Makes a showy
specimen
Zone 4

Used as seasoning,
in perfume, and
medicinally
p. 267

Anthemis
tinctoria

Dyer's chamomile
Height: 2–3 ft.
Blooms in
midsummer
Foliage is fragrant
Zone 3

Makes a yellow
textile dye or hair
coloring
p. 268

Anthoxanthum odoratum

Sweet vernal grass
Height: 2 ft.
(flowers)
Blooms in early
spring
Common in
meadows
Zone 4

Vanilla-scented
dried leaves are
good for potpourri
p. 269

Aralia nudicaulis

Wild sarsaparilla
Height: 2 ft.
Spreads to form
patches
Grows best in
woodlands
Zone 3

Tea from roots
made a pleasant
folk tonic
p. 362

Armoracia rusticana

Horseradish
Height: 4 ft.
(flowers)
Blooms in early summer
Tenacious and long-lived
Zone 3

Ground root is used as a condiment for meats
p. 270

Arnica montana

Arnica
Height: 2 ft.
Tolerates poor soil
Leaves are strong-scented
Zone 4

Used externally to heal sprains and bruises
p. 271

Artemisia abrotanum 'Tangerine'

'Tangerine' southernwood
Height: 6–7 ft.
Evergreen in mild winters
Looks best if pruned hard
Zone 5

Dried leaves are used in moth-repellent sachets
p. 272

Artemisia absinthium 'Lambrook Silver'

'Lambrook Silver' wormwood
Height: 3–5 ft.
Leaves are strongly aromatic
Vigorous and easy to grow
Zone 5

Important historically but not used today
p. 272

Artemisia afra	*African wormwood* *Height: 4 ft.* *Likes hot, dry* *weather* *Strongly aromatic* *Zone 6, with* *protection*	*A popular folk* *medicine in South* *Africa* *p. 272*

Artemisia
dracunculus
var. *sativa*

French tarragon
Height: 2 ft.
Must have good
drainage
Leaves are anise-
scented
Zone 3

Leaves are used to
season salads,
chicken, and fish
p. 273

Artemisia ludoviciana 'Silver King'

'Silver King' artemisia
Height: 2–3 ft.
Evergreen in mild climates
Spreads rapidly by runners
Zone 3

Was used medicinally by Native Americans
p. 274

Artemisia pontica 'Nana'

Dwarf Roman wormwood
Height: 1 ft.
Makes a low ground cover
Foliage is aromatic
Zone 5

Used historically but not today
p. 275

**Artemisia
'Powis Castle'**

*'Powis Castle'
artemisia
Height: 3–4 ft.
Tolerates humidity
better than other
artemisias do
Zone 6*

*Leaves are
aromatic
Grown mostly for
ornament
p. 275*

**Asarum
canadense**

*Wild ginger
Height: 6 in.
Needs a shaded site
Spreads to make a
patch
Zone 2*

*Rhizomes make a
spicy tea, used as a
folk remedy
p. 275*

Asclepias tuberosa   *Butterfly weed*
Height: 1–2 ft.
Tolerates poor, dry soil
Blooms for several weeks
Zone 3

Traditionally, root was used for lung ailments
p. 276

Belamcanda chinensis   *Blackberry lily*
Height: 2–3 ft.
Orange flowers in summer
Pods of shiny black seeds
Zone 5

Root is used in traditional Chinese medicine
p. 277

Calamintha grandiflora

Calamint
Height: 12–18 in.
Blooms in spring and summer
Carefree, often self-sows
Zone 5

Fragrant leaves can be dried for potpourri
p. 279

Calamintha nepeta

Calamint
Height: 2 ft.
Mint-scented leaves
Blooms in summer and fall
Zone 5

Fragrant leaves can be dried for potpourri
p. 280

Caulophyllum thalictrioides

Blue cohosh
Height: 2–3 ft.
Needs part or full shade
A woodland wildflower
Zone 3

Root preparations are used in Native American medicine
p. 285

Chamaemelum nobile

Roman chamomile
Height: 6 in.
Prefers cool summers
Can be used as a lawn
Zone 4

Dried flower heads make a pleasant and soothing tea
p. 287

Chrysanthemum balsamita

*Costmary
Height: 3 ft.
(flowers)
Yellow flowers in
late summer
Spreads to make a
patch
Zone 4*

*Dry pressed leaves
make fragrant
bookmarks
p. 289*

Chrysanthemum parthenium

*Feverfew
Height: 1–3 ft.
Blooms from
spring to fall
Self-sows readily
Zone 5*

*Leaf preparations
are used to relieve
migraines
p. 290*

**Chrysanthemum
pyrethrum**

*Pyrethrum
Height: 18–24 in.
Tolerates poor, dry
soil
Needs full sun
Zone 5*

*Yellow disk florets
have insecticidal
properties
p. 290*

**Cimicifuga
racemosa**

*Black cohosh
Height: 6 ft.
Blooms in
midsummer
Needs rich, moist
soil
Zone 3*

*Extracts of
rhizomes have
medicinal
properties
p. 291*

**Conradina
verticillata**

*Cumberland
rosemary
Height: under 15 in.
Blooms in
midspring
Prefers dry, sandy
soil
Zone 5*

*Mint-scented leaves
can be dried for
sachets
p. 295*

Crocus sativus

*Saffron
Height: 6 in.
Blooms in fall
Needs well-drained
soil
Zone 5*

*Dried stigmas are
used to color and
flavor food
p. 299*

Dianthus caryophyllus

Clove pink
Height: 12–18 in.
Flowers are very
fragrant
Foliage is
semievergreen
Zone 5

Clove-scented
flowers can be used
to flavor wine
p. 301

Dictamnus albus

Gas plant
Height: 2–4 ft.
Glossy leaves are
aromatic
Carefree and long-
lived
Zone 3

Dried leaves make
a pleasant and
soothing tea
p. 302

Echinacea pallida   Pale purple
coneflower
Height: 3–4 ft.
Tolerates poor, dry
soil
A prairie
wildflower
Zone 4

Important
traditionally and
now as a medicinal
herb
p. 304

**Echinacea
purpurea**   Purple coneflower
Height: 3–4 ft.
Blooms for a long
season
Attracts many
butterflies
Zone 4

Important
traditionally and
now as a medicinal
herb
p. 304

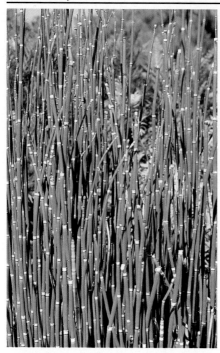

Equisetum hyemale

*Scouring rush
Height: 3–5 ft.
An unusual
specimen but
tenacious and
invasive
Zone 4*

*Tea is used
medicinally and as
a greenhouse
fungicide
p. 306*

Eupatorium perfoliatum

*Boneset
Height: to 4 ft.
Leaves join at the
stem
Blooms in late
summer and fall
Zone 3*

*Historically, leaves
were used to treat
fevers
p. 309*

***Eupatorium
purpureum***

*Joe-Pye weed
Height: 5–9 ft.
A statuesque plant
Blooms in late
summer
Zone 4*

*Used traditionally
for urinary
disorders
p. 309*

***Ferula assa-
foetida***

*Asafoetida
Height: to 6 ft.
Blooms in summer
Easy to grow
Zone 5*

*Resin from roots is
used as a
condiment and
remedy
p. 311*

Filipendula rubra

Queen-of-the-prairie
Height: 6–8 ft.
Prefers moist soil
Blooms for several weeks
Zone 3

Tannin-rich roots have astringent properties
p. 311

Filipendula ulmaria   Meadowsweet   The original source of salicylic acid (aspirin) p. 312

Height: 4–6 ft.
Flowers are sweetly fragrant
Prefers moist soil
Zone 4

Foeniculum vulgare

Fennel
Height: to 6 ft.
Self-sows readily
Seeds are fragrant
Zone 5

Leaves and seeds
are used as
flavoring
p. 312

Foeniculum vulgare var. _rubrum_	Bronze fennel Height: to 6 ft. Leaves are purple-bronze Flowers are yellow Zone 5	Grown mostly for ornament but makes a good garnish p. 312

Galega officinalis

Goat's rue
Height: 3–5 ft.
Tolerates dry spells
Runners can be
invasive
Zone 4

Leaves are used as
a rennet in
cheesemaking
p. 313

Galium odoratum   Sweet woodruff   Dried leaves have a
                      Height: 6 in.   warm vanilla
                      Blooms in spring   fragrance
                      Makes a good   p. 314
                      ground cover
                      Zone 4

Galium verum

Lady's bedstraw
Height: 2–3 ft.
Blooms in summer
Spreads invasively
Zone 4

Flowering tops are
used to color
cheese and butter
p. 314

**Gaultheria
procumbens**

Wintergreen
Height: 4 in.
Part or full shade
Prefers rich, moist
soil
Zone 4

Used as a flavoring
and in home
remedies
p. 315

Glycyrrhiza glabra

Licorice
Height: 3 ft.
Blooms in late summer
Prefers loose, light soil
Zone 5

Root extract is a common flavoring and remedy
p. 317

Heuchera americana

Alumroot
Height: 6 in. (leaves)
Evergreen in mild winters
Needs a well-drained site
Zone 4

Root traditionally was used as an astringent
p. 319

Hierochloe odorata

Sweet grass, vanilla grass
Height: 18–24 in.
Spreads fast by runners
Grows wild in eastern U.S.
Zone 4

Vanilla-scented leaves are used in basketry
p. 320

Humulus lupulus

Hops
Height: to 25 ft.
Needs a strong trellis
Dies down in winter
Zone 3

Dried strobiles of female plants add flavor to beer
p. 321

Hydrastis canadensis

Goldenseal
Height: 1 ft.
Needs full shade
and rich, moist,
woodland soil
Zone 3

Root products are
used as an
antibiotic
p. 322

Hypericum perforatum

St.-John's-wort
Height: 2–3 ft.
Very easy to grow
Good for meadow
gardens
Zone 3

Flower
preparations are
versatile home
remedies
p. 324

Hyssopus officinalis

Hyssop
Height: 18–24 in.
Blooms are blue, white, or pink
Good low hedge or edging
Zone 3

Essential oil from leaves is used in perfumery
p. 324

Inula helenium

Elecampane
Height: to 6 ft.
Blooms in summer
Easy to grow
Zone 4

Root preparations have been used for lung diseases
p. 327

Iris germanica
var. ***florentina***

Orrisroot
Height: 30 in.
(flowers)
Flowers are slightly
fragrant
Needs well-drained
soil
Zone 4

Dried, aged
rhizomes are used
as a fixative for
potpourri
p. 327

Leonurus cardiaca

Motherwort
Height: 4 ft.
Foliage is attractive
Makes a vigorous
clump
Zone 4

Leaf tea is a
versatile and
popular home
remedy
p. 335

Levisticum officinale

Lovage
Height: 4–6 ft.
All parts are fragrant
Prefers rich, moist soil
Zone 3

Fresh or dried leaves have a strong parsleylike flavor
p. 337

Lobelia cardinalis

Cardinal flower
Height: 4 ft.
A slender unbranched plant
Attracts hummingbirds
Zone 2

Used medicinally by Native Americans
p. 341

Lobelia siphilitica

Great blue lobelia
Height: to 3 ft.
Blooms in late
summer
Prefers moist soil
Zone 2

Once considered to
be a cure for
syphilis
p. 341

Marrubium vulgare

Horehound
Height: 18–24 in.
Tolerates heat and
drought
Forms a bushy
mound
Zone 4

Leaf extract is used
for sore throats and
coughs
p. 343

Melissa officinalis

Lemon balm
Height: 2 ft.
Gardeners often cut
off flower stalks
Zone 5

Lemon-flavored
leaves are used for
tea or garnish
p. 344

Mentha spp.

Assorted mints
Height: 2–24 in.
Many mints are
hybrids
Fragrance varies
widely
Zone 5

Fragrant leaves are
used for flavoring
and tea
p. 345

Mentha × piperita

Peppermint
Height: 2 ft.
Propagated by
cuttings only
Doesn't set viable
seed
Zone 5

Used to flavor
candies, toothpaste,
etc.
p. 345

Mentha × piperita
'Grapefruit'

Grapefruit mint
Height: 2 ft.
Small rounded
flower heads
Doesn't bloom
until fall
Zone 5

Smells like a blend
of mint and citrus
p. 345

Mentha pulegium

Pennyroyal
Height: to 12 in.
(flowers)
Creeps near the
ground
Good between
stepping-stones
Zone 6

Used to repel
mosquitoes and
fleas
p. 346

Mentha spicata

Spearmint
Height: 2–3 ft.
Flowers are borne
on long spikes
Forms a dense
patch
Zone 5

Used for tea and to
flavor candies
p. 347

**Mentha
suaveolens**

*Apple mint
Height: 2 ft.
Leaves have a soft
texture
Tolerates fairly dry
soil
Zone 5*

*Mild-flavored
leaves make a
garnish for fruit
salad
p. 347*

**Mentha
suaveolens**

*Pineapple mint
Height: 1 ft.
Beautiful
variegated leaves
Not a very strong
grower
Zone 5*

*Mild-flavored
leaves make a
garnish for fruit
salad
p. 347*

Monarda didyma

Bee balm
Height: 2–4 ft.
Blooms attract
hummingbirds
Spreads fast in
moist soil
Zone 4

Leaf tea was a
traditional remedy
for colds, etc.
p. 348

Monarda fistulosa

Wild bergamot
Height: 2–4 ft.
Tolerates poor, dry
soil
Blooms for several
weeks
Zone 4

Leaf tea has a
milder flavor than
bee balm tea
p. 348

Monarda punctata

Horsemint
Height: 2–4 ft.
Tolerates poor, dry soil
Flowers are unusual
Zone 4

Strong-scented foliage makes a medicinal tea
p. 348

Myrrhis odorata   *Sweet cicely*   *Anise-scented*
                      Height: 3 ft.   *leaves and fruits*
                      Good for shady   *are used as*
                      sites   *seasoning*
                      All parts are edible *p. 350*
                      Zone 4

Nasturtium officinale

*Watercress
Height: 4 in.
Needs plenty of
water
Makes a dense mat
Zone 5*

*Young leaves add a
peppery flavor to
sandwiches
p. 352*

Nepeta cataria

*Catnip
Height: 2–4 ft.
Very easy to grow
Leaves have a
downy texture
Zone 3*

*Used for cat toys
and to make a tea
for colds
p. 353*

Nepeta × faassenii   Catmint
Height: 18–24 in.
Blooms for several
weeks
Needs well-drained
soil
Zone 4

Used for cat toys
but is weaker than
catnip
p. 353

**Origanum vulgare
subsp. *hirtum***

*Greek oregano
Height: 2 ft.
(flowers)
White flowers in
summer
Distinctly pungent
aroma
Zone 5*

*Leaves are an
essential seasoning
for Italian food*
p. 360

Passiflora incarnata

Passionflower, maypop
Height: 15 ft.
Fragrant flowers
Vine can climb or sprawl
Zone 5, with winter mulch

Used medicinally as a sedative
p. 364

Platycodon grandiflorus

Balloon flower
Height: 18–30 in.
Long-lived and carefree
Flowers in midsummer
Zone 3

Root is used in traditional Chinese medicine
p. 370

Polygonatum biflorum

Solomon's-seal
Height: 2–3 ft.
A woodland wildflower
Takes part or full shade
Zone 3

Roots were used medicinally by Native Americans
p. 373

Poterium sanguisorba

Salad burnet
Height: to 3 ft.
Makes a round, bushy clump
Flowers in late spring and summer
Zone 3

Cucumber-flavored leaves are used in salads
p. 376

Primula veris

Cowslip
Height: 6 in.
Flowers are sweet-scented
Best for cool climates
Zone 5

Tea from flowers is used as a sedative in Europe
p. 377

Prunella vulgaris

Heal-all
Height: 1 ft.
Flowers all summer
Easy but often weedy
Zone 4

Leaf tea is a versatile traditional home remedy
p. 378

Pycnanthemum muticum

Mountain mint
Height: 2 ft.
Easy to grow
Leaves turn silvery
in fall
Zone 5

Mint-flavored
leaves make a
pleasant mild tea
p. 380

Rubia tinctorum

Madder
Height: 2 ft.
Spreads to make a
patch
Roots are thick and
red
Zone 4

Roots are an
important source of
red dye
p. 386

Rumex acetosa

*Garden sorrel
Height: 3 ft.
(flowers)
Makes a big clump
of leaves
Carefree and easy
to grow
Zone 3*

*Leaves add a fresh,
tart flavor to salads
and soups
p. 388*

Rumex scutatus

*French sorrel
Height: 6 in.
Spreads by creeping
stems
Leaves have a thick
texture
Zone 3*

*Leaves add a fresh,
tart flavor to salads
and soups
p. 388*

Ruta graveolens

Rue
Height: 2–3 ft.
Leaves are
semievergreen
Flowers in
midsummer
Zone 5

Important
historically but
little used today
p. 389

Salvia officinalis

Garden sage
Height: 2 ft.
Flowers in early
summer
Foliage is
semievergreen
Zone 5

Leaves are used as
seasoning
Leaf tea is
therapeutic
p. 392

Salvia officinalis 'Icterina'

Gold-variegated sage
Height: 1 ft.
Needs well-drained soil
Grows well in a pot
Zone 8

Can be used as seasoning but is used mostly for ornament
p. 392

Salvia officinalis 'Tricolor'

Tricolor sage
Height: 1 ft.
Foliage is outstanding
Flowers are blue-violet
Zone 8

Can be used as seasoning but is used mostly for ornament
p. 392

Sanguinaria canadensis

*Bloodroot
Height: 6–8 in.
A woodland
wildflower
Blooms in early
spring
Zone 4*

*Used medicinally
by Native
Americans
p. 395*

*Santolina
chamaecyparissus*

*Lavender cotton,
gray santolina
Height: 2 ft.
Good for clipped
edgings
Yellow flowers in
summer
Zone 6, with
protection*

*Foliage has a
pungent,
penetrating aroma
p. 396*

Santolina virens

Green santolina
Height: 2 ft.
Good for clipped
edgings
Yellow flowers in
summer
Zone 6

Foliage has a
pungent, resinous
aroma
p. 396

**Saponaria
officinalis**

Soapwort,
bouncing Bet
Height: 2–3 ft.
A roadside
wildflower
Blooms for many
months
Zone 2

All parts make
soaplike suds when
mixed in water
p. 397

Satureja montana

*Winter savory
Height: 2 ft.
Flowers in late
summer
Leaves are
evergreen
Zone 5*

*Fresh or dried
leaves are used as
seasoning
p. 399*

**Smilacina
racemosa**

*False Solomon's-
seal
Height: 2–3 ft.
Flowers in spring
Forms wide
colonies
Zone 3*

*Root tea was a
traditional remedy
for constipation
p. 400*

Solidago odora

Sweet goldenrod
Height: 3 ft.
Blooms from July
to September
Leaves smell like
anise
Zone 5

Leaf tea is a
pleasant beverage
p. 401

Stachys byzantina

Lamb's-ears
Height: 8 in.
Needs good
drainage
Often planted as
edging
Zone 5

Leaves are
sometimes used to
bandage minor
wounds
p. 402

Stachys officinalis

Betony
Height: 2–3 ft.
Easy to grow
Blooms in summer
Zone 4

Fresh or dried
leaves are used as a
sedative
p. 403

Symphytum officinale

Comfrey
Height: 2 ft.
Blooms all summer
A tough, tenacious
plant
Zone 3

Leaves and roots
are used externally
as a poultice
p. 404

Tanacetum vulgare

Tansy
Height: 3–4 ft.
Tolerates poor, dry soil
Foliage is strong-scented
Zone 4

Now used mostly as an insect repellent
p. 406

Teucrium chamaedrys

Germander
Height: 1–2 ft.
Blooms in summer
Foliage is evergreen
Zone 5

In the past, leaf tea was used medicinally
p. 407

**Teucrium
majoricum**

*Majoricum
Height: 6 in.
Does well in
containers
Pineapple-scented
flowers
Zone 5*

*Foliage has a
pungent odor, like
creosote
p. 408*

**Thymus ×
citriodorus
'Aureus'**

*Golden lemon
thyme
Height: 6–8 in.
Forms a dense mat
Leaves have a
lemony aroma
Zone 5*

*Fresh or dried
leaves are a
versatile seasoning
p. 411*

Thymus herba-barona

Caraway thyme
Height: 4 in.
Makes a good
ground cover
Leaves taste like
caraway
Zone 4

Fresh or dried
leaves add flavor to
meat dishes
p. 411

Thymus praecox
subsp. *arcticus*
'Coccineus'

Creeping thyme
Height: 3–4 in.
Remarkable for its
blooms
One of many fine
cultivars
Zone 4

Edible but grown
mostly for its
beautiful flowers
p. 411

Thymus
pseudolanuginosus

Woolly thyme
Height: 3 in.
Needs a well-
drained site
Blooms in early
summer
Zone 5

Edible but grown
mostly for its
woolly foliage
p. 412

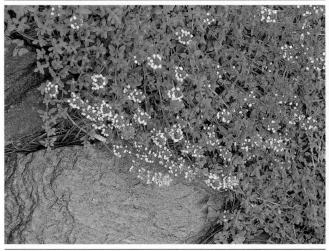

Thymus
pulegioides

Mother-of-thyme
Height: 8 in.
Grows easily from
seed
Makes a good
ground cover
Zone 4

Leaves are used as
seasoning, for tea,
and in potpourri
p. 412

Thymus vulgaris

Common thyme
Height: to 12 in.
A bushy, erect plant
Good for clipped
edgings
Zone 4

A versatile culinary
herb
Leaf tea is used
medicinally
p. 413

Tussilago farfara   *Coltsfoot*   *Formerly used in*
                       Height: 6 in.   *cough remedies*
                       Flowers in spring,   *p. 418*
                       before leaves
                       develop
                       Zone 4

Valeriana officinalis

Valerian
Height: to 5 ft.
Flowers are very
sweet-scented
Carefree and long-
lived
Zone 3

Root preparations
are an important
herbal sedative
p. 419

Viola odorata

Sweet violet
Height: 4–6 in.
Intensely sweet
flowers
Spreads fast by
runners
Zone 5

Essential oil from
flowers is used in
perfumes
p. 422

Xanthorhiza simplicissima

Yellowroot
Height: 2–3 ft.
Prefers rich, moist
soil
Grows well in part
shade
Zone 3

Tea from rhizomes
was a Native
American remedy
p. 424

Yucca filamentosa

Yucca
Height: 5 ft.
(flowers)
Tough and long-
lived
Slowly forms a
dense patch
Zone 5

Roots make a suds,
usable as soap or
shampoo
p. 425

Tender
Perennials

Aloe vera

*Burn plant
Height: 18 in.
(leaves)
Needs well-drained
soil
Grows well in a pot
Zone 9*

*Leaf gel soothes
dry skin and minor
burns
p. 263*

Alpinia galanga

*Galangal
Height: 3–6 ft.
Goes dormant in
winter
Leaves are fragrant
Zone 9*

*Spicy rhizomes are
used as a flavoring
p. 265*

Cedronella canariensis

*Balm of Gilead
Height: 2–3 ft.
Leaves have a
lemony aroma
A slender, upright
plant
Zone 10*

*Fresh or dried
leaves are used for
tea
p. 286*

Coleus amboinicus

*Cuban oregano
Height: 2–3 ft.
Thrives in hot
weather
Prefers sandy soil
Zone 10*

*Fresh leaves are
used as a seasoning
p. 295*

**Curcuma
domestica**

*Turmeric
Height: 2–4 ft.
Grows well in a
pot
Flowers in early
winter
Zone 8*

*Dried rhizomes are
used in curry
powders
p. 300*

**Cymbopogon
citratus**

*Lemon grass
Height: to 6 ft.
Leaves are
evergreen
Strong lemony
aroma
Zone 10*

*Used in tea, in Thai
food, and
medicinally
p. 301*

Elettaria cardamomum

Cardamom
Height: 2–4 ft.
Grows well in a pot
Leaves are aromatic
Zone 10

Seeds are used in Indian food and baked goods
p. 305

Helichrysum angustifolium

Curry plant
Height: 2–4 ft.
Leaves smell like curry
Needs well-drained soil
Zone 9

Fragrant leaves are used medicinally in Europe
p. 319

Hydrocotyle asiatica

Gotu kola
Height: about 4 in.
Spreads 3–4 ft.
wide
Grows indoors
in winter
Zone 10

Highly esteemed as
a medicinal herb in
India
p. 323

Lippia dulcis

Sweet herb
Height: 1–2 ft.
Good for hanging
baskets
Can flower year-
round
Zone 9

Remarkably sweet
leaves can
substitute for sugar
p. 339

Lippia graveolens

*Mexican oregano
Height: 3–6 ft.
Thrives in hot
weather
Needs regular
pruning
Zone 8*

*Oregano-flavored
leaves are used as
seasoning
p. 339*

Mentha requienii

*Corsican mint
Height: under 1 in.
Clings to the
ground
Spreads 1 ft. or
more
Zone 8*

*Fragrant leaves
make a tasty tea or
garnish
p. 346*

Nashia inaguensis

*Moujean tea
Height: 1–2 ft.
Grows well in a pot
Makes a good
standard
Zone 10*

*Fresh or dried
leaves make a
pungent tea*
p. 352

**Ocimum
'African Blue'**　　'African Blue' basil　　*Spicy leaves can be
Height: 3 ft.　　　　dried for potpourri
Foliage is very　　　p. 358
showy
Flowers are pale
purple
Zone 10*

Ocimum kilimandscharicum

Camphor basil
Height: to 5 ft.
Makes a bushy
specimen
Leaves smell like
camphor
Zone 10

Used as an insect
repellent and a cold
remedy
p. 357

Origanum dictamnus

Dittany of Crete
Height: to 1 ft.
Needs excellent
drainage
Good for hanging
baskets
Zone 8

Leaves have a mild
oregano flavor
p. 361

Origanum × majoricum

*Hardy sweet marjoram
Height: 12–18 in.
Shrubby and evergreen
Flowers in early summer
Zone 7*

*Fresh or dried leaves are used as seasoning
p. 360*

Origanum syriacum

*Bible hyssop
Height: to 2 ft.
Grows well in pots
Used since biblical times
Zone 10*

*Leaves have a good oregano flavor and pleasant aroma
p. 361*

***Pelargonium capitatum* 'Attar of Roses'**

*Rose-scented geranium
Height: 2 ft.
Flowers in spring
Makes a nice edging
Zone 10*

*Rose-scented leaves can be added to potpourri
p. 365*

***Pelargonium crispum* 'Prince Rupert'**

*Prince Rupert geranium
Height: 1–2 ft.
Avoid overwatering
Needs careful pruning
Zone 10*

*Lemon-scented leaves are an attractive garnish
p. 365*

Pelargonium ×
fragrans

Nutmeg-scented
geranium
Height: 1 ft.
Tends to sprawl
Good for hanging
baskets
Zone 10

Leaves have a spicy
nutmeg aroma
p. 365

Pelargonium
graveolens
'Lady Plymouth'

Lady Plymouth
geranium
Height: 3 ft.
A bushy, upright
plant
Can make a
standard
Zone 10

Leaves smell like
sun-warmed roses
p. 366

Pelargonium graveolens 'Rober's Lemon Rose'	*Rober's lemon rose geranium* *Height: to 3 ft.* *A full, bushy plant* *Flowers in spring* *Zone 10*	*Leaves can be used to flavor pound cakes* *p. 366*

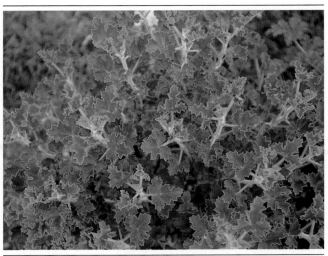

Pelargonium × nervosum 'Torento'	*Ginger-scented geranium* *Height: 2 ft.* *Stems are stiff and erect* *Needs careful pruning* *Zone 10*	*Leaves have a spicy aroma, like ginger* *p. 366*

Pelargonium quercifolium 'Fair Ellen'

Fair Ellen oakleaf geranium
Height: 2–3 ft.
A bushy, spreading plant
Flowers in spring
Zone 10

Leaves have a piney, resinous aroma
p. 366

Pelargonium tomentosum

Peppermint-scented geranium
Height: 1 ft.
Can sprawl to 4 ft. wide
Leaves are very fuzzy
Zone 10

Leaves have a pleasant peppermint aroma
p. 366

Pelargonium tomentosum 'Chocolate Mint'

Chocolate mint geranium
Height: 1 ft.
Can sprawl to 4 ft. wide
Zone 10

Leaves have a pleasant candylike aroma
p. 366

Plectranthus sp.

Menthol plant
Height: 1 ft.
Grows well in a pot
Leaves are very succulent
Zone 10

Inhaling the menthol helps a stuffy nose
p. 371

Pogostemon cablin

Patchouli
Height: 3 ft.
Leaves have a strong aroma
Grows well in a pot
Zone 10

Dried leaves are used in sachets
p. 372

Poliomintha longiflora

Mexican oregano
Height: 4 ft.
Thrives in hot weather
Tolerates dry soil
Zone 8

Leaves have a strong oregano flavor
p. 372

Polygonum odoratum

Vietnamese coriander
Height: under 1 ft.
Sprawling stems
Can grow as a houseplant
Zone 8, with protection

Fresh leaves have the flavor of cilantro
p. 373

Salvia clevelandii

Cleveland sage
Height: 4 ft.
Tolerates poor, dry soil
Blooms from spring to summer
Zone 8

Aromatic leaves are used mostly in potpourri
p. 390

Salvia dorisiana

Fruit-scented sage
Height: 4 ft.
Gets big and bushy
Pink flowers in fall
Zone 10

Aromatic leaves are
used for tea and in
potpourri
p. 391

Salvia elegans   *Pineapple sage*   *Fresh leaves make a*
                             Height: 4 ft.   *tasty hot or iced tea*
                             Red flowers in fall   *p. 391*
                             Good houseplant
                             in winter
                             Zone 8

Satureja viminea

*Costa Rican mint
bush
Height: 2–3 ft.
A good winter
houseplant
Prune to keep it
bushy
Zone 10*

*Leaves have a
strong aroma, like
pennyroyal
p. 399*

Stevia rebaudiana

*Sweet herb of
Paraguay
Height: 1 ft.
Must have good
drainage
Goes dormant in
winter
Zone 10*

*Leaves have an
incredible
sweetness
p. 403*

Tagetes lemmonii   *Mexican bush marigold*
Height: 3–6 ft.
Leaves are evergreen
Blooms almost all year
Zone 9

Leaves make a pleasant aromatic tea
p. 405

Tagetes lucida

Mexican mint marigold
Height: to 3 ft.
Leaves smell like anise
Yellow flowers in fall
Zone 8

Leaves are used as seasoning and for a fragrant tea
p. 405

| *Teucrium marum* | Cat thyme
Height: 1 ft.
Grows well in a pot
Needs good drainage
Zone 8 | Leaves have a strong odor that appeals to cats
p. 408 |

| *Thymbra spicata* | Za'tar
Height: 1–2 ft.
Has a pleasant spicy aroma
Flowers in summer
Zone 8 | An important seasoning for Middle Eastern food
p. 410 |

***Tulbaghia
violacea* 'Tricolor'**

*Society garlic
Height: 1 ft.
A good winter
houseplant
Blooms mostly in
summer
Zone 9*

*Used medicinally,
not as seasoning
p. 417*

***Vetiveria
zizanioides***

*Vetiver
Height: 3–4 ft.
Makes dense
clumps
Rarely flowers in
U.S.
Zone 9*

*Dried roots have a
very pleasant
fragrance
p. 420*

Withania somnifera

No common name
Height: 2 ft. or more
Grows well as an annual
Can overwinter indoors
Zone 10

An important medicinal plant from India
p. 424

Zingiber officinale

Ginger
Height: 2 ft.
Needs warm, humid weather
Grows well in a pot
Zone 9

Aromatic rhizome is a very important seasoning
p. 427

*Annuals and
Biennials*

**Anethum
graveolens**

Dill
Height: 3–5 ft.
Leaves are
threadlike
Blooms in
midsummer
All zones

All parts are edible
Used as seasoning
p. 266

Artemisia annua

Sweet Annie
Height: 6–8 ft.
Has a strong, sweet
aroma
Self-sows readily
All zones

Used medicinally
and for making
wreaths
p. 273

Borago officinalis

Borage
Height: 2 ft.
Prefers cool
weather
Usually self-sows
All zones

Used to flavor
salads and in folk
remedies
p. 278

Brassica hirta

Yellow mustard
Height: 3 ft.
Easy to grow
Seeds ripen in
summer
All zones

Seeds are ground to
make a condiment
p. 279

*Calendula
officinalis*

*Calendula
Height: 1–2 ft.
Flowers can be
yellow, orange,
gold, or cream
All zones*

*Used as a food
coloring and a
remedy for sores
p. 280*

*Capsicum
annuum*

*Chili pepper,
paprika
Height: 2–3 ft.
Dozens of varieties
Prefers hot weather
All zones*

*Fresh or dried
fruits are used as
seasoning
p. 282*

Carthamus tinctorius

*Safflower
Height: 3 ft.
Leaves are prickly
Easy to grow
All zones*

*Dried florets are
used for food
coloring and dye
p. 283*

Carum carvi

*Caraway
Height: 2 ft.
Biennial; blooms
the second year
Zone 4*

*Seeds are used as
seasoning and in
tea
p. 283*

Chenopodium ambrosioides

Epazote
Height: 4–5 ft.
Has a pungent aroma
Can be weedy
All zones

Used to season Mexican food, especially beans
p. 288

Chenopodium botrys

Ambrosia
Height: 2 ft.
Smells like turpentine
Blooms in late summer
All zones

Dried flower spikes are used in wreaths and potpourri
p. 289

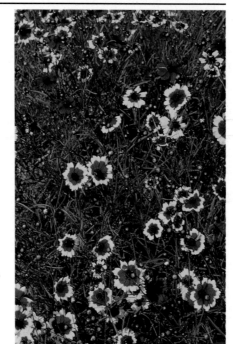

**Coreopsis
tinctoria**

*Dyer's coreopsis
Height: 1–3 ft.
Easy to grow
Blooms all summer
All zones*

*Flowers provide a
bright gold dye
p. 296*

| **Coriandrum sativum** | *Cilantro, coriander Height: 1–3 ft. Matures quickly Prefers cool weather All zones* | *Both leaves and seeds are used as seasoning p. 297* |

Digitalis purpurea

*Foxglove
Height: 3–5 ft.
Usually biennial
Blooms for weeks
Zone 4*

*Source of an
important heart
medicine
p. 303*

**Dipsacus
sylvestris**

*Fuller's teasel
Height: 3–6 ft.
Biennial; easy to
grow
Has a prickly
texture
Zone 4*

*Used by weavers
to make fabrics like
flannel
p. 303*

Euphorbia lathyris

Mole plant
Height: 3–4 ft.
Annual or biennial
Has milky white
sap
Zone 5

Used medicinally
and reputed to
repel moles
p. 310

Gossypium hirsutum

Cotton
Height: 3–5 ft.
Makes a pretty
specimen
Needs a long, hot
summer
Zone 7

Seed fibers are spun
to make cotton
fabrics
p. 317

Hibiscus
sabdariffa

Roselle
Height: 6 ft.
Blooms in fall
Needs a long, hot
summer
Zone 7

Calyxes make a
tasty hot or iced tea
p. 320

Indigofera
suffruticosa

Indigo
Height: 3–5 ft.
A shrubby plant
Very tender to cold
Zone 10

Leaves produce a
blue pigment used
in dyeing
p. 326

Isatis tinctoria

Woad
Height: 2–4 ft.
Biennial; blooms in
spring
Seedlings can be
weedy
Zone 4

Leaves produce a
blue pigment used
in dyeing
p. 328

Linum usitatissimum

Flax
Height: 3–4 ft.
Sow in early spring
Prefers cool
weather
All zones

Source of linseed
oil and linen fabric
p. 338

Matricaria recutita

German chamomile
Height: 24–30 in.
Easy to grow
Foliage is fragrant
All zones

Flowers make a
pleasant tea and
folk remedy
p. 343

Nicandra physaloides

Shoo-fly plant
Height: 5 ft.
Blooms all summer
Self-sows freely
All zones

Traditionally said
to repel flies
p. 354

Nicotiana rustica

Indian tobacco
Height: 2–4 ft.
Leaves are very
sticky
Easy to grow
All zones

High in nicotine,
used as an
insecticide
p. 355

Nigella sativa

Black cumin
Height: 1–2 ft.
Leaves are very
delicate
Interesting pods
All zones

Dried seeds are
used as seasoning
p. 356

Ocimum basilicum

*Sweet basil
Height: 2–3 ft.
Tender to cold
Leaves are very
fragrant
All zones*

*Leaves are used in
pesto and as
seasoning
p. 356*

Ocimum basilicum

*Cinnamon basil
Height: 2–3 ft.
Stems are reddish
Leaves are very
fragrant
All zones*

*Leaves are used in
tea and as
seasoning
p. 357*

Ocimum basilicum

Lettuce-leaf basil
Height: 2–4 ft.
Leaves are larger
than those of
common sweet
basil
All zones

Leaves are used to
wrap and season
food
p. 357

Ocimum sanctum

Sacred basil, holy
basil
Height: 2 ft.
Leaves are slightly
hairy
Spicy, clovelike
aroma
All zones

Leaves are used in
rituals, cooking,
and medicine
p. 358

Oenothera biennis

*Evening primrose
Height: 4–6 ft.
Flowers are
fragrant
Self-sows readily
Zone 4*

*Seeds, especially,
are used
medicinally
p. 359*

**Origanum
majorana**

*Sweet marjoram
Height: 1–2 ft.
Has a delicious
fragrance
Overwinters in
zone 9
Annual in all zones*

*Leaves are used in
cooking, tea, and
perfumery
p. 360*

Papaver somniferum

Opium poppy, breadseed poppy
Height: 2–4 ft.
Flowers come in many colors
Interesting seedpods
All zones

Seeds are used as flavoring
Sap is source of opium
p. 363

Perilla frutescens

Perilla
Height: 3–4 ft.
Leaves can be green, red, or dark purple
All zones

Leaves are used to flavor Oriental food
p. 367

Petroselinum crispum

Curly parsley
Height: 2–3 ft.
Makes a pretty
edging
Biennial, can self-
sow
All zones

Leaves are a
popular seasoning
and garnish
p. 368

Petroselinum crispum

Flat-leaf parsley
Height: 2–3 ft.
Leaflets are flat
Biennial, can self-
sow
All zones

Tastier than curly
parsley
p. 368

Polygonum tinctorium

*Japanese indigo
Height: 3 ft.
Blooms in late
summer
Very tender to cold
All zones*

*Leaves produce a
blue pigment used
in dyeing
p. 374*

Reseda luteola

*Weld
Height: 2–4 ft.
Hardy biennial;
makes a flat first-
year rosette
Zone 4*

*Makes a pretty
yellow dye for
textiles
p. 381*

Salvia sclarea

*Clary sage
Height: 3–4 ft.
Biennial; makes a
rosette the first year
Zone 4*

*Essential oil is used
in perfumery
p. 392*

Salvia sclarea
'Turkestanica'

*Clary sage
Height: 3–4 ft.
Has especially large
and pretty flowers
Zone 4*

*Essential oil is used
in perfumery
p. 392*

Satureja hortensis   *Summer savory*
Height: 12–18 in.
A slender plant
with a mild,
pleasant aroma
All zones

Leaves are used to
season beans and
other foods
p. 399

Tropaeolum
majus

Nasturtium
Height: 2–4 ft.
Can sprawl or
climb
Blooms all summer
All zones

Used as seasoning
Has a peppery
flavor
p. 415

Encyclopedia
of Plants

Abies

Ay′bees
Pinaceae. Pine family

Description
Evergreen conifers that thrive in moist or mountainous habitats. About 40 species, native to the north temperate zone.

■ *balsamea* p. 112
Balsam fir. This symbol of the North Woods is valued for its fragrance. The shiny dark green needles, under 1 in. long, spread on both sides of the twigs like the pages of an open book. Seedlings grow into perfect Christmas trees; older specimens develop irregular shapes. Can reach 40–60 ft. tall. 'Nana' is a dwarf selection that slowly forms a compact sphere. Zone 3.

How to Grow
Full or part sun. Needs constant soil moisture. Grows best where summers are cool and humid. Mulch generously and water regularly. In the South or Midwest, plant *A. fraseri,* the southern balsam fir. It looks similar and is almost as fragrant, but it is more tolerant of warm, dry summers.

Herbal Use
Dried needles retain their fragrance for years and make pleasant sachets for perfuming drawers and closets. Resin from the bark is used as an antiseptic in hemorrhoid preparations and root-canal sealers. Leaf tea is a folk medicine for colds and asthma.

Achillea

A-kil-lee′a
Compositae. Composite family

Description
Perennials with aromatic foliage, often finely divided. About 80 species, native to the north temperate zone.

■ *millefolium* p. 150 *Pictured opposite*
Common yarrow. A traditional European herb that grows as a wildflower throughout the United States, with flat clusters of small white flowers and pungent, gray-green, fernlike leaves. Flower stalks can reach 2–3 ft. tall; a patch can spread 2–3 ft. wide. The foliage is evergreen in mild climates, nearly so in cold climates. A natural for meadow gardens, it also tol-

erates mowing and light traffic and spreads to make a surprisingly versatile ground cover. Perennial nurseries offer several new cultivars and hybrids with flowers in a wide range of bright and pastel colors. Zone 3.

How to Grow
Full or part sun. Ordinary soil and watering. Cut flowers as they fade to prolong blooming. Easily propagated by seed or division. Pest-free, but leaves may rot in hot, humid weather.

Herbal Use
Traditionally used as a folk medicine for colds, fevers, digestive problems, and internal bleeding. Fresh flowers or leaves are applied externally to stop bleeding. Caution: Internal use is now discouraged. External application may cause dermatitis.

Acorus
Ak´o-rus
Araceae. Arum family

Description
Rhizomatous perennials with upright fans of slender leaves and tiny flowers in a thumblike cluster. Only 2 species, native to wetlands in Eurasia and North America.

■ *calamus* p. 150
Sweet flag. Spreads 2 ft. or more to form a dense patch of slender leaves, 4 ft. tall, that resemble cattails but have pronounced midribs. The leaves release a spicy fragrance when crushed. A variegated form with creamy white stripes on the leaves is especially attractive. Zone 3.

How to Grow
Sun or shade. Prefers fertile soil and constant moisture but will grow in ordinary soil with regular watering. Propagate by division in spring or fall. Long-lived and trouble-free.

Herbal Use
Fresh or dried leaves traditionally were strewn on floors to deodorize and perfume stuffy rooms. Tea of the dried rhizome was formerly used for indigestion, heartburn, colds, and fevers. Native Americans chewed the rhizome as a stimulant.

Agastache
A-guh-sta´key
Labiatae. Mint family

Description
Perennials with strong upright stems topped with dense spikes of small flowers. Many species have fragrant leaves. About 30 species, native to North and Central America and to Asia.

■ *foeniculum p. 151*
Anise hyssop. A prairie wildflower. Forms a clump of stiffly upright stalks, up to 4 ft. tall, topped with dense, finger-sized spikes of small blue-purple flowers that attract bees, butterflies, and hummingbirds from July to September. The heart-shaped leaves have a soft texture and pleasant licorice aroma and flavor. Zone 4.

How to Grow
Full or part sun. Ordinary soil. Pest-free and easy to grow. Self-sows readily, but the seedlings are easily uprooted. Good for meadow or prairie gardens. Transplant seedlings or propagate by dividing large clumps in early spring.

Herbal Use
Fresh or dried, the leaves make a tasty hot or iced tea. Used as a folk remedy for fevers, colds, and coughs.

■ *hybrids p. 151*
Hybrid agastache. These recently introduced plants are becoming very popular. They have wonderfully fragrant leaves and bear colorful flowers, 1–1½ in. long, from June to frost, on stalks about 2 ft. tall. 'Firebird' has bright coppery orange flowers. 'Tutti Fruti' has raspberry pink-purple flowers. There are several more cultivars with different color flowers; hummingbirds love them all. Hardiness uncertain.

How to Grow
Like *A. foeniculum*. Also grows well in a pot on the patio.

Herbal Use
Fresh or dried leaves make a tasty tea.

■ *rugosa* *p. 152*
Korean mint, hyssop. This Asian species resembles our native anise hyssop, but it grows larger (to 5 ft. tall) and has a mintier aroma and taste. Small rosy purple flowers bloom from early summer through fall. Zone 5.

How to Grow
Like *A. foeniculum*.

Herbal Use
Leaves are used in traditional Chinese medicine to relieve the pain of angina. Root has been used for coughs and lung ailments.

Alchemilla
Al-ke-mill′a
Rosaceae. Rose family

Description
Perennials with lobed or compound leaves and sprays of tiny greenish yellow flowers. About 200 species, most native to the north temperate zone.

■ *mollis* *p. 152*
Lady's-mantle. An easy and adaptable perennial, lovely as an edging plant or massed around a birdbath or sundial. The pleated and scalloped 6-in.-wide leaves unfold to make a soft gray-green clump in early spring; frothy clouds of chartreuse flowers on 2-ft. stalks spill over the top later in season. The flowers last a long time in the garden, and they also dry well. Zone 3.

How to Grow
Sun (North) or shade (South). Tolerates poor conditions but does better with good soil and regular watering. Cut back after flowering to encourage a flush of new foliage that looks good all fall. Propagate by division in spring or after bloom. May self-sow but isn't weedy. Space 2 ft. apart for ground cover or edging.

Herbal Use
Leaves and roots are high in tannin and historically were used as an astringent and styptic to stop bleeding or profuse menstruation.

Allium
Al′li-um
Amaryllidaceae. Amaryllis family

Description
Bulb-forming perennials with flat or hollow leaves and round clusters of small flowers. Many, including onion and garlic, have pungent leaves and bulbs, but the flowers may smell quite sweet. About 700 species, all native to the Northern Hemisphere.

■ *sativum* p. 153
Garlic. Makes a clump of long flat leaves in spring and a single 18-in. stalk topped with a ball of small white flowers in summer, then forms a bulb with many individually wrapped cloves. Rocambolė or stiffneck garlic (*A. sativum* var. *ophioscorodon*) is similar but has a stiff stalk that forms a neat coil topped with a cluster of red-skinned bulblets (as well as an underground bulb). Elephant garlic (*A. ampeloprasum*) grows larger and has very large cloves with a mild flavor. Zone 4.

How to Grow
Full sun. Fertile, well-drained soil. Plant individual cloves 2 in. deep and 6 in. apart in fall or very early spring. Harvest in late summer when the tops turn tan and tip over. Spread or hang in a sheltered spot until the tops wither, then store the bulbs in a cool, dry place.

Herbal Use
Minced garlic cloves are an essential ingredient in countless recipes. The chopped leaves can also be used for flavoring. Fresh garlic is a favorite home remedy for colds, fevers, bronchitis, high blood pressure, diarrhea, and many other ailments. Clinical studies confirm its medicinal value.

■ *schoenoprasum* p. 153
Chives. This hardy perennial makes a pincushion-like clump of slender, hollow leaves, 12–18 in. long, with a mild oniony flavor. New growth starts in early spring. The leaves are very

hardy and don't die back in fall until killed by hard frost. Round 1-in. heads of fragrant, edible, lilac-purple flowers are showy for about a month in late spring. Zone 3.

How to Grow

Full or part sun. Average soil and watering. Shear after flowering to promote new growth. In cold climates, pot up part of a clump to keep on a cool sunny windowsill in winter. Easily raised from seed. Divide in early spring or after flowering.

Herbal Use

Pick fresh leaves to chop them for seasoning and garnish. Freeze in water or oil for winter use.

■ *tuberosum* p. 154

Garlic chives. A hardy perennial that makes a more slender, erect clump than regular chives. Thin, flat leaves have a mild garlic flavor. Bears lovely round clusters of white flowers on 2–3-ft. stalks in late summer or early fall. Zone 3.

How to Grow

Full or part sun. Average soil and watering. Easy to grow; just remove faded flowers to prevent rampant self-sowing.

Herbal Use

Same as for *A. schoenoprasum*.

Aloe

Al'oh, al'o-ee
Liliaceae. Lily family

Description

Succulents with thick fleshy leaves that are sometimes spiny and clusters of brightly colored, long-lasting flowers on tall stalks. More than 360 species, most native to Africa.

■ *vera* p. 212 Pictured on p. 264

Burn plant. A tender perennial that forms a rosette of plump dagger-shaped leaves up to 18 in. long, with soft teeth along the edges. Leaves are usually light to medium green but may be mottled with pale spots or tinged with red. New plants arise around the base of the parent plant and spread gradually to fill an area. Rarely blooms in containers, but outdoor plantings in mild climates bear yellow flowers in 3-ft. racemes in spring. Sometimes listed as *A. barbadensis*. Zone 9.

How to Grow
Full or part sun. Needs well-drained soil and can tolerate prolonged dry spells or lapses in watering. Grows very well in a
clay pot filled with porous, sandy soil. Put it outdoors in light
shade for the summer, but be sure to bring it indoors before
fall frost. Keep it on a bright windowsill for the winter.

Herbal Use
The slippery gel from a broken leaf helps soothe dry skin,
minor burns, sunburn, frostbite, small scratches, and razor
nicks. Recent studies confirm that compounds in the gel relieve pain and contribute to wound and burn healing.

Aloysia
A-loyz´ee-a
Verbenaceae. Verbena family

Description
Deciduous or evergreen shrubs with fragrant leaves. About
30 species, native to Central and South America.

■ *triphylla* p. 136
Lemon verbena. A tender shrub valued for its leaves, which
release an intense lemony fragrance at the slightest touch.
Borne in whorls of 3 or more, the papery-thin leaves are pale
green, about 3 in. long and $1/_2$ in. wide, with a rough surface
and brittle texture. Old plants develop woody trunks. Makes
a shrub up to 10 ft. tall outdoors in mild regions and bears
lacy clusters of small pinkish white flowers in early summer,
but specimens grown in containers or as annuals usually get
only 3–5 ft. tall and don't bloom. Normally drops its leaves
briefly in winter, indoors or outdoors. Sometimes listed as
Lippia citriodora. Zone 8.

How to Grow

Full sun. Needs well-drained soil and regular watering during active growth. Looks best with frequent pruning, which promotes bushiness. Can be trained into a standard or espaliered. In cold climates, buy a new plant each spring to treat as an annual, or grow one in a pot and bring it into a bright, cool, dry place for the winter. Water sparingly and prune it back when dormant; it will resprout shortly. Often infested with spider mites, whiteflies, aphids, or mealybugs.

Herbal Use

Gather leaves at any season. They retain their fragrance well when dried and are popular for sachets or potpourris. Tea made from fresh or dried leaves tastes pleasant and is recommended for colds, headaches, colic, dyspepsia, and fever. Rub leaves in pets' fur to repel fleas and on yourself to repel mosquitoes.

Alpinia
Al-pin´ee-a
Zingiberaceae. Ginger family

Description

Tender perennials with ginger-scented rhizomes, leafy stems, and long-lasting flowers. About 250 species, native to Asia.

■ *galanga* p. 212
Galangal. Makes an upright clump of stiff stalks 3–6 ft. tall, with large, smooth, fragrant leaves that are held horizontally. Rarely blooms in containers, but plants established outdoors bear loose clusters of spidery flowers, white with red veins, in late summer. Spreads by creeping rhizomes. Zone 9.

How to Grow

Full sun. Average soil and watering. Plant in a sheltered site outdoors in zones 9 and 10. It will recover if frost kills back the tops. In colder regions, grow it in a container. Water freely and fertilize often during active growth, but hold back during winter dormancy. Propagate by dividing the rhizomes in spring.

Herbal Use

The aromatic rhizomes are harvested when dormant and used as a flavoring in Southeast Asian cooking. Has a spicy, gingerlike flavor. Also used to flavor liqueurs and medicines.

Anaphalis
A-naf′a-lis
Compositae. Composite family

Description
Low-growing perennials with clusters of everlasting flowers.
About 100 species, native to the north temperate zone.

■ *margaritacea p. 154*
Pearly everlasting. A hardy perennial that spreads 12–18 in.
wide, making a low mat of dark green-gray foliage that lasts
late into the fall. Blooms for a long season in summer, with
stalks 12 in. tall that branch near the top, holding clusters
of small rounded blossoms like little white strawflowers.
Zone 4.

How to Grow
Full sun. Does best in well-drained soil with regular watering. Tolerates sandy soil and dry spells; grows as a roadside
wildflower on rough exposed sites. Foliage may rot in hot,
wet, or humid conditions. Easily propagated by seed or division.

Herbal Use
Dried flowers look decorative in potpourri. Leaf tea is used
as a folk medicine for diarrhea, dysentery, colds, coughs,
and throat infections; leaves are applied externally to
bruises and sores. Traditional uses have not been scienti-
fically confirmed.

Anethum
A-nee′thum
Umbelliferae. Carrot family

Description
Annual herbs with fragrant threadlike leaves and tasty seeds.
Only 2 species, native to the Old World.

■ *graveolens p. 236 Pictured opposite*
Dill. A fast-growing annual. Seedlings grow quickly to make
a low rosette of grayish green, finely divided leaves with
wonderful flavor and fragrance. The stalks shoot up 3–5 ft.
tall in midsummer, each branch topped with an umbel of tiny
yellow flowers that ripen into flat round seeds. New cultivars such as 'Dukat' and 'Tetra' don't rush into bloom. All
zones.

How to Grow

Full sun. Ordinary soil. Does best in cool weather and can't take extreme heat or drought. Sow seeds where they are to grow in early spring and again in midsummer for a fall crop. After the first year, watch for volunteer seedlings.

Herbal Use

Finely chopped leaves, flower heads, and dry seeds are all used as seasoning in salads, pickles, bread, casseroles, and other dishes. The leaves are sweet and mild; the seeds have a more penetrating flavor. The seeds are chewed as a digestive aid.

Angelica

An-jel'i-ka
Umbelliferae. Carrot family

Description

Perennials or biennials that form large upright clumps. Many species are used medicinally in Asia. About 50 species, native to the Northern Hemisphere and New Zealand.

■ *archangelica* *p. 155*

Angelica. A dramatic sculptural plant, up to 6 ft. tall and 3 ft. wide. Makes a rosette of compound leaves with dark, glossy, toothed leaflets the first year, then dies down in the winter. The second year, it sends up stout ribbed stalks bearing large round compound umbels of greenish white flowers. Zone 4.

How to Grow

Part sun. Prefers rich soil with plenty of moisture; grows well but doesn't get as big in ordinary or dry soil. Usually performs as a biennial. Buy one plant to start with the first spring. Let it self-sow the next year, or gather the seeds and sow them immediately after ripening in late summer. Doesn't like hot summers, wet or dry.

Herbal Use

Add fresh leaves to salads. The stems can be candied to flavor desserts, and the fragrant seeds are used in perfumery. Preparations of the roots, seeds, and leaves traditionally were used for indigestion, menstrual disorders, fevers, colds, and the like.

Anthemis

An´the-mis
Compositae. Composite family

Description

Annuals or perennials with toothed or divided leaves and rounded or daisylike flower heads. Many have aromatic foliage; some are weedy. About 100 species, native to Europe and Asia.

■ *tinctoria* *p. 155*

Dyer's chamomile, golden marguerite. A hardy perennial that's showy in midsummer, with masses of yellow or gold blossoms on stalks 2–3 ft. tall. Makes a 2-ft. mound of fragrant, lacy, gray-green foliage. Perennial nurseries carry several cultivars selected for pale or bright flower colors. *A. sancti-johannis* is a similar plant with orange flowers. Zone 3.

How to Grow

Full sun. Average well-drained soil with regular watering. Does best where summers are mild; can't tolerate extreme heat or drought. Blooms the first year from seed sown early indoors. Deadhead to prolong bloom, and cut back after flowering is done. Divide every few years in spring.

Herbal Use

Simmering the flowers yields a yellow dye for wool, silk, or cotton yarns. It can also be used as a hair coloring.

Anthoxanthum
An-tho-zan´thum
Gramineae. Grass family

Description
Annual or perennial grasses with flat, slender, fragrant leaves. About 15 species, native to the Old World.

■ *odoratum* p. 156
Sweet vernal grass. A hardy perennial grass that forms a dense mounded clump of long narrow leaves. Odorless when green, they release a spicy vanilla fragrance when cut, and dried leaves remain fragrant for years. Spikes of small, yellow, sweet-scented flowers are held above the leaves on 2-ft. stalks in early summer. (The pollen can irritate hayfever sufferers.) Although native to Eurasia, sweet vernal grass now grows wild in meadows, pastures, and lawns in the eastern United States. Zone 4.

How to Grow
Full or part sun. Average or damp soil. Propagate by seed or division in spring or fall. Carefree once established.

Herbal Use
Dried leaves are useful in potpourri. The vanilla-like fragrance comes from the compound coumarin.

Arctostaphylos
Ark-toe-staff´i-los
Ericaceae. Heath family

Description
Evergreen shrubs with small leathery leaves and fruit like tiny apples. About 50 species, most native to western North America, and several hybrids and cultivars.

■ *uva-ursi* p. 112 Pictured on p. 270
Bearberry, kinnikinnick. A hardy native evergreen shrub that makes a fine ground cover for rocky or sandy slopes. It stays under 1 ft. tall but spreads more than 5 ft. wide. The leathery round leaves are glossy green in summer, bronzy reddish purple in winter. Has pale pinkish white flowers in spring, lustrous red fruits in fall. Named cultivars such as 'Point Reyes', 'Vancouver Jade', and 'Massachusetts' are especially desirable. Zone 3.

How to Grow
Full or part sun. Needs well-drained soil. Plant 2 ft. apart for ground cover, and use mulch to control weeds until it fills in. Can take infrequent foot traffic. Needs virtually no care.

Herbal Use
Tea made from the dried leaves is used for urinary disorders.

Armoracia
Ar-mor-ay´see-a
Cruciferae. Mustard family

Description
Perennials with deep roots, large leaves, and clusters of tiny flowers. Only 3 species, native to Eurasia.

■ *rusticana* p. 157
Horseradish. A hardy perennial that forms a clump of oblong dark green leaves up to 15 in. long, with crinkled edges. Blooms in early summer, with small pale flowers clustered on stalks up to 4 ft. tall. A variegated form has pretty white markings on its leaves. Formerly listed as *Cochlearia armoracia*. Zone 3.

How to Grow
Full sun. Average soil. Choose the site carefully; once you plant horseradish, you'll always have it. Plant a pencil-sized root cutting in early spring. Harvest by digging the root in fall. Any bits of broken root will resprout the next year. Flea beetles may bite holes in the leaves. Can't take extreme heat.

Herbal Use

The root is grated and mixed with vinegar to make a sharp-flavored condiment for beef, other meats, and fish. Medicinally, the root has been used for bronchitis and coughs or applied externally for rheumatism. Caution: Large amounts may irritate the digestive system, and external use may cause skin blisters.

Arnica

Ar′ni-ka
Compositae. Composite family

Description

Perennials with thick rootstocks, simple leaves, and composite flowers on single or branched stalks. About 32 species, native to the north temperate and Arctic regions.

■ *montana*   p. 157

Arnica. A hardy perennial that forms a clump of basal leaves with a rough texture and strong scent. Stalks up to 2 ft. tall hold bright yellow daisylike blossoms about 2 in. wide. Native to Europe and Siberia. *A. chamissonis* and *A. cordifolia* are similar species from western North America. Zone 4.

How to Grow

Full sun. Needs good drainage. Tolerates poor, sandy soil. Native to high altitudes and can't take extreme heat. Propagate by seed or division.

Herbal Use

Used (mostly in Europe) in ointments applied to sprains and bruises. Caution: May cause dermatitis. Do not take internally.

Artemisia

Ar-te-miss′ee-a
Compositae. Composite family

Description

Evergreen or deciduous shrubs or perennials. Most have aromatic foliage, often silver or gray, and rather inconspicuous small flowers. About 300 species, native to the Old and New World. In addition to the species listed below, many other artemisias are raised as ornamentals.

■ *abrotanum* *p. 158*
Southernwood, old-man, lad's-love. A hardy perennial,
woody at the base, with many stems 3–5 ft. tall. The finely
divided, almost feathery leaves are light gray-green. Tiny yellowish flowers may appear in fall. 'Tangerine' has citrus-
scented leaves with a greener color and has a more sprawling
habit. It can reach 6–7 ft. tall and wide. Camphor wormwood, *A. camphorata*, has camphor-scented gray foliage and
a spreading habit. It grows 2 ft. tall and 6 ft. wide. All are
hardy to zone 5.

How to Grow
Full or part sun. Well-drained average soil. Tolerates dry
spells. Evergreen in mild winters; dies back in cold winters.
Prune hard in early spring. Easily shaped into a compact ball
or sheared into a neat low hedge. Propagate by layering or
cuttings.

Herbal Use
Dried foliage makes fragrant sachets, said to repel clothes
moths. Formerly used in Europe as a seasoning and a folk
remedy. Caution: Can be toxic.

■ *absinthium* *p. 158*
Wormwood. A hardy perennial with soft-textured gray-green
leaves, 2–5 in. long, divided into many slender segments.
Makes a bushy specimen 3–5 ft. tall, topped with sprays of
tiny yellow flowers in summer. The foliage has a very strong,
penetrating fragrance. 'Lambrook Silver' has more finely divided leaves that are especially silky and silvery. Zone 5.

How to Grow
Like *A. abrotanum*. Vigorous and easy to grow. Can be invasive.

Herbal Use
Historically used as a medicinal herb, to expel worms; as an
insect repellent; and to flavor the alcoholic beverage absinthe.
Caution: Contains thujone, which even in small doses may
cause nervous disorders, convulsions, insomnia, and other
symptoms.

■ *afra* *p. 159*
African wormwood. A hardy perennial with upright, sparsely
branched stems, 4 ft. tall, topped in summer with loose clusters of tiny pale green flowers. The lacy, finely cut leaves are
green above, white below, 3 in. long, and strongly aromatic.
Zone 6, with protection.

How to Grow

Like *A. absinthium*. Thrives in hot, dry weather. Mulch for winter protection in zone 6.

Herbal Use

One of the most popular folk medicines in South Africa. Made into tea, with sugar added, for treating colds, coughs, dyspepsia, stomachaches, and other conditions. Caution: Can be toxic.

■ *annua* *p. 236*

Sweet Annie, sweet wormwood. A fast-growing annual that makes an upright, branching pyramid 6–8 ft. tall and 4 ft. wide. Both the finely divided, 4-in.-long leaves and the small round yellow-green flowers have a strong, sweet aroma. All zones.

How to Grow

Full sun. Average or dry soil. Easily started from seed. Self-sows freely and may become a pest.

Herbal Use

Leaves gathered before flowering are used as a tea for colds, fevers, and diarrhea. Dry branches are made into wreaths. Used for hundreds of years in treating malaria, and still the subject of intense research. Contains artemisinin, one of the best malaria treatments since quinine. Caution: Can be toxic.

■ *dracunculus* var. *sativa* *p. 159*

French tarragon. A hardy perennial, usually reaching about 2 ft. tall and 2 ft. wide. Forms a slowly spreading colony of upright stems clothed with slender dull green leaves. Rarely bears small greenish flowers. Sniff a leaf before you buy a plant; true French tarragon is a sterile variety that must be propagated from cuttings or by division. Russian tarragon, *A. dracunculus*, is cheaply raised from seed and often sold, but it has no flavor and is useless for culinary (or any other) purposes. Zone 3.

How to Grow

Full sun. Grows best in a raised bed. Needs well-drained soil with regular watering during active growth. Soggy soil will kill it, summer or winter. Divide in early spring.

Herbal Use

Fresh leaves have a wonderful anise flavor, popular in salad dressings and tasty with chicken or fish. Generally considered safe if ingested in small amounts as flavoring.

■ *ludoviciana* p. 160

A hardy perennial, native to the western United States, with silvery gray stems and foliage that have a pleasant fragrance. Stems reach 2–3 ft. tall, leaves about 2 in. long. 'Silver Queen' has attractive foliage but tends to be floppy. 'Silver King' is almost as pretty and stands up better. Looks good year-round in mild climates. Zone 3.

How to Grow
Full sun. Average soil. Spreads rapidly by underground runners and can make a large patch or invade adjacent plantings. Use a bottomless pot to confine it, or divide and replant every spring.

Herbal Use
Cut stems before the flower buds open to make dried arrangements or wreaths. Traditionally used by Native Americans in sweat baths for rheumatism, fever, colds, and flu. Caution: Can be toxic.

■ *vulgaris*

Mugwort. A hardy perennial native to Eurasia but naturalized along roadsides and riverbanks in the eastern United States. Spreads underground to make a patch of upright branching stems, 4–6 ft. tall, topped with dense clusters of small reddish brown or yellowish flowers in summer. The deeply lobed leaves are dark green above, woolly white below, with a pleasant aroma. Zone 4.

How to Grow
Full or part sun. Average soil and watering. Will invade adjacent plantings unless you watch it. Divide in spring or fall.

Herbal Use
Traditionally an important herb in Europe and Asia, used to flavor beer, as a condiment, and medicinally. Also valued as a magic plant or charm. Caution: Can be toxic.

■ other artemisias

Herb and perennial nurseries offer several other artemisias. Most are easy to grow in well-drained soil and have attractive white or silvery foliage. Several are used for medicine or fragrance.

Threadleaf sage, *A. filifolia,* is a semievergreen shrub, 3–4 ft. tall and wide. The very fine, threadlike, semievergreen leaves are silver-blue in summer, silver-gray in winter, and the whole plant is sweetly pungent. Zone 4.

White mugwort, *A. lactiflora,* is a perennial that forms a

clump of stems 4–5 ft. tall and 2–3 ft. wide. Creamy plumes of sweetly fragrant flowers top the stems in summer and dry well for winter wreaths. The foliage is dark green. Zone 4.

Dwarf Roman wormwood, *A. pontica* 'Nana' (p. 160), has finely dissected gray-green leaves with a mildly sweet scent and small yellowish flowers in early summer. Spreads underground and can be used as a 1-ft.-tall ground cover. The essential oil has been used like that of *A. absinthium*. Zone 5.

A. 'Powis Castle' (p. 161) is the best artemisia for the South, where summers are hot and humid. It forms a 3–4-ft. mound of beautiful silvery filigree foliage. Sometimes called fringe tree. Zone 6.

A. schmidtiana 'Silver Mound' is widely sold but not highly recommended. Only in cool, dry summers does it mound into a silky, silvery dome; exposed to heat and humidity, it flops apart into a soggy gray doughnut. Zone 5.

Asarum

Ass'a-rum
Aristolochiaceae. Birthwort family

Description

Low, spreading perennials with evergreen or deciduous leaves and unusual dark flowers. About 70 species, native to the north temperate zone.

■ *canadense* p. 161

Wild ginger. A perennial that spreads by creeping rhizomes. Forms a 6-in.-tall mat of deciduous, heart-shaped leaves, 6 in. wide, with a dull surface and a thick texture. You won't notice the odd red-brown flowers unless you look for them, at ground level in early spring. Grows wild in eastern woodlands. *A. caudatum,* native to the West, is similar but has glossier leaves. Zone 2.

How to Grow

Filtered sun to dense shade. Needs well-drained, organic soil and prefers constant moisture. Plant 12 in. apart for ground cover. Propagate by division at any time during the period of active growth. Carefree but subject to slugs and snails.

Herbal Use

Tea from the spicy-scented rhizomes was a folk remedy for indigestion, coughs, colds, and the like. Rhizome is edible but rarely used in cooking.

Asclepias
As-klee´pee-us
Asclepiadaceae. Milkweed family

Description
Perennials with milky sap, simple leaves, showy flowers, decorative pods, and silky-plumed seeds. About 120 species, most native to North America.

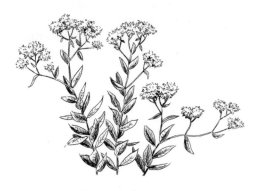

■ *tuberosa* p. 162 *Pictured above*
Butterfly weed. A perennial wildflower, native to the prairies and eastern United States. Grows 1–2 ft. tall and spreads 1–2 ft. wide. Forms a clump of upright stems surrounded with narrow green leaves and topped with flat clusters of bright orange flowers in summer and slender pods in fall. Zone 3.

How to Grow
Full sun. Tolerates poor or dry soil. Sow fresh seeds in fall for bloom in 2–3 years. Choose a site and leave it there; older plants have large brittle roots, which makes transplanting difficult. Susceptible to aphids and powdery mildew.

Herbal Use
Traditionally used for inflammations of the lung lining (pleurisy) and for asthma and bronchitis.

Belamcanda
Bel-am-kan´da
Iridaceae. Iris family

Description
Perennials with stout rhizomes, irislike leaves, colorful flowers, and seed clusters that resemble blackberries. Only 2 species, native to eastern Asia.

■ *chinensis* p. 162
Blackberry lily, leopard lily. An interesting perennial with flat sheaves of leaves on zigzag stalks, topped in summer with dark-spotted orange flowers. Grows 2–3 ft. tall. The pods of shiny black seeds resemble blackberries. Zone 5.

How to Grow
Full sun. Average well-drained soil. Easy from seed, and blooms the first or second year. Remove all debris in fall to reduce problems with iris borers and foliar leafspot.

Herbal Use
The root is prescribed in traditional Chinese medicine for tonsillitis, laryngitis, and stomachache and is a traditional folk remedy for breast cancer. Caution: Considered toxic.

Betula
Bet´you-la
Betulaceae. Birch family

Description
Deciduous trees or shrubs, most fast-growing but short-lived. Some have white or colored peeling bark. About 60 species, most native to cool northern climates.

■ *lenta* p. 113
Sweet birch, black birch. A deciduous tree native to eastern North America. Grows 50 ft. tall, usually with a single trunk. The young trees and twigs have shiny reddish black bark; older trunks have dark scaly bark. The leaves are oval with toothed edges, 3–6 in. long, glossy green in summer and golden yellow in fall. Has catkins of flowers in early spring. Zone 4.

How to Grow
Full sun. Prefers rich, well-drained soil but grows well in average garden soil. Subject to various insect pests and fungal diseases, especially if stressed by heat or drought.

Herbal Use
The bark contains methyl salicylate, the compound with the fragrance of wintergreen. It was formerly used medicinally and for flavoring. Twigs can be simmered to make wintergreen-flavored tea. The trees are sometimes tapped in spring, like maple trees, to collect the sap, which can be boiled down into a sweet syrup or fermented into an alcoholic beer.

Borago
Bo-ray´go
Boraginaceae. Borage family

Description
Annuals or perennials with hairy leaves and stems and star-shaped blue flowers. Only 3 species, native to the Mediterranean region.

■ *officinalis p. 237 Pictured below*
Borage. An annual that grows about 2 ft. tall and wide, with beautiful, starry, sky blue flowers ¾ in. wide. The large oblong leaves and stems are covered with stiff hairs that sparkle in the sun. Declines quickly after flowering. All zones.

How to Grow
Full sun. Average soil. Start seeds in peat pots or direct-sow in the garden, but do not cover, as they need light to germinate. Once started, borage usually self-sows in subsequent years. Does best in cool weather and falters in hot, humid summers.

Herbal Use
The flowers make a beautiful garnish, and the tender new leaves add a cucumber flavor to salads. The leaves were used in many folk remedies, and oil from the seeds is currently being studied (especially in Japan) for several medicinal applications.

Brassica
Bras′si-ka
Cruciferae. Mustard family

Description
A large group of mostly annuals or biennials, including the many forms of cabbage, kale, collards, and mustards. About 30 species, native to Europe and Asia, and hundreds of cultivars.

■ *juncea*
Brown mustard. An annual with erect branching stems 3–4 ft. tall. The rough, deeply lobed leaves, 6 in. long, have a pungent odor and flavor and are eaten raw or cooked. Masses of yellow flowers in early summer are followed by slender pods filled with small round seeds. Black mustard (*B. nigra*) grows taller and has smaller seeds with a sharper flavor. Yellow mustard (*Sinapis alba,* also listed as *B. alba* or *B. hirta,* p. 237), grows shorter and has larger seeds. All zones.

How to Grow
Easy to grow in full sun and average soil. Sow seeds in early spring. If flea beetles attack the leaves, dust with rotenone. Harvest before the seedpods open, or it will self-sow like a weed. Dry whole stalks in large paper bags to catch the seeds.

Herbal Use
Whole or ground seeds are used as a seasoning, especially in Indian food. Ground seeds are mixed with vinegar and other ingredients to make the familiar condiment. Poultices and tonics made from the seeds and leaves are popular folk remedies. Caution: Mustard oil is a powerful irritant.

Calamintha
Kal-a-minth′a
Labiatae. Mint family

Description
Perennials, sometimes woody at the base, with scented leaves and clusters of many flowers. Only 7 species, native to Eurasia.

■ *grandiflora* p. 163
Calamint. A hardy perennial that's easy and handsome. Makes a mound of foliage, 12–18 in. tall and 24 in. wide, crowned by showy whorls of slender bright pink flowers in

spring and summer. The brittle, deep green leaves are oval with notched edges. A variegated form (not as hardy) has beautiful white marbling on the leaves. Zone 5.

How to Grow
Full sun or afternoon shade. Needs well-drained soil. Cut back long stems in fall and mulch with pine boughs where winters are cold. Often self-sows. Carefree, with no serious pests or diseases. Does well in a container outdoors.

Herbal Use
The leaves have a pleasant fruity aroma and can be dried for sachets or potpourri.

■ *nepeta*   *p. 163*
Calamint. A hardy perennial. Makes a mound of gracefully arranged gray-green foliage topped with a hazy cloud of tiny white or lilac flowers for weeks in summer and fall. Bees love it. The shiny leaves are mint-scented. Grows up to 2 ft. tall and wide and combines beautifully with shrub roses. Sometimes listed as *C. nepetoides*. Zone 5.

How to Grow
Like *C. grandiflora*.

Herbal Use
Same as for *C. grandiflora*.

Calendula
Ka-len´dew-la
Compositae. Composite family

Description
Annuals or perennials with slightly hairy leaves and long-stemmed daisylike blossoms. About 20 species, most native to the Mediterranean region.

■ *officinalis*   *p. 238*
Calendula. Bright and cheerful blossoms on long stalks top this easy-to-grow annual. Flower colors range from pale cream to yellow, gold, and orange. Grows 1–2 ft. tall. The oblong leaves are pale green, with a soft texture. All zones.

How to Grow
Full sun. Ordinary soil and watering. The seeds are big enough to handle easily. Direct-sow or set out transplants;

space 12 in. apart. Often attacked by aphids or slugs. Does best in cool weather and tolerates light frosts. Grow for summer bloom in the North, for fall to spring bloom where winters are mild. Deadhead to prolong blooming. May self-sow.

Herbal Use

Traditionally called pot marigold, the flowers are edible and can be used fresh or dried to add color and a mild flavor to salads, soups, or rice. In Europe, preparations of the flowers and leaves are applied externally to burns, wounds, sores, and the like.

Camellia

Ka-mee'lee-a
Theaceae. Tea family

Description

Evergreen shrubs or trees with leathery leaves. Many have showy waxlike flowers in fall, winter, or spring. About 80 species, native to eastern Asia, and thousands of cultivars.

■ *sinensis* p. 113

Tea. An evergreen shrub with compact, upright, rounded growth. Makes a good hedge or can be trained as a standard or espalier. Normally grows about 6 ft. tall and wide but can be kept smaller by pruning. The leaves are oval, about 3 in. long, with a glossy dark green color and leathery texture. The flowers are single, about 1 in. wide, with white or pale pink petals and a tuft of gold stamens. Blooms in early fall, then makes acorn-sized capsules with a few large seeds inside. Zone 6.

How to Grow

Part sun or filtered shade. Needs well-drained soil amended with plenty of peat or compost, and a thick layer of organic mulch such as ground bark or pine needles. Water regularly to keep the soil moist. Use an acid-type fertilizer. Grows well in a large pot that can be moved to a cool bright room in winter.

Herbal Use

Tea is a popular beverage that serves as a stimulant and diuretic. Only the tender new leaves are picked. Quick drying makes a mild-flavored green tea. Carefully controlled fermentation adds the richer flavor to black tea.

Capsicum

Kap′si-kum
Solanaceae. Nightshade family

Description

Shrubby perennials with simple alternate leaves, 5-petaled flowers, and bright-colored fruits with many seeds. About 10 species, native to Latin America.

■ *annuum p. 238 Pictured above*
Chili pepper, paprika. There are dozens of varieties with peppers of different size, shape, flavor, and potency. Most are bushy plants 2–3 ft. tall, with sturdy, upright, branching stems. The leaves are smooth pointed ovals, thin as paper. Small white flowers soon develop into dry or fleshy fruits that ripen to bright red. Tender to frost but is grown as an annual in all zones.

How to Grow

Full sun. Average garden soil with regular watering. Start seeds indoors 8–10 weeks before last frost. Wait until the soil is warm before setting out transplants. Chili peppers thrive in heat: the hotter the weather, the hotter the flavor. Easy to grow, with no serious pests.

Herbal Use

Fresh or dried chili peppers are essential for Mexican food and are also used in Chinese and Indian cuisine. Paprika, ground from dried sweet peppers, is popular in eastern European cooking. Medicinally, chili peppers have been taken internally for various ailments and applied externally for rheumatism and arthritis. Organic gardeners spray a chili pepper solution on garden plants to deter aphids and other pests. Capsaicin is the compound in chili peppers that produces a burning sensation.

Carthamus

Kar-tham´us
Compositae. Composite family

Description
Annuals with spiny foliage and thistlelike flower heads. About 14 species, native to the Mediterranean region and Asia.

■ *tinctorius* *p. 239*
Safflower. An upright annual, about 3 ft. tall, with stiff stems that branch near the top. The scant foliage is lobed and prickly, like thistles. The flower heads, about 1 in. wide, have a tuft of gold-orange florets surrounded by spiny bracts. All zones.

How to Grow
Full sun. Average or dry soil. Sow directly in the garden in late spring. Sow the rice-sized seeds about $\frac{1}{2}$ in. deep and 8–12 in. apart. Carefree and easy to grow.

Herbal Use
The seeds are pressed for a salad and cooking oil. Dried florets can be substituted for saffron as a food coloring or can be used to dye cotton or silk fabrics shades of yellow or red. (The colors are pretty but fade quickly.) The flowers have many medicinal uses, including the treatment of ear disorders and menstrual problems.

Carum

Kay´rum
Umbelliferae. Carrot family

Description
Annuals or perennials with finely divided leaves and umbels of small flowers. About 30 species, native to the Old World.

■ *carvi* *p. 239*
Caraway. A biennial, it makes a rosette of feathery leaves like carrot tops the first year. The second year, it sends up a 2-ft. stalk topped with white flowers, like Queen-Anne's-lace, then goes to seed. Zone 4.

How to Grow
Full sun. Average soil with regular watering. Plant in spring. Mark planting sites 9–12 in. apart and sow a few seeds at

each site. Thin to the strongest seedling. Mulch to control weeds in summer, and use a covering of boughs to protect from winter cold.

Herbal Use
Cut whole stalks when they turn yellow or tan and dry the seed heads in a paper bag. The seeds are used to flavor breads, potatoes, cabbage, and other foods; they are chewed or made into tea to soothe an upset stomach, relieve menstrual pain, and stimulate milk secretion.

Catha
Ka′tha
Celastraceae. Staff-tree family

Description
An evergreen shrub. Only 1 species, from East Africa.

■ *edulis* p. 136
Chat, khat, Arabian tea. A bushy evergreen shrub that grows 20–30 ft. tall in the wild or 4–5 ft. tall in pots. Oval leaves, to 4 in. long, are smooth glossy green. The bark has a reddish tinge. May bear clusters of tiny white flowers. Zone 8.

How to Grow
Full sun. Average soil and watering. Tolerates dry spells. Where hardy it makes a fine specimen or hedge and can be pruned or trained to shape. Grows well in a container and seems to like being pot-bound. Put it in a bright sunny window for the winter.

Herbal Use
In the Middle East, where chat use predates coffee by a thousand years, the fresh leaves are chewed or brewed into tea and taken as a stimulant. Must be used fresh; the active ingredient deteriorates within a few days of picking. Caution: Can cause numerous disquieting symptoms, including high blood pressure, headache, and hyperthermia.

Caulophyllum
Kaul-oh-fill'um
Berberidaceae. Barberry family

Description
Perennial woodland wildflowers. Only 2 species, one from eastern North America and the other from eastern Asia.

■ *thalictrioides* *p. 164*
Blue cohosh, squawroot. A perennial wildflower, 2–3 ft. tall, native to shady woodlands. The compound leaves with lobed leaflets have a smooth texture and blue-green color that is quite distinctive. The starry clusters of small yellow-green flowers are inconspicuous in spring, but the shiny blue berries are pretty in late summer. Zone 3.

How to Grow
Needs part or full shade. Prefers rich, fertile soil and steady moisture. Spreads slowly by rhizomes. Divide every few years.

Herbal Use
Root preparations were used by Native Americans and early settlers to aid in childbirth and to treat urinary infections, abdominal cramps, profuse menstruation, and uterine disease. Research confirms its effectiveness. Caution: Avoid during pregnancy.

Ceanothus
See-a-no'thus
Rhamnaceae. Buckthorn family

Description
Deciduous or evergreen shrubs or small trees, usually with dense foliage and profuse clusters of tiny blue, violet, or white flowers. About 55 species, all native to North America.

■ *americanus* *p. 114*
New Jersey tea. A small (3–4 ft. tall and wide) deciduous shrub, native to eastern North America, where it grows on sandy banks and roadcuts. Makes a thick, deep root that enables it to survive dry spells. The dark green leaves are simple ovals, 2–3 in. long. Fluffy clusters of creamy white flowers catch your attention in early summer. Zone 4.

How to Grow
Full sun. Needs good drainage. A good choice for difficult

sites with sandy or gravelly soil. Prune back by one-third in spring to encourage denser, more compact growth.

Herbal Use
Dried leaves were used as a tea substitute in colonial days. Thick roots, with a distinct red color, were used in folk remedies for colds, fevers, and sore throats and as a sedative.

Cedronella
See-dro-nee´la
Labiatae. Mint family

Description
A tender perennial with fragrant leaves. Only 1 species, native to the Canary Islands.

■ *canariensis* *p. 213*
Balm of Gilead, Canary balm. A slender, airy plant with upright stems reaching 2–3 ft. or taller. Compound leaves have 3 small leaflets with a pleasant lemony-fruity aroma. Spikes of tiny pale flowers are inconspicuous. Also listed as *C. triphylla*. Zone 10.

How to Grow
Full sun. Prefers sandy soil and frequent watering; wilts quickly if it dries out. Prune often to encourage branching and to keep it bushy. Plant outdoors when the soil is warm. It will make a sizable specimen in one season, but frost kills it. Cut back and pot up to overwinter indoors, or buy a new plant each year.

Herbal Use
Fresh or dried leaves make a pleasant tea. Reputed to work as a mosquito repellent, like citronella candles, but only if direct sun releases the essential oil from the leaves. Rub leaves on pets' fur to repel fleas.

Ceratonia
Ser-ra-tone´ee-a
Leguminosae. Pea family

Description
Evergreen trees with pinnate leaves and pods filled with sweet edible pulp. Only 2 species, native to Arabia and Somalia.

■ *siliqua* p. 137
Carob, St.-John's-bread. A stout shrub or tree with shiny, leathery, evergreen compound leaves. Male and female flowers are produced on separate trees. If pollinated, female trees produce long beanlike pods with sugary pulp and hard seeds inside. Grows up to 40 ft. tall and wide, but can be kept smaller by pruning. Zone 9.

How to Grow
Full sun. Tolerates poor soil, heat, and drought once established. Where hardy, it makes a dense screen or specimen tree. Otherwise, it can be grown in a large pot as a handsome foliage plant, but it won't bloom or make pods.

Herbal Use
Fresh pulp from the pods is soft, sticky, and tasty. Powder ground from dried pods is used as a substitute for chocolate.

Chamaemelum
Kam-e-mel′um
Compositae. Composite family

Description
Perennial herbs with aromatic foliage and daisylike blossoms. Only 3 or 4 species, native to Europe and the Mediterranean region.

■ *nobile* p. 164 *Pictured below*
Roman chamomile. A hardy perennial that makes a flat, spreading, branching mat of finely dissected leaves that release a pungent fragrance when bruised. Grows about 6 in. tall and 12 in. wide. Blossoms like tiny daisies open from summer to fall. 'Grandiflora' has larger flowers; 'Flore-Pleno'

has double flowers; 'Treneague' is a flowerless form used for lawns. Zone 4.

How to Grow
Full sun. Average soil. Prefers cool summers and can't take extreme heat, whether humid or dry. Can be planted between flagstones or used as an herbal lawn or ground cover. To start a chamomile lawn, prepare the soil well in advance, then plant seedlings or divisions 6–12 in. apart and mulch to control weeds. Established plantings tolerate mowing and light foot traffic.

Herbal Use
Pick flower heads regularly and dry them on a paper or screen. They make a soothing tea with an applelike fragrance, popular as a folk remedy for colds, flus, upset stomach, and insomnia; or to wash irritated skin or sore gums. Also used as a rinse to lighten blond hair. Organic gardeners spray the tea on seed flats to protect seedlings from damping-off.

Chenopodium
Key-no-po´dee-um
Chenopodiaceae. Goosefoot family

Description
Annuals or perennials, often weedy, sometimes used for medicine or food. About 150 species, native to temperate zones.

■ *ambrosioides* *p. 240*
Epazote, wormseed, Mexican tea. A bushy upright annual, 4–5 ft. tall. Looks like a little tree, with a woody trunk, many branches, coarsely toothed leaves, and dense spikes of tiny flowers in late summer. All aboveground parts have an extremely pungent odor. All zones.

How to Grow
Full sun. Average or dry soil. Easily started from seed. One plant is enough. Uproot it before it goes to seed or you'll have hundreds to pull up next year. Sometimes overwinters.

Herbal Use
A pinch of dried leaves is a popular seasoning in Mexico, added to bean dishes to reduce flatulence. Essential oil from the flowers and seeds was formerly used as a treatment for intestinal parasites and skin fungi. Caution: The oil is highly toxic. Handling the plant can cause dermatitis.

■ *botrys*   *p. 240*

Ambrosia, Jerusalem oak. An annual that makes a mound about 2 ft. tall and wide, with sticky, hairy, light green leaves that are shaped like oak leaves and smell pungent, like turpentine. Bears long, dense, cylindrical clusters of tiny yellow-green flowers in late summer. An unusual and interesting accent plant. All zones.

How to Grow

Like *C. ambrosioides.*

Herbal Use

Dried flower spikes are used in wreath making and potpourri. Used medicinally like *C. ambrosioides;* similar cautions apply.

Chrysanthemum

Kri-san´thee-mum
Compositae. Composite family

Description

A diverse group of annuals, perennials, and subshrubs, most with daisylike blossoms. Classification of these plants is in flux. The genus used to include some 100–200 species, but there have been various attempts to regroup the species into other genera, so the entries below have many synonyms.

■ *balsamita*   *p. 165*

Costmary, bibleleaf, alecost. A hardy perennial that spreads a carpet of basal leaves in spring and sends up floppy 3-ft. stalks topped with small yellow buttonlike flowers in late summer. The basal leaves are oblong, about 6 in. long, with toothed edges and silvery hairs. Fresh or dried, they have a pleasant fragrance. Also listed as *Tanacetum balsamita.* Zone 4.

How to Grow

Full sun. Well-drained soil and regular watering. May spread invasively. Confine it, or divide and replant every few years. Cut flower stalks to the ground after bloom fades.

Herbal Use

The leaves, which have a pleasant aroma but a bitter flavor, historically were used to flavor ale, in potpourri, as a moth repellent, and as bookmarks in Bibles.

■ *parthenium* p. 165   *Pictured above*
Feverfew. A popular and carefree perennial, 1–3 ft. tall, that
bears masses of small daisies off and on from late spring to
early winter. There are single and double forms, with yellow
or white flowers. Makes a soft mound of ferny-looking, compound leaves that are evergreen in mild winters. 'Aureum' has
golden yellow foliage. Also listed as *Matricaria capensis* or
Tanacetum parthenium. Zone 5.

How to Grow
Full sun. Well-drained soil with regular watering. Not reliably
winter-hardy in the North or summer-hardy in the South, but
it self-sows. Cut back after flowering. Subject to aphids.

Herbal Use
Traditionally used as a medicinal herb. Recent studies show
that preparations of the dried leaves can reduce the frequency
and duration of migraine headaches and associated nausea.

■ *pyrethrum* p. 166
Pyrethrum. A hardy perennial that makes an airy clump
18–24 in. tall. Has finely cut, fernlike foliage and daisylike
blossoms, 2 in. wide, with yellow disks and white rays. Also
listed as *C. cinerariaefolium*. Painted daisy, listed as *C. coc-
cineum* or *Pyrethrum roseum*, is a popular perennial with red,
pink, or white daisies. It is easier to grow than pyrethrum,
because it tolerates more soil moisture, and has similar but
weaker insecticidal properties. Zone 5.

How to Grow
Full sun. Grows best in lean, dry soil; flops over in rich, moist
soil. Cut back after flowering. Propagate by seed or division.
Needs good drainage and light mulch to survive cold wet
winters.

Herbal Use

The yellow disk florets produce compounds that kill insects on contact but are harmless to mammals and birds. Dried, powdered flowers have been used for centuries and were once sold as "Dalmation insect powder" or "insect dust." Now the active ingredients are extracted from the flowers to make aerosol house and garden insecticides.

Cimicifuga

Sim-i-cif´u-ga
Ranunculaceae. Buttercup family

Description

Perennials with upright stems, large compound leaves, and white flowers. About 15 species, native to rich woodlands in the north temperate zone.

■ *racemosa*   p. 166

Black cohosh, bugbane, black snakeroot. A long-lived, easy-to-grow perennial, common in eastern woodlands. Spreads underground with thick black rhizomes. The glossy green leaves are divided into many toothed segments. Wiry stems up to 6 ft. tall carry long tapered wands of starry white flowers for a month or more in summer. The flowers have a strong odor, said to repel insects. Zone 3.

How to Grow

Needs full or part shade, rich organic soil, and constant moisture. Top-dress with aged manure or compost every year. Plant in spring or fall, spaced 2 ft. apart. Divide only when the clump gets too big. Despite its height, it doesn't need staking.

Herbal Use

Alcohol extracts of the rhizomes traditionally were used for bronchitis, nervous disorders, and menstrual irregularities and to aid childbirth. Caution: Avoid during pregnancy.

Cinnamomum

Sin-na-mo´mum
Lauraceae. Laurel family

Description

Evergreen tropical trees or shrubs with aromatic leaves and bark, providing camphor, cinnamon, and fragrant timber.

About 250 species, native to eastern and southeastern Asia and Australia.

■ *camphora p. 137*
Camphor tree. A tropical tree with shiny, smooth, pale green leaves about 3 in. long, shaped like peach leaves. New growth is flushed with red. Clusters of tiny yellow flowers in spring are followed by small shiny black fruits in fall. All parts are fragrant. Often planted as a shade tree in Florida and California, where it can grow up to 50 ft. tall, but also does well in a container. As a houseplant, it makes an interesting alternative to the ubiquitous *Ficus benjamina* and can be kept 6–8 ft. tall. Zone 9.

How to Grow
Full or part sun. Ordinary or sandy soil. Prefers regular watering but tolerates lapses. Can be shaped as a tree or shrub. Subject to aphids and scale.

Herbal Use
The wood, bark, and leaves are distilled to yield camphor, used in medicines and as an insect repellent. The barks of several related species constitute different kinds of cinnamon, widely used as a spice and flavoring.

Cistus
Sis′tus
Cistaceae. Rock rose family

Description
Mostly evergreen shrubs of low spreading habit, with simple opposite leaves and wide, open flowers. Some yield fragrant resins. About 17 species, native to the Mediterranean region, and a few cultivated hybrids.

■ *ladanifer p. 138 Pictured opposite*
Crimson-spot rock rose. An evergreen shrub that makes a mound 3–5 ft. tall and wide. Narrow dark green leaves are dotted with sticky glands that release a wonderful incenselike fragrance on warm, still days. Round flowers 2 in. wide have a crimson dot at the base of each white petal. Var. *immaculatus* has spotless white flowers. Zone 8.

How to Grow
Full sun. Ordinary or lean, gravelly soil. Loves heat; tolerates drought once established. Pinch tips to fatten young plants.

Thin old branches from established plants. Pest-free and easy to grow. Does well in a large clay pot and will bloom in a sunny window.

Herbal Use
Fragrant resin extracted from the leaves and twigs is used in flavoring and perfumery. It was used in traditional medicine as an expectorant for catarrh, an astringent for diarrhea, a styptic for bleeding, and a mild nerve sedative.

Citrus
Sit´rus
Rutaceae. Citrus family

Description
Evergreen trees or shrubs, usually spiny, with glossy leaves, richly fragrant flowers, and aromatic juicy fruit. This genus includes oranges, lemons, grapefruits, limes, and other citrus fruits. About 16 species, native to Asia.

■ *limon* *p. 138*
Lemon. Lemons are beautiful little trees with shiny, leathery, bright green leaves; powerfully fragrant blossoms; and showy, tasty fruit. Full-size trees reach 20–25 ft. tall and wide. Dwarf forms start bearing when only a few feet tall and eventually reach 10–12 ft. Don't plant a seed—you'll just get a thorny bush that won't flower for years. Buy a named cultivar from a nursery, and it will start producing good fruit in just a year or two. The 'Ponderosa' lemon has fruits the size of grapefruits, with thick rinds. 'Meyer' and 'Improved Meyer' make small, rounded, very juicy, not-too-sour fruits with thin rinds and tolerate more cold than other lemons. 'Eureka' has excellent flavor and keeps bearing all year long. Zone 9.

How to Grow

Full sun. Outdoors, lemons need ordinary or better soil and deep, infrequent watering. Feed regularly with an acid-type fertilizer that supplies iron and other micronutrients. In cold climates, you can keep a dwarf lemon tree for many years in a 12-in. pot, taking it outdoors for the summer and over-wintering it in a cool sunroom or greenhouse, or a sunny window. Subject to aphids, spider mites, and scale.

Herbal Use

Lemon juice and peel are indispensable flavorings. Lemon oil is used in furniture polish, paints, household cleansers, and detergents. Compounds from lemon and other citrus rinds are the active ingredients in new flea and mosquito repellents.

Coffea
Kof´ee-a
Rubiaceae. Madder family

Description

Evergreen shrubs or trees with opposite leaves, fragrant white flowers, and fleshy berries that hold 2 large seeds. About 40 species, most native to tropical Africa.

■ *arabica* p. 139
Coffee. A small evergreen tree. Glossy leaves with wavy edges are arranged in pairs on slender branches. Clusters of very fragrant small white flowers open in the leaf axils in spring and summer, followed by berries that slowly ripen to ruby red. Grows to 20 ft. or more outdoors but about 4 ft. as a houseplant. Other species of *Coffea* are also grown to produce coffee. Zone 10.

How to Grow

Part-day or filtered sun. Rich organic soil with regular watering. Prefers humid air. Makes a rewarding houseplant. Set it outdoors under a tree in the summer, in a bright place (but out of direct sun) indoors in winter. Nurseries usually sell seedlings that start flowering and making berries in 3–5 years. Subject to scale, mealybugs, and spider mites.

Herbal Use

Seeds removed from the berries are dried, roasted, and ground to make the beverage. Caffeine, the famous stimulant in coffee, is also an ingredient in cold, allergy, and weight-control products.

Coleus

Ko'lee-us
Labiatae. Mint family

Description

Perennials or annuals, usually succulent, with square stems, opposite leaves, and small white or pale lavender flowers. About 150 species, native to the Old World tropics.

■ *amboinicus* p. 213

Cuban oregano, Spanish oregano. A tender perennial that makes a spreading mound 2–3 ft. tall and 3–4 ft. wide. Rounded leaves, 2–3 in. wide, are thick and succulent and have a velvety surface and pale green color. They smell and taste like oregano. Flowers are insignificant. There's a gorgeous variegated form with white-edged leaves, and another with mottled green and gold leaves. Also listed as *Plectranthus amboinicus*. Zone 10.

How to Grow

Full sun. Prefers sandy soil that drains quickly. Thrives in hot, dry weather. Treat it as an annual in the summer garden, or grow it in a pot or hanging basket. Prune to keep it compact and bushy. Easy to propagate: root tip cuttings in a glass of water or a pot of moist soil. Sensitive to cold and may rot in wet weather, but virtually pest-free.

Herbal Use

Use fresh leaves for seasoning, as an oregano substitute. Doesn't preserve well, but you can pick it year-round.

Conradina

Kon-ra-dee'na
Labiatae. Mint family

Description

Low shrubs with aromatic needlelike leaves. Only 4 species, native to the southeastern United States.

■ *verticillata* p. 167

Cumberland rosemary. A small evergreen shrub, usually under 15 in. tall. Forms a spreading mound of thin stems with fine, dark green leaves that resemble rosemary foliage but have a strong minty aroma. Small pale pink-purple flowers appear in midspring. Rare and endangered in its native habitat—sandy riverbanks in eastern Tennessee and Kentucky—but nursery-propagated plants are popular in gardens from New England to Texas. Zone 5.

How to Grow
Full or part sun. Needs good drainage and does best on dry, sandy sites. Can be pruned to shape. Makes a neat edging or specimen. Recently introduced to cultivation but is now offered by many nurseries.

Herbal Use
Not a traditional herb, but dried leaves can be used in sachets.

Coreopsis
Ko-ree-op´sis
Compositae. Composite family

Description
Perennials or annuals, most with abundant displays of yellow daisylike blossoms. More than 100 species, native to the New World and Africa.

■ *tinctoria* *p. 241*
Dyer's coreopsis. An annual prairie wildflower, popular in meadow gardens and prairie plantings. Slender stalks 1–3 ft. tall combine well with grasses. Foliage is scant, but the upright branching stalks carry scores of bright yellow, maroon, and/or bicolor blossoms. Blooms all summer if deadheaded. Also listed as *Calliopsis tinctoria*. All zones.

How to Grow
Full sun. Tolerates poor or dry soil and heat. Easy to grow from seed sown in fall or spring. Self-sows readily.

Herbal Use
Fresh or dried flowers yield gold, orange, and rust dyes for wool and other fibers.

Coriandrum
Ko-ree-an´drum
Umbelliferae. Carrot family

Description
Annual herbs with strong-scented leaves, umbels of pale flowers, and fragrant seeds. Only 2 species, native to Eurasia.

■ *sativum* *p. 241*

Cilantro, coriander, Chinese parsley. A fast-growing annual. Forms a low rosette of lobed or pinnately compound leaves, then stalks of white or pale rosy lavender flowers bolt 1–3 ft. tall. Soon goes to seed and dies. New slow-bolting varieties yield a longer harvest of larger leaves. All zones.

How to Grow

Full sun. Not fussy about soil. Sow small patches at 2–4-week intervals, starting in early spring. Sow seeds where the plants are to grow, and thin seedlings to 6 in. apart. Grows well in cool weather.

Herbal Use

The fresh leaves are a staple in Mexican and Oriental cookery, and the aromatic seeds are used in curries and ground as a spice.

Cornus

Kor´nus
Cornaceae. Dogwood family

Description

Deciduous trees or shrubs with attractive bark, leaves, flowers, and fruits. About 45 species, native to the north temperate zone.

■ *florida* *p. 114*

Flowering dogwood. A native tree beloved throughout the eastern United States, and an excellent choice for small gardens. Blooms in early spring, just before the leaves expand. Each cluster of small flowers is framed by 4 large white or pink bracts. Pointed oval leaves are rich green all summer, then turn dark red or maroon in fall, when the bright red berries ripen. There are many cultivars. Zone 5.

How to Grow

Part sun or shade, especially where summers are hot. Prefers well-drained, acidic soil with a thick layer of organic mulch. Needs watering during dry spells. Susceptible to borers, various leafspots, and a fungal disease called anthracnose. Don't try to transplant a wild tree; one from a nursery will grow much better.

Herbal Use

During the Civil War, the bark of flowering dogwood was

used as a substitute for quinine to treat malaria. Dogwood twigs have been used as "chewing sticks"—the forerunners of modern toothbrushes.

Cotinus
Kot´i-nus, ko-ty´nus
Anacardiaceae. Sumac family

Description
Deciduous shrubs or small trees. Only 3 species, native to the southeastern United States and Asia.

■ *obovatus* *p. 115*
American smoke tree. A small tree, 30 ft. tall, that grows wild on rocky limestone ledges from the Appalachians down into Texas. Leaves shaped like ping-pong paddles turn vivid shades of red, orange, and gold in fall. The flowers are small and drop soon, but the much-branched flower stalks expand into hairy puffs that last all season. *C. coggygria*, smoke bush, is a popular garden shrub, usually under 12 ft. tall, with green or purple leaves and cream, pink, or purple "smoke." Both species are hardy to zone 4.

How to Grow
Full or part sun. Tolerates poor soil, acidic or alkaline, and summer dryness. Blooms on new growth, so prune in early spring. Cutting the stems back to the ground each year forces tall straight shoots with larger leaves. No serious pests or diseases.

Herbal Use
Twigs and wood from both American smoke tree and smoke bush make permanent yellow dyes for wool and other fibers.

Crataegus
Kra-tee´gus
Rosaceae. Rose family

Description
Deciduous small trees or shrubs, usually thorny, with white flowers in spring and small gold, red, or purplish fruits in fall and winter. At least 300 species, native to the north temperate zone, and many hybrids and varieties.

■ *phaenopyrum*   *p. 115*
Washington hawthorn. An excellent small tree with multiple trunks, spreading branches, and thorny twigs. Grows about 25 ft. tall. Clusters of small white flowers open in June. Bright red fruits color in late summer and hang on through winter. The glossy triangular or oval leaves turn bright red in fall. Many other kinds of hawthorn are also good garden trees. Zone 3.

How to Grow
Full or part sun. Very tolerant of poor soil conditions, such as alkalinity, compaction, low organic matter, and seasonal wetness or dryness. Needs minimal pruning. Has few pests.

Herbal Use
Hawthorn fruits and flowers have been used in Native American, Chinese, and European traditions as a heart tonic and are still used clinically in Europe for hypertension and angina pectoris.

Crocus
Kro´kus
Iridaceae. Iris family

Description
Small perennials with rounded corms, grassy leaves, and bright white, yellow, blue, or purple flowers in spring or fall. About 80 species, native from the Mediterranean region to China.

■ *sativus*   *p. 167*
Saffron. A hardy perennial that starts growing in early fall and dies back in late spring. Makes a small tuft of grasslike leaves, 6 in. tall, and pale lavender flowers that open about 2 in. wide on sunny fall days. Don't confuse saffron with meadow saffron, *Colchicum autumnale,* a poisonous plant that blooms at the same time but has much larger flowers and wider leaves. Zone 5.

How to Grow
Full sun. Needs well-drained soil that dries out quickly; can't take constant moisture, especially during summer dormancy. Plant purchased corms in early fall. Can be divided after a few years. Grows well in containers; set in a warm, dry place for the summer.

Herbal Use

The slender, 3-lobed, reddish orange stigmas are the spice saffron, which gives color and flavor to paella, risotto, and other dishes. Use tweezers to pluck them from open flowers, dry on a sheet of paper, and store in an airtight container.

Curcuma

Kur-koo'ma
Zingiberaceae. Ginger family

Description

Tender perennials with thick rhizomes, cornlike leaves, and large showy flowers. About 40 species, native to tropical Asia.

■ *domestica* p. 214

Turmeric. An exotic-looking perennial that spreads to make a patch of leafy stalks 2–5 ft. tall. Bears spikes of pinkish yellow flowers, 1 in. wide, in early winter. All parts have a spicy fragrance. Also listed as *C. longa*. Zone 8.

How to Grow

Full or part sun. Prefers rich soil and frequent watering. Outdoors, protect from severe cold. Where not hardy, grows well in a container. Put it outdoors in summer and fertilize liberally. Bring to a cool, dry place and withhold water in winter. Cut off old stalks and divide rhizomes in spring.

Herbal Use

Dormant rhizomes are harvested, dried, ground, and used as the main ingredient in most curry powders and many mustards. Makes a yellow dye on fabric or paper that is pretty at first but soon fades. Also used medicinally.

Cymbopogon

Sim-bo-po'gon
Gramineae. Grass family

Description

Tropical grasses with slender arching leaves. Many are very aromatic, used for fragrance and flavoring. More than 50 species, native to tropical climates in the Old World.

■ *citratus* p. 214
Lemon grass. A vigorous but frost-tender perennial grass. Makes a clump of evergreen leaves, 1 in. wide and up to 6 ft. long, with a stiff midrib and sharp edges. The leaves have a strong lemon aroma. Rarely flowers in temperate gardens. Zone 10.

How to Grow
Full sun. Average or moist soil. Can't stand frost and is hardy outdoors only in the mildest regions. In most of the United States, a plant set in the ground after frost will make a nice clump by midsummer. Dig and divide it in fall to pot up a start for overwintering indoors, or buy new plants every spring.

Herbal Use
Harvest leaves from the outside of the clump to make hot or iced tea or to season Thai food. Used medicinally to reduce fever, relieve cold symptoms, ease headaches, and soothe upset stomaches. The insect repellent citronella comes from a related and similar-looking species, *C. nardus.*

Dianthus
Dy-an´thus
Caryophyllaceae. Pink family

Description
Annuals, biennials, or perennials, usually with grassy leaves and fragrant flowers. About 300 species, most from Europe and Asia.

■ *caryophyllus* p. 168
Clove pink. A short-lived perennial with grassy blue-green leaves in tufts at the base and paired on the stems. Flower stalks 12–18 in. tall carry single or double blossoms about 1 in. wide with red, pink, or white petals and a rich spicy fragrance. Scented forms of cottage pinks, *D. plumarius,* and Allwood pinks, *D. × allwoodii,* are similar and equally desirable. For fragrance, don't bother with the large-flowered forms of *D. caryophyllus* grown as florist's carnations. Zone 5.

How to Grow
Full sun. Prefers fertile soil with plenty of lime. Needs good drainage, especially to survive the winter. Easily raised from seed; usually starts flowering the second year. Cut back stalks after blooming. Divide every few years in late summer.

Herbal Use
Clove-scented petals traditionally were used to flavor wine or were brewed with sugar and water to make a tasty syrup for fruit salads. Dried flowers retain their color and fragrance in potpourri. Used as a diuretic in traditional Chinese medicine.

Dictamnus
Dik-tam′nus
Rutaceae. Citrus family

Description
A hardy perennial with pinnately compound leaves and white or pink flowers. The foliage releases an aromatic oil; legend says that you can touch a match to a leaf and ignite this oil without harming the plant. Only 1 species, native to Eurasia.

■ *albus* *p. 168*
Gas plant. An erect perennial that makes a clump 2–4 ft. tall. The leaves are glossy dark green and have a strong citrusy or medicinal fragrance. In summer, the sturdy stems are topped with striking clusters of pure white flowers, followed by ornamental seedpods. Selected forms have rose or purple flowers. Zone 3.

How to Grow
Full sun. Prefers fertile, well-drained soil. Starts slowly from seed and resents transplanting, so buy a container-grown plant and put it in its permanent location. Lives for decades, very gradually developing into a large clump, and never needs division. Carefree. Does best where summer nights are cool.

Herbal Use
Dried leaves make a pleasant tea, used traditionally to calm the nerves and reduce fevers.

Digitalis
Di-ji-tal′is
Scrophulariaceae. Foxglove family

Description
Perennials or biennials with a basal rosette of large simple leaves and upright stalks crowded with bell-shaped flowers. About 19 species, native to Europe and Asia.

■ *purpurea* p. 242
Common foxglove. Usually grows as a biennial. Makes a
first-year rosette up to 2 ft. wide of furry, oblong leaves. The
second year, several stalks 3–5 ft. tall carry dozens of thim-
ble-sized flowers in shades of magenta, rosy pink, or white.
Bloom continues for several weeks or more in summer.
Gather the dry stalks of round seedpods for winter arrangements. Zone 4.

How to Grow
Part shade; avoid afternoon sun, especially where summers
are hot. Needs fertile, well-drained soil and regular watering.
Space 2 ft. or more apart, establishing plants by fall for
bloom the following year. Cut spent flower stalks to the
ground to prolong the bloom season. Easily started from seed
and self-sows readily. Prone to slugs.

Herbal Use
A traditional herb of lasting importance. Doctors use compounds extracted from the leaves to treat several heart conditions. Caution: Ingesting the leaves can be fatal. Do not
self-medicate.

Dipsacus
Dip´sa-kus
Dipsacaceae. Teasel family

Description
Biennials or perennials with prickly leaves, stems, and flower
heads. About 15 species, native to Eurasia and Africa.

■ *sylvestris* p. 242
Fuller's teasel. A hardy biennial. The first year, oblong leaves
with toothed edges and a prickly surface make a rosette 1–2
ft. wide (depending on soil fertility and moisture). The second year, stiff prickly flower stalks bolt 3–6 ft. tall. Paired
leaves join across the stalk, making shallow cups where water
collects; that water traditionally was considered to have
magic properties. The flower heads are cylindrical, 3–5 in.
long, covered with springy down-curved bracts and ringed
with small, pale violet flowers. Often confused (partly because Linnaeus mixed up the Latin names) with *D. fullonum*,
a roadside weed with similar foliage and habit but with floral
bracts that are straight and brittle, useless for brushing fabric. Zone 4.

How to Grow
Full sun. Average soil and watering. Raised from seed sown in spring or summer for bloom the next year. Easy to grow.

Herbal Use
The dried flower heads were used from the days of the Romans through the 20th century to brush the surface of woven fabrics, making a soft flannellike finish. Washing with tea made from the leaves was an Iroquois folk remedy for acne.

Echinacea
Ek-i-nay´see-a
Compositae. Composite family

Description
Hardy perennials with rough or hairy leaves and daisylike blossoms with prominent cone-shaped disks and drooping rays. About 10 species, native to the eastern United States.

■ *purpurea* p. 169 *Pictured below*
Purple coneflower. A popular perennial with coarse-textured dark green leaves, at the base and on tough stalks 3–4 ft. tall. Daisylike blossoms, 3–4 in. wide, have rose or pink rays and orange disks. Blooms all summer and attracts many butterflies. 'Bright Star' has deep pink rays and a maroon cone. 'White Swan' has white rays and a bronze cone. *E. angustifolia* and *E. pallida* (p. 169) are less commonly planted but are just as important medicinally. Zone 4.

How to Grow

Full sun. Tolerates poor or dry soil and heat. Easy from seed and may bloom the first year. Divide older plants in spring or fall. Deadheading prolongs bloom in summer, but let the seed heads ripen in fall to feed the birds and to provide winter interest.

Herbal Use

Echinacea species were used by the Plains Indians for more medicinal purposes than any other plant group. Now echinacea preparations are used, especially in Europe, as a nonspecific immune-system stimulant that can help reduce the severity and duration of cold and flu symptoms. Caution: Not recommended for anyone with diabetes, AIDS, multiple sclerosis, lupus, or other immune-system disorders.

Elettaria
El-e-tay´ree-a
Zingiberaceae. Ginger family

Description

Tender perennials with thick aromatic rhizomes and tall leafy stalks. About 6 species, native to Southeast Asia.

■ *cardamomum* p. 215

Cardamom, grains-of-paradise. A gingerlike plant that spreads by rhizomes to make a dense clump of erect shoots. Grows quite tall outdoors in frost-free regions but usually 2–4 ft. in pots. The long smooth leaves release a pleasant fragrance when you touch them. Where established in the ground, it bears small flowers on short separate stalks, followed by bean-sized pods filled with fragrant, tasty seeds. It rarely flowers in pots. Zone 10.

How to Grow

Part or full shade. Usually grown in a container. Prefers loose, peaty soil and regular watering. Very easy to grow and always looks tidy. Put it in a shady place outdoors for the summer. One of the best (and only) herbs for a north window indoors in winter. Easily propagated by division. Subject to red spider mites.

Herbal Use

The seeds are an important flavoring for curries and other Indian foods; also used to flavor breads and baked goods. Seeds are chewed as a digestive aid and breath freshener.

Ephedra
E-fee´dra
Ephedraceae. Ephedra family

Description
Shrubby plants, almost leafless, with conspicuous green twigs. About 40 species, native to the Old and New World.

■ *sinica* p. 116
Chinese ephedra, joint fir. An unusual evergreen shrub from China. It makes a spreading mound, 2 ft. tall and 3 ft. wide, of slender green twigs that resemble long crooked pine needles. At the joints or nodes are tiny scalelike leaves and male and female flowers in small separate cones. *E. viridis* and *E. nevadensis*, both called Mormon tea, are native to arid sites in the Southwest. They grow 4–6 ft. tall but generally resemble Chinese ephedra and have similar properties. Zone 6.

How to Grow
Full sun. Not fussy about soil but needs good drainage. In a container, let it dry out between waterings. In cold climates, bring it indoors to a cool bright room for winter. Propagate by seed or layering. Can be used as a ground cover, low hedge, edging, or accent plant. Easy to grow and trouble-free.

Herbal Use
Used in China for more than 2,000 years to treat colds, flus, fevers, chills, coughs, and the like. The effects are due to the alkaloid ephedrine, present in over-the-counter products for colds and asthma. The American species contain little ephedrine, but twigs brew into a pleasant tea. Caution: In excess, ephedra can cause edginess, visions, and high blood pressure.

Equisetum
Ek-wi-see´tum
Equisetaceae. Horsetail family

Description
An ancient group of primitive plants, mostly perennial, with creeping rhizomes, hollow stems, whorls of thin leaves, and spore-bearing cones. About 30 species, found worldwide.

■ *hyemale* p. 170
Scouring rush. An unusual perennial, hardy and evergreen. Spreads underground to make a dense thicket of hollow dark

green stems, $1/4$ in. thick and 3–5 ft. tall, with a rough texture of stiff vertical ridges. Tiny leaves make a ring of chaff at each node. Makes an ornamental accent, like bamboo, but confine the roots so it doesn't get out of control. Horsetail, *E. arvense,* has bright green stems 1 ft. tall that branch at the nodes, making a fluffy mound of foliage. It is valued as a medicinal plant, but it spreads invasively, especially in damp, sandy soil. Zone 4.

How to Grow
Part sun. Average soil and watering. One plant is enough. Use a bottomless 5-gal. pot to keep it from spreading. Hard to eradicate, even with herbicides. Cut old stems to the ground in spring, and divide every few years.

Herbal Use
Tea brewed from the stems has been widely used for kidney and bladder ailments and is also proving effective as a greenhouse fungicide. The stems are unusually high in silica and can be used to scour pots and pans or to sand wood. Caution: Toxic to livestock.

Eucalyptus
You-ka-lip´tus
Myrtaceae. Myrtle family

Description
Evergreen trees, some small and shrubby and others very tall. Most have leathery foliage, which is sometimes very aromatic. The brushy flowers are often very brightly colored and are followed by curious woody pods. About 450 species, almost all from Australia.

■ *cinerea* *p. 139*
Silver-dollar eucalyptus. Seedlings grow quickly into broad bushy plants, reaching 3 ft. or more the first year, and eventually mature into trees, 25–40 ft. tall, with fibrous, reddish brown bark. The stems are crowded with rounded leaves, 1–2 in. wide, in shades of green, blue, and silver. They feel sticky or waxy, have a penetrating resinous aroma, and are very popular for dried arrangements. The flowers are inconspicuous. Zone 9.

How to Grow
Full sun. Average well-drained soil. Tolerates dry spells once established. Start seeds early indoors to grow as an annual.

Makes an excellent container plant. Put it outdoors in summer, in a sunny window in winter. Keep pot-bound, and prune in spring to restrain growth.

Herbal Use
Dried branches are used in floral arrangements. Leaves give red and gold dyes on wool and other fibers.

■ *citriodora p. 140*
Lemon-scented gum. A narrow, upright tree, planted as a lawn tree in California, where it grows 60 ft. or taller with a magnificent straight white trunk. Fast enough from seed to use as an annual, and can be kept in a pot for several years, reaching 6 ft. or more. Narrow oblong leaves are 3–6 in. long and have a strong lemon scent when crushed. The leaves are thin and fuzzy on young plants or new growth, smooth and leathery on older plants. Flowers are inconspicuous. Zone 9.

How to Grow
Like *E. cinerea.*

Herbal Use
Dried leaves retain their fragrance in sachets. Leaf tea has been used for colds and fevers.

■ *globulus p. 140*
Blue gum eucalyptus. A common tree in California, where it reaches 200 ft. tall. Slender, lance-shaped, 6-in. leaves have a leathery texture and a strong aroma. Old trees outdoors are messy, always dropping leaves, twigs, bark, flowers, or pods, but a young potted plant makes a neat and fragrant houseplant. Zone 9.

How to Grow
Like *E. cinerea.*

Herbal Use
Oil from the leaves is used as an antiseptic and in cough drops.

Eupatorium
You-pa-toe′ree-um
Compositae. Composite family

Description
Perennials with opposite or whorled leaves on upright stalks

topped with showy clusters of small flowers. About 40 species, native to the eastern United States and Eurasia.

■ *perfoliatum* p. 170

Boneset, thoroughwort, feverweed. A hardy native perennial that makes one or more upright stalks topped with flat clusters of small white flowers in late summer and fall. Pairs of slightly aromatic, hairy, wrinkled, pointed leaves join at the base, enclosing the stem. Don't confuse boneset with white snakeroot, *E. rugosum*, a poisonous plant that looks generally similar but has smooth, heart-shaped leaves with distinct petioles. Zone 3.

How to Grow

Full sun. Prefers rich, damp soil but grows okay with average soil and watering. Propagate by seed or make divisions in spring.

Herbal Use

Leaves gathered just before flowering historically were used to treat fevers during flu epidemics. German research shows it may stimulate the immune system. Caution: Contains compounds that can cause liver damage.

■ *purpureum* p. 171 *Pictured below*

Joe-Pye weed, gravel root. A hardy native perennial that grows bigger than many shrubs. Established clumps produce 20 or more strong stalks 5–9 ft. tall, punctuated with whorls of 3–5 large, toothed, vanilla-scented leaves. Broad (12–18-in.) domed clusters of tiny pinkish purple flowers top the stalks in late summer, gradually fading to pinkish beige and lasting through fall. *E. fistulosa* and *E. maculatum* are similar plants, also called Joe-Pye weed. Zone 4.

How to Grow
Full sun. Does best in fertile, organic, moist soil. Cut stems back by one-third in late spring to encourage branching and to reduce overall height. Increase by division in early spring.

Herbal Use
Tea from the leaves and roots historically was used as a diuretic, to eliminate stones in the urinary tract, and to treat urinary incontinence in children.

Euphorbia
You-for'bee-a
Euphorbiaceae. Spurge family

Description
A giant and diverse group of herbaceous annuals and perennials, succulents, shrubs, and trees. All have a milky sap. The actual flowers are usually small but may be surrounded with large colorful bracts. About 1,600 species, native worldwide.

■ *lathyris* p. 243
Mole plant, gopher purge. A variable plant; can be annual or biennial, branched or unbranched. In any form, it has a distinctive appearance and usually grows 3–4 ft. tall. Opposite leaves are narrow and pointed, 6 in. long, blue-green with a pale midrib. Clusters of small, crescent-shaped, yellow-green flowers bloom in late summer and fall. All parts of the plant exude a sticky white latex when broken. Zone 5.

How to Grow
Full sun. Average soil and watering. Grows easily from seed and often self-sows. Protect with mulch where winters are cold.

Herbal Use
Reputed to repel moles from the garden and also to remove skin moles and warts. Used in traditional Chinese medicine, but the plant is considered toxic and the sap causes skin irritation.

Ferula

Fer-oo´la
Umbelliferae. Carrot family

Description
Robust perennials with thick roots, large compound leaves, and umbels of small flowers. More than 170 species, native to Eurasia.

■ *assa-foetida* p. 171
Asafoetida, Devil's dung, food-of-the-gods. A legendary and intriguing plant that's uncommon but easy to grow. One plant makes an attractive clump of stalks up to 6 ft. tall, with large, bright green leaves that are divided into many segments, like lovage or angelica. The leaves have a somewhat fetid odor. Umbels of tiny yellow-green flowers top the stems in summer. The thick roots ooze a smelly, gummy, reddish resin when cut. Zone 5.

How to Grow
Full sun. Average soil and watering. Tolerates dry spells. Easily raised from seed. Occasionally self-sows. Lives for years in a bed with no special care, and grows well in a large (1–3-gal.) planter if you fertilize regularly. Cut old flower stalks to the ground in fall or spring.

Herbal Use
Resin from the roots is dried and ground into a powder, highly esteemed in India and Asia as a condiment and remedy.

Filipendula

Fil-i-pen´dew-la
Rosaceae. Rose family

Description
Hardy perennials with compound leaves and fluffy clusters of flowers. About 10 species, native to the north temperate zone.

■ *rubra* p. 172
Queen-of-the-prairie. A statuesque perennial with stalks 6–8 ft. tall, topped with fluffy plumes of flowers, like pink cotton candy. Blooms for weeks in July or August. The foliage—dark green pinnately compound leaves with jagged leaflets—is almost as beautiful as the blossoms. Native to moist, sunny sites in the eastern United States. Zone 3.

How to Grow
Full or part sun. Prefers fertile, organic soil and steady moisture. Won't grow very tall in dry soil. Give it plenty of room—2–3 ft. on all sides—to begin with. It will spread to fill the space but isn't invasive. The sturdy stalks usually don't need staking. Cut back after flowering. Pest-free.

Herbal Use
The tannin-rich roots are a folk remedy used as an astringent to stop bleeding, diarrhea, or dysentery. In modern Europe the leaf tea and other preparations are used as an antacid.

■ *ulmaria* p. 172
Meadowsweet, queen-of-the-meadow. A hardy perennial, native to Europe but naturalized in the northeastern United States. Has compound leaves with toothed leaflets that are green above, woolly white below. Stalks 4–6 ft. tall are topped with fluffy clusters of sweetly fragrant white flowers that perfume the garden for a month or more in summer. Zone 4.

How to Grow
Like *F. rubra*.

Herbal Use
Salicylic acid, a chemical forerunner of aspirin, was first extracted from this plant about 150 years ago. Long used as a folk remedy for fevers and flus and as an astringent.

Foeniculum
Fee-nick'you-lum
Umbelliferae. Carrot family

Description
A perennial with compound leaves divided into fine needle-like segments, umbels of yellow flowers, and aromatic seeds. Only 1 species, native to Europe and the Mediterranean region.

■ *vulgare* p. 173
Fennel. There are three varieties of fennel. Common fennel is a perennial with delicate, threadlike, yellow-green foliage. Stout but hollow stalks up to 6 ft. tall hold broad umbels of yellow flowers followed by fragrant rice-sized seeds. Var. *rubrum* or 'Purpurascens', bronze fennel, is similar but has

beautiful purple-bronze foliage. Var. *dulce,* Florence fennel, is a cool-weather annual; it makes a bulb that is eaten as a vegetable. Zone 5.

How to Grow
Full sun. Ordinary soil and watering. Sow seeds in early spring. Cut off seed heads before they mature. Plants usually die after a few years, but they self-sow readily and may even be weedy.

Herbal Use
Chopped leaves are used to flavor fish, potatoes, and salads. Seeds are used in cakes, breads, sausage, Italian food, and other dishes. Seeds also are chewed to aid digestion, relieve flatulence, and sweeten the breath.

Galega
Ga-lee′ga
Leguminosae. Legume family

Description
Perennials with pinnately compound leaves and showy clusters of pealike flowers. Only 6 species, native to the Old World.

■ *officinalis p. 174*
Goat's rue. A bushy perennial with many branching stems, 3–5 ft. tall. The compound leaves have smooth, pale green leaflets about 1 in. long, with an unpleasant odor when crushed. The erect spikes of pealike purple or white flowers are quite showy in summer. Spreads by underground runners. Zone 4.

How to Grow
Full sun. Average soil and watering. Tolerates dry spells. Propagate from seed or by dividing crowns in early spring. Easy to grow but can be invasive. Confine the roots, divide it often, or plant it in a meadow or natural garden.

Herbal Use
Leaves are used as a rennet to curdle milk for making cheese and also to stimulate milk flow in dairy animals and nursing mothers.

Galium

Gay´lee-um
Rubiaceae. Madder family

Description
Perennials with spreading rhizomes, prickly stems, whorled leaves, and small 4-petaled flowers. About 400 species, native worldwide. Some European species are weedy in the United States.

■ *odoratum* *p. 174*
Sweet woodruff. A hardy perennial that makes a tough ground cover. Once it gets going, it will form a solid thick mat, about 6 in. tall, of pretty whorled leaves, dotted in spring with starry white flowers. When cut or dried, the leaves smell like vanilla. In cool climates, the foliage is deep green all summer, dies and dries to a warm tan in winter. In the South, it is evergreen in winter and may die back in summer. Runners creep underground and spread relentlessly, competing well with tree roots. Previously called *Asperula odorata*. Zone 4.

How to Grow
Part sun or shade. Ordinary soil and watering. Space 1 ft. apart for ground cover. Pull up runners that go out of bounds. Propagate by dividing clumps in spring or fall.

Herbal Use
Fresh shoots are used to flavor white wine for May Day celebrations in Europe. Dried leaves make a pleasant sachet for perfuming drawers or for a soothing sleep pillow.

■ *verum* *p. 175*
Lady's bedstraw. A hardy perennial, native to Europe but established as a roadside weed in the northeastern United States. Makes a tangle of slender prickly stems, 2–3 ft. tall, with tiny needlelike leaves and hazy masses of little gold flowers. A carefree plant for sunny meadow gardens. Zone 4.

How to Grow
Like *G. odoratum*. Spreads invasively; confine it in a bottomless pot if planted in a formal garden.

Herbal Use
The flowering tops are used to curdle milk for cheesemaking and also make a yellow food coloring for cheese or butter. The roots give a red dye on wool yarn. Leaf tea is used as a diuretic.

Gaultheria

Gal-thee´ree-a
Ericaceae. Heath family

Description

Evergreen shrubs with glossy foliage, pink or white flowers, and fleshy fruits. Many species produce methyl salicylate, the basis of wintergreen flavoring. About 150 species, native worldwide.

■ *procumbens* p. 175
Wintergreen. A low, creeping shrub native to woodlands in eastern North America. Smooth oval leaves, 1 in. long, are dark green in summer, turning burgundy in cold weather. Pea-sized bright red berries ripen in summer and last until the next spring, when the small pink flowers open. One plant makes a clump 4 in. tall, gradually spreading up to 2 ft. wide. Zone 4.

How to Grow

Part or full shade. Can't take hot summers. Prefers rich, moist, acidic, woodland soil and a mulch of decomposed leaves. Needs no care once established in a favorable spot. Propagate by division in spring. Seeds are slow to germinate.

Herbal Use

Used as a flavoring for gum, candy, and toothpaste. Tea made from fresh leaves or berries is a traditional remedy for colds, fevers, and headaches. A poultice of crushed leaves relieves sore muscles. Caution: Be careful of the essential oil. It's too concentrated for safe use. The active ingredient, methyl salicylate, is toxic and can be absorbed through the skin.

Ginkgo

Gink´o
Ginkgoaceae. Ginkgo family

Description

A deciduous tree with delicate leaves borne in clusters on stubby branchlets. Introduced from China in the 1700s and widely cultivated, but now rare or extinct in the wild. Judging from the fossil record, ginkgo trees existed 200 million years ago, looking just as they do today. Only 1 species.

■ *biloba* p. 116 *Pictured on p. 316*
Ginkgo, maidenhair tree. A hardy deciduous tree, 50–80 ft.

tall. Forms an upright pyramid when young, spreading irregularly with age. The fan-shaped leaves, divided into 2 lobes
at the broad end, move in the slightest breeze. Bright green
all summer, they turn clear yellow in fall. Avoid seedling trees.
They might be females, which produce messy, smelly fruits.
Nurseries carry fruitless male cultivars selected for good fall
color and upright, conical, or spreading habit. Zone 4.

How to Grow
Full or part sun. An excellent tree for difficult conditions. Tolerates infertile or alkaline soil, air pollution, and hot city
streets. Has no pests and needs no special care. A good can-
didate for underplanting with perennials—it doesn't cast too
much shade, and the roots aren't too greedy.

Herbal Use
The leaves are used in traditional Chinese medicine. Modern
clinical studies show that leaf extracts increase blood flow
and improve circulation. Caution: Gingko fruits are eaten in
China, but the pulp can cause dermatitis and the seeds can
be toxic.

Glycyrrhiza
Gli-si-rye´za
Leguminosae. Legume family

Description
Shrubby perennials with creeping rhizomes, compound
leaves, and small pealike flowers. About 20 species, native
worldwide.

■ *glabra* *p. 176*

Licorice. A hardy perennial with arching or upright stems about 3 ft. tall. Compound leaves with many small oval leaflets have a sticky texture. Short spikes of blue-purple flowers form at the leaf axils in late summer. Wild licorice, *G. lepidota,* is a similar plant native to the western United States. Zone 5.

How to Grow

Full or part sun. Does best in light, loose, fertile, well-drained soil. Needs regular watering. Propagate by dividing the roots in spring. It isn't invasive, but it is difficult to eradicate, as any bits of overlooked roots survive to make new plants.

Herbal Use

Commercially, the roots are harvested in autumn after 4 years of growth. Extracts of the dried roots are used to flavor candy and beverages, to treat coughs and sore throats, and as a mild laxative. Licorice is one of the most widely used medicinal plants in the world. Caution: Prolonged use can cause potassium loss and sodium retention. Avoid during pregnancy.

Gossypium

Go-sip´ee-um
Malvaceae. Mallow family

Description

Annuals, shrubs, or trees with hollyhock-like flowers, woody pods, and hairy seeds. About 35 species, native to tropical regions in the Old and New World.

■ *hirsutum* *p. 243*

Cotton. A shrubby plant, tender to frost. Millions of acres are planted as a crop, but one plant makes an attractive and interesting specimen in a home herb garden. It grows 3–5 ft. tall, with strong branching stems, large lobed leaves, pretty yellow and pink flowers, and egg-sized bolls that puff open like popcorn, releasing locks of fluffy white cotton fiber attached to bean-sized seeds. Zone 7.

How to Grow

Needs full sun, deep fertile soil, and regular watering. Grows best where summers are sunny and hot. Sow seeds outdoors when the soil is warm. Where the growing season is short, plant one in a large container and bring it indoors before frost.

Herbal Use
Cotton is the most important natural textile fiber. Cottonseed oil is a common cooking and salad oil. Gossypol, extracted from the seeds and roots, is being investigated as a male contraceptive, because of its ability to decrease sperm count.

Hamamelis
Ha-ma-mell′is
Hamamelidaceae. Witch hazel family

Description
Deciduous shrubs or small trees with sweet-scented flowers in fall, winter, or early spring. Only 5 or 6 species, native to eastern Asia and eastern North America.

■ *virginiana* p. 117
Common witch hazel. A deciduous shrub or tree native to woodlands in eastern North America. Grows about 20 ft. tall, usually with multiple trunks. Blooms in fall, about the same time as the leaves turn gold. The fragrant flowers have 4 slender yellow petals. The leaves are rounded, with scalloped edges. The dry woody pods pop open to shoot the seeds several feet into the air. Zone 4.

How to Grow
Part sun. Prefers rich, moist soil but grows fine in average garden soil with regular watering. Prune out suckers and extra shoots to train it into a tree, or let it grow naturally as a big bush. Pest-free and easy to grow.

Herbal Use
Witch hazel water, distilled from the twigs and branches, is available at every pharmacy and is used to treat itchy or irritated skin, nicks and bruises, sore muscles, and hemorrhoids.

Helichrysum
Hell-i-kry′zum
Compositae. Composite family

Description
A big genus of annuals, perennials, and shrubs, most with rounded flower heads composed of stiff, papery bracts. About 500 species, most native to South Africa and Australia.

■ *angustifolium* *p. 215*
Curry plant. A tender perennial, usually treated like an annual. Grows upright, reaching 2–4 ft. tall by fall. The stems are crowded with needlelike leaves, 1 in. long, that are coated with a dense felt of silvery hairs and have a fragrance uncannily similar to curry powder. Yellow flower heads are not showy. 'Nana' is a dwarf form that's just as fragrant. *H. petiolare* 'Limelight' isn't used herbally, but it's very popular because its soft, velvety, lime green leaves are a perfect complement for herbs with blue or lavender flowers. Zone 9.

How to Grow
Full sun. Needs loose, sandy, very well drained soil. Tolerates drought. Grows well in a container outdoors. Prune hard to encourage branching. Prone to aphids and mealybugs.

Herbal Use
The fragrant leaves are not used as a seasoning, but they are used for many medicinal purposes in Europe.

Heuchera
Hew´ker-a
Saxifragaceae. Saxifrage family

Description
Perennials with thick rhizomes, a tuft of rounded or lobed basal leaves, and many tiny cup-shaped flowers on slender stalks. About 55 species, native to North America.

■ *americana* *p. 176*
Alumroot. A hardy perennial native to eastern woodlands. Makes a compact mound, about 6 in. tall, of thick, leathery leaves with lobed edges and dark reddish purple markings along the veins. The leaves are evergreen in mild winters. Wiry stalks hold tiny pale flowers well above the foliage in late spring. Spreads by creeping rhizomes. Use it as an edging plant or ground cover. *H. sanguinea* is a southwestern species with red flowers. The popular garden plants called coralbells are *Heuchera* hybrids that grow larger and bear clouds of pink, red, or white flowers. All have similar herbal value. Zone 4.

How to Grow
Part shade. Needs well-drained soil and regular watering. Don't plant too deep—put the crown level with the soil surface. Divide every few years in early spring. May die back in hot summers but recovers in fall.

Herbal Use
Used like alum as an astringent and styptic, hence the common name. Root tea was a folk remedy for sore throats, diarrhea, and hemorrhoids.

Hibiscus
Hy-bis′kus
Malvaceae. Mallow family

Description
A diverse group of annuals, perennials, shrubs, and trees, most with showy flowers. About 200 species, native worldwide.

■ *sabdariffa p. 244*
Roselle. A tropical annual that makes a bushy clump of erect branching stems, up to 6 ft. tall. The large leaves have 3–5 blunt lobes. Needs a long growing season, because it doesn't start blooming until days get shorter in fall. Then it bears lots of small yellow flowers with plump red calyxes. Makes a good backdrop or centerpiece for a tea garden. Zone 7.

How to Grow
Full sun. Average soil and watering. Sow seeds when the soil is warm, or start early indoors. Like its relative okra, roselle grows best where summers are hot.

Herbal Use
The fleshy calyxes make a very refreshing hot or iced tea. In Egypt the leaves are used for treating heart and nerve diseases. Fibers from the stem are woven into fabric like burlap.

Hierochloe
Hy-er-ok′low-ee
Gramineae. Grass family

Description
Perennial grasses with creeping runners. About 15 species, native to temperate and tropical climates.

■ *odorata p. 177*
Sweet grass, vanilla grass. A perennial grass that spreads by underground runners. Shiny bright green leaves contain coumarin and release a vanilla fragrance when dried. Basal

leaves grow up to 18 in. long; stem leaves are shorter. Blooms in May, with loose flower clusters on 2-ft. stalks. Grows wild in the eastern United States. Zone 4.

How to Grow
Full or part sun. Average soil and watering. Easily propagated by root divisions. Start a patch in a meadow where you can let it spread. Mow or cut back in early spring. Carefree.

Herbal Use
Dried leaves retain their scent for years and are used in basketry. Also burned as incense in Native American rituals. Leaf tea has been used in the past for coughs, sore throats, and venereal infections, but now coumarins are considered potentially carcinogenic.

Humulus
Hew'mew-lus
Cannabidaceae. Hemp family

Description
Vigorous twining vines. Only 2 species, a perennial native to Europe and North America and an annual from Asia.

■ *lupulus* *p. 177* *Pictured below*
Hops. A vigorous perennial vine that grows up to 25 ft. tall in a single growing season, then dies down in winter. Twining stems and large leaves with several toothed, pointed lobes have a scratchy texture. Male plants make catkins of small yellow-green flowers. Female flowers and seeds are tucked inside fragrant, puffy, conelike structures called strobiles, green at first, turning rosy tan as they mature. Beer brewers have

selected several cultivars for outstanding flavor. 'Aureus' is grown for its pretty yellow foliage. Zone 3.

H. japonicus, Japanese hops, is the annual species. It has similar foliage, flowers, and properties but is used much less. There's a white-variegated form of Japanese hops with beautiful foliage; it comes true from seed.

How to Grow

Full sun. Average soil and watering. Buy dormant roots to plant in early spring. Provide a strong trellis or support, or let it scramble over a shed, fence, or hedge. Wear long sleeves and gloves to protect your arms when you clean up the dead stalks.

Herbal Use

Dried strobiles add the bitter flavor to beer. Stuffed into pillows, they act as a sedative. Hops tea is used in Europe for insomnia, nervous tension, restlessness, and lack of appetite.

Hydrastis

Hi-dras´tis
Ranunculaceae. Buttercup family

Description

Low-growing perennial woodland wildflowers. Only 2 species, one from eastern North America and the other from eastern Asia.

■ *canadensis* p. 178
Goldenseal. A hardy perennial about 1 ft. tall. Each upright stalk holds a few leaves with 5–7 toothed lobes. Right in the center is a tuft of small greenish white flowers in spring and a raspberry-like cluster of red fruits in fall. The tough roots have a bright yellow color and a bitter taste. Spreads underground to make a dense patch. Zone 3.

How to Grow

Full shade. Rich, moist, organic soil with regular watering. Slow-growing; seeds can take 18 months to germinate. Buy nursery-propagated stock to plant in early spring. Harvest and divide the roots every third year in fall, after the tops die down.

Herbal Use

Goldenseal root products are sold at health food stores as a popular antibiotic for various infections. Historically used to treat inflammations of the eye, mouth, throat, and digestive tract. Caution: Avoid during pregnancy, and avoid prolonged use.

Hydrocotyle
Hi-dro-kot′le
Umbelliferae. Carrot family

Description
Low-growing perennials that creep over the ground. Many species have parasol-like leaves. About 75 species, native worldwide.

■ *asiatica* p. 216
Gotu kola. A tender perennial from Asia that spreads by aboveground runners, reaching 3–4 ft. wide in a single growing season. Smooth, olive green leaves are almost round, 1–2 in. wide, on stalks about 4 in. tall. Insignificant little green flowers appear nearly year-round, followed by clusters of disk-shaped seeds. Sometimes listed as *Centella asiatica*. Zone 10.

How to Grow
Sun or shade. Prefers constant moisture but tolerates average garden soil. Easy to grow and pest-free. Makes a versatile low ground cover that can't take frost but often self-sows. Pull up runners that go too far. Propagate by replanting rooted runners. Does fine in hanging baskets or other containers, and grows easily indoors in winter, even in a north window.

Herbal Use
Has a remarkable history of use in Asia and now in Europe. Preparations of the leaves accelerate the healing of skin diseases, wounds, and burns. In India, where leaves are made into tea or chopped fresh into salads, this herb is claimed to increase intelligence and stimulate the brain. Various studies on animals and humans suggest that it may indeed help improve memory.

Hypericum
Hy-per′i-kum
Hypericaceae. St.-John's-wort family

Description
A big group of perennials and shrubs, most with yellow

flowers. About 370 species, native to the Old and New World.

■ *perforatum* *p. 178*

St.-John's-wort, Klamath weed. A hardy perennial, native to Europe but widely naturalized in the United States. Grows 2–3 ft. tall, with many upright branching stems. Small oval leaves are pale green, dotted with tiny oil glands. Bright yellow flowers, 1 in. wide, have a tuft of stamens and 5 petals with black dots along the edges. Blooms for several weeks in summer, starting around June 24th, St. John's Day. Zone 3.

How to Grow

Full sun. Average or dry soil. Starts easily from seed or division in spring. Once established, needs no care. Best for meadows and informal gardens, where it can sprawl and spread.

Herbal Use

Fresh flowers are steeped in olive oil or alcohol to make a home remedy for sores, wounds, cuts, bruises, burns, and the like. Hypericin, a pigment in the petals, turns the preparations a bright red color. Flower tea is also taken internally as a folk remedy, shown to have sedative, anti-inflammatory, antibacterial, and antidepressant effects. Has been researched for possible AIDS treatment. Caution: Used externally or taken internally, hypericin can cause photodermatitis—welts on the skin after exposure to direct sunlight—in humans or grazing livestock.

Hyssopus

Hi-so´pus
Labiatae. Mint family

Description

Perennials or small shrubs with square stems, opposite leaves, and 2-lipped flowers. Only 5 species, native to Eurasia.

■ *officinalis* *p. 179*

Hyssop. A shrubby perennial, 18–24 in. tall. Leafy upright stems hold regularly spaced pairs of narrow dark green leaves, about 1 in. long. The foliage is semievergreen and strongly aromatic. Starts blooming in summer and continues into the fall, with showy spikes of small blue, white, or pink flowers. A single plant makes a colorful, showy specimen. Can also be used for a low clipped hedge or edging. Zone 3.

How to Grow

Full sun. Does best in well-drained, sandy, neutral or limy soil. Tolerates dry heat but not high humidity. Propagate by division or seed. Flowers the first year from seed. Space 1 ft. apart for a hedge. Prune to the ground in spring and shear after flowering. Grows well in a container. Pest-free.

Herbal Use

Makes a good honey plant—bees love the flowers. Essential oil from the leaves is used commercially in liqueurs and perfumes. The leaf tea has been used for sore throats and stomachaches.

Ilex

Eye'lecks
Aquifoliaceae. Holly family

Description

Mostly evergreen (some deciduous) trees or shrubs, usually with thick leathery leaves, sometimes spiny, and round red, gold, or black fruits. About 400 species, native worldwide, and many hybrids and cultivars.

■ *paraguariensis p. 141*

Yerba maté, Paraguay tea. A bushy, upright shrub, about 4–5 ft. tall, with evergreen foliage and deep red berries. Dark green leaves, $1/2$ in. wide and 3–4 in. long, have a nutty aroma when bruised. Small pale flowers are inconspicuous. Zone 7.

How to Grow

Full sun. Average soil and watering. Branches readily and responds well to pruning. Makes a large specimen or could be used for hedging. Grows well in containers but soon outgrows the average windowsill. Subject to mealybugs and aphids.

Herbal Use

Dried leaves make a stimulating tea, high in caffeine.

■ *vomitoria p. 141*

Yaupon holly. A native evergreen shrub or tree with short, narrow, dark green leaves and huge crops of small, juicy-looking red berries. Easily trained as a small multitrunked tree 15–20 ft. tall. Dwarf cultivars such as 'Nana' make compact mounds of foliage and can be sheared into any desired shape. Zone 7.

How to Grow
Full or part sun. Not fussy about soil; tolerates alkaline conditions, clay, sand, and wet or dry sites. Responds well to pruning. Good for hedges or edging. No serious pests.

Herbal Use
The only North American plant that contains appreciable amounts of caffeine. Native Americans used a strong leaf tea to induce ceremonial vomiting.

Indigofera
In-di-gof′er-a
Leguminosae. Legume family

Description
Shrubs or perennials with compound leaves and pealike flowers. About 700 species, native to tropical and warm climates.

■ *suffruticosa p. 244 Pictured above*
Indigo. A tropical shrub, grown as an annual. Seedlings reach 3–5 ft. tall in one season. Upright stems are tough and woody. Compound leaves are 3 in. long with many pairs of small oval leaflets. Spikes of pale pink flowers and clusters of short curved pods are held close to the stems. Zone 10.

How to Grow
Full sun. Average soil and watering. Thrives in hot weather and is very sensitive to cold. Start indoors or sow direct after danger of frost. Space 12 in. apart.

Herbal Use
The leaves produce an excellent blue pigment, long used in Latin America as a textile dye. Leaf tea was also taken medicinally.

nula

n´you-la
Compositae. Composite family

Description

Robust perennials or annuals with rough stalks, large leaves, and yellow flowers. About 90 species, native to the Old World.

helenium p. 179

Elecampane, elf dock, velvet dock. A hardy perennial with erect stalks up to 6 ft. tall. Basal leaves can be 6 in. wide and 2 ft. long; stem leaves clasp the furrowed stalks; all have rough tops and downy undersides. Sunflower-like blossoms are showy in summer, but it looks worn and shabby by fall. Zone 4.

How to Grow

Full sun. Average soil and watering. Cut back after flowering. Easily raised from seed, or divide crowns in early spring.

Herbal Use

Root preparations traditionally were used for lung diseases such as pneumonia, asthma, and bronchitis and also to quiet coughing. Science confirms that the root has sedative, antispasmodic, anti-inflammatory, antibacterial, and fungicidal properties.

Iris

Eye´ris
Iridaceae. Iris family

Description

Perennials with rhizomes or bulbs, long flat leaves, and characteristic flowers with 6 segments. About 300 species, most native to the north temperate zone.

germanica var. *florentina* p. 180

Orrisroot, Florentine iris. A hardy iris with short stout rhizomes. Makes an upright clump of gray-green, sword-shaped leaves up to 18 in. tall. Blooms in spring, just before most iris hybrids, with 2–3 flowers per stalk, on stalks up to 30 in. tall. Large showy flowers are slightly fragrant, silvery white with an iridescent sheen and conspicuous yellow beards. *I. pallida* is a similar species, also used as a source of orrisroot. It has purple flowers. Variegated forms with gold- or white-striped leaves are especially popular. Zone 4.

How to Grow
Full sun. Needs well-drained soil. Established plants tolerate hot, dry weather. Divide every few years, after flowering. Be sure the top of the rhizome is exposed to sun—that encourages flowering. Use slug bait to protect it from slugs.

Herbal Use
Rhizomes are peeled, sliced, dried, and aged for 2 years to develop a violet-like fragrance, then used as a fixative for potpourris. Orris powder was once a major ingredient in face powders and other toiletries, but it caused allergic reactions and is no longer used commercially.

Isatis
Eye-sat′is
Cruciferae. Mustard family

Description
Herbaceous plants with simple leaves and masses of small yellow flowers. About 30 species, native to Eurasia.

■ *tinctoria p. 245*
Woad. A hardy biennial. Makes a mound of smooth oblong basal leaves up to 1 in. wide and 8 in. long the first year. Blooms with the daffodils the second year, bearing hundreds of yellow flowers on stalks 2–4 ft. tall, followed by decorative, dangling, flat black fruits. Showy but invasive, because it self-sows prolifically. Considered a serious roadside or rangeland weed in several states. Zone 4.

How to Grow
Full sun. Average soil and watering. Sow seeds in spring or summer. Thin to 12 in. apart. Cut off flower stalks immediately after bloom to prevent self-sowing. Very easy to grow.

Herbal Use
The leaves produce indigo, a blue dye. Traditionally used as a body paint in ancient Europe and as an important textile dye until the 19th century.

Jasminum

Jas´mi-num
Oleaceae. Olive family

Description
Deciduous or evergreen shrubs or vines with white, yellow, or pink flowers, often sweetly fragrant. About 450 species, almost all native to the Old World tropics.

■ *officinale* *p. 142*
Jasmine, poet's jasmine. A vigorous woody vine with twining stems up to 15 ft. long. Glossy compound leaves have 5 or 7 oval leaflets. They may drop in winter. Fragrant white flowers, 1 in. wide, bloom off and on throughout the summer. Var. *grandiflorum* has larger, double flowers. Zone 9.

How to Grow
Full or part sun. Average soil and watering. Readily climbs a trellis or fence. Prune in early spring to control size. Propagated by tip cuttings. Subject to mealybugs; treat with oil spray. Can be grown in containers but soon fills a 10-in. pot.

Herbal Use
Essential oil from the flowers is widely used in perfumes and as a flavoring for confections.

■ *sambac*
Indian tea jasmine or Arabian jasmine. An evergreen shrub with glossy undivided leaves. Can reach 3–5 ft. tall. Blooms year-round, with small clusters of especially fragrant flowers. 'Maid of Orleans' is a compact, bushy cultivar with bunches of 5 or 6 flowers that open one at a time. They are semi-double, 1 in. wide, white at first and fading to cranberry, with a very pleasant aroma that intensifies at dusk. Blooms year-round. 'Belle of India' is similar, but the flowers are star-shaped, with pointed petals. 'Arabian Nights' is more compact than 'Maid of Orleans', with darker foliage and larger flowers. 'Grand Duke of Tuscany' has double flowers, like carnations, that are very intensely perfumed, but it's a leggy plant unsuitable for windowsills. Zone 7.

How to Grow
Like *J. officinale*. Grows slowly, so prune sparingly. Most cultivars grow well in an east or west window in winter, but put them outside for the summer. Where hardy, can be planted as a specimen or hedge, or trained against a trellis or building as a loose, leaning vine.

Herbal Use

The dried flowers are used to flavor tea. In Asia, fresh flowers are strewn at weddings and used as a calmative and an aphrodisiac.

Juniperus

Jew-nip´er-us
Cupressaceae. Cypress family

Description

Evergreen conifers, including low, spreading shrubs and upright trees. Leaves are needlelike or scalelike. Female cones are berrylike. Wood, foliage, and fruits are often very fragrant. About 50 species, native to the Old and New World.

■ *communis* *p. 117* *Pictured above*

Common juniper. A hardy small tree or shrub, usually under 10 ft. tall, with many upright or spreading branches. Twigs are crowded with short spiny needles, gray-green in summer, bronze in winter. Grows wild across North America and Eurasia. There are low-growing cultivars that stay green all winter. Zone 2.

How to Grow

Full sun. Not fussy about soil and watering. Thrives on sterile sandy or rocky sites. Very hardy. Easy to grow. Prune as desired.

Herbal Use

Dark blue berries are used to flavor gin and as a seasoning for game and other meats, and are eaten as a digestive aid and diuretic. Vapor of hot leaf or berry tea helps relieve colds and bronchitis. Caution: Avoid use during pregnancy or if suffering from kidney disease.

■ *virginiana* *p. 118*

Eastern red cedar. A common tree on abandoned pastures and vacant land everywhere east of the Mississippi. Grows fast into a slender cone 30 ft. tall. Young shoots are prickly; older branches have flat fans of scalelike foliage. Foliage is rich green in summer but often turns dull brown in winter. Small silvery fruits are sometimes abundant enough to give the tree a sparkly, frosted appearance. Selected cultivars have distinct shapes and better foliage color. Zone 2.

How to Grow
Full or part sun. Not fussy about soil; tolerates acidic or alkaline, wet or dry sites. Responds well to pruning and can be sheared into formal shapes for hedges or specimens.

Herbal Use
The fragrant reddish purple heartwood is used to make cedar chests that protect woolens from clothes moths. Native Americans used tea from the berries to induce sweating and cure colds.

Laurus
Law'rus
Lauraceae. Laurel family

Description
Evergreen trees with aromatic leaves. Only 2 species, native to the Mediterranean region and adjacent Atlantic islands.

■ *nobilis* p. 142
Bay laurel, sweet bay. A dense evergreen shrub or tree, often pruned into formal shapes and used as a specimen or planted as a hedge. Grows up to 30 ft. tall in the ground, about 6 ft. in pots. The pointed oval leaves are stiff, leathery, dark green, and pleasantly fragrant when crushed. Tight clusters of small greenish yellow flowers are inconspicuous in early spring, but you'll probably notice the shiny black fruits in fall. Zone 8.

How to Grow
Full sun or afternoon shade. Ordinary soil and watering; tolerates dry spells once established. Grows well in a pot. Bring indoors when the weather gets cold. Shape with hand pruners, not hedge shears, to avoid mutilating the foliage. Use horticultural oil spray to control scale, a common pest.

Herbal Use
Garlands of laurel leaves symbolized honorable achievement in ancient Greece. Now we speak of "resting on one's laurels." Leaves are important for flavoring sauces and stews; remove before serving. Use leaves to repel pantry insects.

Lavandula
La-van′dew-la
Labiatae. Mint family

Description
Perennials or shrubs, mostly evergreen in mild climates, with very fragrant foliage and flowers. About 20 species, native to the Mediterranean region.

■ *angustifolia*   pp. 118–119   *Pictured below*
Lavender. Prized for the legendary fragrance of its small lavender-purple flowers, which form crowded spikes on slender stalks in early summer. Makes a compact rounded subshrub, usually about 2 ft. tall, with many erect stems. The closely spaced leaves are stiff and slender, 1–2 in. long, with a fuzzy gray surface. Makes a soft low hedge or edging, or can be massed with other drought-tolerant shrubs to fill a dry sunny slope. Evergreen only in mild climates; it discolors and then freezes back where winters are cold. There are dozens of cultivars, differing in size, flower color and fragrance, and season and duration of bloom. 'Hidcote' has dark purple flowers, 'Jean Davis' has pale pink, and 'Munstead' has lavender-blue. 'Nana Alba' is a compact plant with white flowers. 'Lavender Lady' is a recent introduction that blooms the first year from seed. Previously known as *L. officinalis* and *L. vera*. Zone 5.

How to Grow
Best in full sun. Ordinary, sandy, or alkaline soil. Needs good drainage and tolerates drought once established. Where the

soil is heavy, plant "high" by positioning the crown above the surrounding grade so that water will run away from the plant. In cold areas, prune back frozen shoots in late spring. Remove old stalks as flowers fade to encourage reblooming later in the season. Don't prune after midsummer, or soft new shoots will be killed in winter. In mild regions, prune as desired. Can be cut back hard to renew leggy, untidy plants.

Pest-free but subject to fungal diseases. Prevent by siting plants to provide good air circulation and lots of sunlight.

Can be grown in a container for one season outdoors but goes downhill when it gets pot-bound. Doesn't do well as a houseplant; gets leggy and is prone to aphids.

Herbal Use
The fresh flowers are sometimes used to flavor ice cream, confections, and baked goods. Dried flowers, gathered in full bloom for best fragrance, are excellent for potpourris and sachets. Miniature pillows stuffed with dried lavender flowers can relieve insomnia and restlessness. The essential oil is used in perfumery, cosmetics, insect repellents, furniture polish, candles, and the like. Lavender extracts are used medicinally as an antiseptic; taken for fever and headaches; and applied to burns, cuts, and eczema.

■ × *intermedia* *p. 120*
Lavandin. A hardy lavender that makes a bushy mound up to 3–4 ft. tall and wide, with slightly woolly silver, gray, or green leaves up to $2\frac{1}{2}$ in. long. Long stalks hold large spikes of very fragrant white, lavender, or blue flowers in summer. There are several fine cultivars; 'Grosso' is especially fragrant and has lovely silvery foliage. *L.* × *intermedia* is a hybrid between *L. angustifolia* and *L. latifolia*. Zone 5.

How to Grow
Like *L. angustifolia*. Doesn't set seed, so must be propagated by cuttings or layering.

Herbal Use
Same as for *L. angustifolia*. The long spikes are excellent for making lavender wands. Several cultivars are raised for commercial lavender oil production in France.

■ *latifolia* *p. 143*
Spike lavender, aspic. An upright shrub, 3 ft. tall, with leaves that are longer and broader than those of common lavender. Lavender flowers open in late summer. Foliage and flowers have a slightly camphorous lavender aroma. Zone 7.

How to Grow

Like *L. angustifolia* but is more sensitive to cold and dampness. Comes true from seed.

Herbal Use

Spike oil is used to perfume cheaper goods such as soap, disinfectants, and shampoo and in artist's paints and varnishes. Flowers are used medicinally as an antispasmodic.

■ *stoechas* p. 143

Spanish lavender, French lavender. A mounded subshrub, 18–24 in. tall. Narrow 1-in. gray-green leaves have a pleasant fragrance reminiscent of both lavender and rosemary. Compact flower spikes like little pinecones or corncobs are packed with dark purple flowers and topped with 2 bracts that look like rabbit ears. Selected forms have larger or smaller heads and bracts in purple, dark purple-black, or white. Zone 7.

How to Grow

Like *L. angustifolia*. Extremely drought-tolerant and good for rock gardens or gravelly sites.

Herbal Use

Flowers were used medicinally and in perfumes. The essential oil is antibacterial and antiseptic.

■ tender lavenders

L. dentata, French or fringed lavender, is a tender subshrub 2–3 ft. tall, with narrow green leaves 2–3 in. long that are toothed all around the edge. Deep lavender flowers pack a plump compressed spike, topped by a tuft of large, upright, lavender-colored bracts. Can bloom in all seasons. Var. *candicans,* gray French lavender, is larger and more vigorous, with silvery gray foliage. Makes a good hedge or mass planting outdoors in mild climates. Otherwise, grow it in a pot and bring it indoors for winter. It needs a window as sunny and warm as possible and regular pruning to keep it bushy. Dried flowers and leaves are used in sachets and potpourris. Zone 10.

   L. heterophylla, sweet lavender, grows about 3 ft. tall and has silver-gray leaves, 2 in. long, sometimes toothed on the edges. Dark lavender flowers pack 2-in. spikes on 12-in. stalks. Blooms in summer and fall outdoors; continues in winter indoors if given plenty of sunlight and warmth. Foliage and flowers have a warm fragrance, like lavender with a hint of camphor. Hardy to zone 9 or 8.

Lawsonia

Law-son´ee-a
Lythraceae. Loosestrife family

Description
A tender tropical shrub or tree. Only 1 species, native to the Old World.

■ *inermis* (*inerma*) *p. 144*
Henna, mignonette tree. A shrubby plant with semievergreen foliage. Can grow to 25 ft. in the ground but usually stays 4–6 ft. tall in pots. The pale green leaves are smooth ellipses, about 2 in. long. Blooms in midwinter with profuse clusters of small, white, deliciously fragrant flowers. Zone 10.

How to Grow
Full sun. Average soil and watering. Grows well in a pot. Fertilize regularly. Can be pruned into formal shapes. Propagate from tip cuttings in early spring. Subject to spider mites.

Herbal Use
The dried powdered leaves are used as a hair and skin dye and also as treatment for skin problems, jaundice, headaches, and other ailments. They have analgesic and antibacterial properties. The flowers are used to make a very sweet-scented perfume.

Leonurus

Lee-oh-nur´us
Labiatae. Mint family

Description
Biennials or perennials with square stems and opposite leaves. Only 4 species, native to Eurasia.

■ *cardiaca* *p. 180*
Motherwort. A hardy perennial European herb, widely naturalized on disturbed sites in North America. Grows erect, with branching stems up to 4 ft. tall and interesting foliage. The opposite leaves are dark green, dusted with white hairs; they have jagged teeth or lobes, distinct purplish veins, and a bitter flavor. Whorls of tiny pinkish flowers are spaced along the top parts of every stem and are followed by prickly fruits. Makes a vigorous clump. Zone 4.

How to Grow
Full or part sun. Average soil. Grows easily from seed. Often self-sows and can be invasive. Good for a meadow, natural garden, or hedgerow.

Herbal Use
An important medicinal herb. Leaf tea traditionally was used to promote and regulate menstruation, aid in childbirth, calm heart palpitations, overcome insomnia, relieve sciatica, lower fevers, and ease stomachache. Scientific tests confirm many of these benefits. A well-documented Chinese species is used similarly.

Leptospermum
Lep-to-sper´mum
Myrtaceae. Myrtle family

Description
Evergreen shrubs or small trees, most with small or slender leaves. About 30 species, most native to Australia.

■ *scoparium* *p. 144*
New Zealand tea tree. A fine-textured evergreen shrub with small wiry or needlelike leaves. Single or double white, pink, or red flowers $\frac{1}{2}$ in. wide are crowded along the branches over a long season in spring and summer. Makes an exuberant display of bloom. There are several cultivars, with dwarf, spreading, or upright habit. Can grow 6–10 ft. tall. Easily pruned to shape or trained as a single-stemmed standard, in the ground or in a pot. *L. laevigatum,* Australian tea tree, grows to 30 ft. tall, with stiff, oval, gray-green leaves and round white flowers. Zone 9.

How to Grow
Full sun. Takes ordinary soil and watering, but good drainage is essential; succumbs to root rots in soggy soil. Pinch tips of young plants to encourage dense growth. Shear mature plants to shape. Don't prune back to bare wood. Pest-free.

Herbal Use
The fragrant leaves make a pleasant, tasty tea.

Levisticum

Le-vis´ti-kum
Umbelliferae. Carrot family

Description

A robust perennial herb with fragrant seeds, foliage, and roots. Only 1 species, native to southern Europe.

■ *officinale* p. 181

Lovage. A handsome plant for the back of the border, with glossy thrice-compound leaves on long hollow stalks. Makes a big clump, 4–6 ft. tall. Broad umbels of greenish yellow flowers top the stalks in June, followed by decorative seed heads. All parts are fragrant and edible. Zone 3.

How to Grow

Full or part sun. Does best in rich, moist soil. Sow freshly gathered seeds in fall. Goes on for years with no special care. Can be moved or divided in spring. You'll be surprised at how big the roots are, and how good they smell.

Herbal Use

The fresh or dried leaves taste like strong celery or parsley and are used in soups, stuffings, and salads. The ground seeds are tasty in cakes or breads. The root traditionally was used for digestive problems, flatulence, coughs, and menstrual problems.

Lindera

Lin-dair´a
Lauraceae. Laurel family

Description

Trees or shrubs with fragrant evergreen or deciduous leaves, yellow flowers, and 1-seeded berries. About 80 species, native to North America and Asia.

■ *benzoin* p. 120 *Pictured on p. 338*

Spicebush. A hardy deciduous shrub, native throughout the eastern United States. All parts are fragrant. Grows upright or bushy, about 8–10 ft. tall. Simple alternate leaves are plain green in summer, gold in fall. Plants are either male or female. Both sexes bear showy clusters of small golden flowers in early spring. Female plants bear bright red berries that attract waxwings and other birds in fall. Zone 5.

How to Grow

Full or part sun. Prefers moist, fertile soil but will grow in average garden beds. Don't try to transplant from the wild; it's better to buy container-grown plants at a nursery. Prune early to encourage branching.

Herbal Use

The leaf tea makes a tasty beverage. Dried, ground fruits can substitute for allspice in baked goods. In the past, the fruits, bark, and twig tea were all widely used as folk remedies for various ailments.

Linum

Lie´num
Linaceae. Flax family

Description

Annuals, perennials, or subshrubs with slender stems, narrow leaves, and round 5-petaled flowers in red, yellow, blue, or white. About 200 species, native to the Old and New World.

■ *usitatissimum* *p. 245*

Flax. An annual with slender erect stems 3–4 ft. tall. Pale green leaves are soft and slender, about 1 in. long. Round blue flowers with 5 petals open ½ in. wide on sunny mornings and close in early afternoon. Pea-sized fruits hold several shiny brown seeds. *L. perenne* is a hardy perennial species that makes an arching fountain of stems and blooms every morning for week after week. It's easy to grow and beautiful. All zones.

How to Grow

Full sun. Prefers rich, moist soil. Sow seeds in very early

spring, as soon as the ground can be worked. Plants develop quickly and grow best in cool weather. For fiber production, plants are densely spaced to produce tall, unbranched stems.

Herbal Use
Flax stems produce long, strong, fine fibers that are woven into linen fabrics. Linseed oil, pressed from the seeds, is used in paint, wood finishes, and linoleum. Flax seeds were a traditional folk remedy for skin and mouth cancer, colds, coughs, and lung ailments and were also taken as a laxative and made into a poultice for inflammations.

Lippia
Lip´ee-a
Verbenaceae. Verbena family

Description
Perennials or shrubs with opposite simple leaves, some aromatic. About 200 species, native to Latin America and Africa.

■ *dulcis* *p. 216*
Sweet herb. A tender shrub native to Mexico, usually grown here as an annual or a houseplant. Sprawling stems reach 1–2 ft. tall and spread 2–3 ft. wide. The heavy-textured leaves, pale green with darker edges, have a unique musky or fetid scent and a remarkably sweet flavor. Small white flowers appear year-round if plants are grown in good light. Also called *Phyla scaberrima*. Zone 9.

How to Grow
Full sun. Well-drained soil. Tolerates hot, dry conditions and makes a good ground cover for sandy banks. Easily rooted from tip cuttings. Prune young plants to encourage branching. One of the best herbs for a hanging basket. Thrives in a sunny window. Subject to mealybugs and aphids.

Herbal Use
Leaves are sweeter than saccharine and are used as a substitute for sugar. Caution: Consuming larger amounts might cause infertility in males.

■ *graveolens* *p. 217*
Mexican oregano. A tender shrub with slender upright stems 3–6 ft. tall. Dark green leaves, 1–2 in. long, have a rough surface and pungent fragrance. Small pale flowers are borne in axillary clusters throughout the summer. Zone 8.

How to Grow
Full sun. Well-drained soil. Tolerates hot, dry weather and sandy sites. Usually propagated by cuttings. Tends to sprawl unless you prune it often and hard. Where hardy, may die back in winter but recovers in spring. Can be overwintered indoors as a houseplant.

Herbal Use
Fresh or dried leaves are used like oregano in Mexico. The "oregano" on grocery-store spice racks is often this species. Its flavor is nice and spicy. Several other species of *Lippia* are also used as flavorings throughout Central America. *L. alba* is one of the best; its leaves have a pleasant lemony flavor that makes a tasty tea.

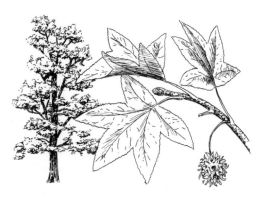

Liquidambar
Li-quid-am´bar
Hamamelidaceae. Witch hazel family

Description
Deciduous trees with lobed leaves and prickly round fruits. Only 4 species, native to North America and Asia.

■ *styraciflua* p. 121 *Pictured above*
Sweet gum. An easy-to-grow tree with outstanding fall color. The star-shaped leaves, 6 in. wide, turn bright orange, red, or purplish. Forms a narrow pyramid when young, spreading wider with age. Can reach 60 ft. or more. The twigs have interesting corky wings, and the trunk has ridged bark. The 1-in. fruits dangle like Christmas decorations on the bare limbs in early winter, but they make a rough litter when they drop on the lawn or sidewalk. 'Rotundifolia' is a desirable cultivar that doesn't set fruit. Its leaves have rounded, rather than pointed, lobes. Zone 6.

How to Grow
Full sun. Ordinary soil and watering. Tolerates heat and dryness. Surface roots can heave sidewalks or interfere with lawns; occasional deep soaking helps promote deeper roots. Prune only to remove lower limbs as needed. Pest-free.

Herbal Use
The fragrant, sticky sap can be chewed like gum. It was traditionally used in cough preparations and applied externally to wounds, sores, and skin infections.

Lobelia
Lo-bee´lee-a
Campanulaceae. Bellflower family

Description
A diverse genus of herbaceous and woody plants. About 365 species, most native to tropical and warm climates.

■ *cardinalis* p. 181
Cardinal flower. A hardy perennial wildflower native to moist sites in eastern North America. It blooms in late summer, with dense clusters of crimson flowers on leafy unbranched stalks up to 4 ft. tall. Zone 2.

How to Grow
Sun or part shade. Prefers damp, fertile soil but grows okay in ordinary soil with regular watering. Plants are generally short-lived but self-sow freely. Divide every 2–3 years.

Herbal Use
Lobelias were very significant historically, used to induce vomiting and profuse sweating in asthma, bronchial congestion, and other conditions. Until 1993, lobeline, an alkaloid from the annual *L. inflata,* was used in antismoking preparations, to appease the craving for nicotine. Caution: May be toxic.

■ *siphilitica* p. 182
Great blue lobelia. A perennial similar to cardinal flower, but with blue flowers on 3-ft. stalks. Zone 2.

How to Grow
Like *L. cardinalis.*

Herbal Use
Like *L. cardinalis.*

Magnolia
Mag-no´lee-a
Magnoliaceae. Magnolia family

Description
Deciduous or evergreen shrubs or trees, often with large, showy flowers. About 125 species, most native to eastern Asia or eastern North America, and many hybrids and cultivars.

■ *virginiana p. 121*
Sweet bay magnolia. A variable plant native to wet sites along the eastern seaboard from Massachusetts to Mississippi. Southern specimens are evergreen trees up to 60 ft. tall. Northern forms are deciduous shrubs, often no more than 20 ft. tall. In either case, the leaves are leathery-textured, 3–5 in. long, dark green above and silvery below, with a spicy fragrance when crushed. Cup-shaped creamy white flowers, 2–3 in. wide, have a lemony fragrance and open in June and July, sometimes repeating through the summer. Grows slowly and makes a graceful specimen. Zone 5.

How to Grow
Part sun. Prefers rich, constantly moist soil but grows in average garden soil with regular deep watering and a thick layer of mulch. Tolerates poorly drained soil, even boggy conditions. Can't take dryness. Plant container-grown or balled-and-burlapped plants in spring, after new growth starts. Don't disturb the roots by underplanting with annuals. It's fine if perennial ground covers planted around the edge creep toward the trunk. Needs minimal pruning—simply remove dead or damaged shoots.

Herbal Use
The leaves can be used as a substitute for bay laurel in cooking. Formerly used by Native Americans as a cold and fever remedy.

Marrubium
Ma-roo´bee-um
Labiatae. Mint family

Description
Perennials with square stems, furry opposite leaves, and small flowers. About 30 species, native to Eurasia.

■ *vulgare* *p. 182*

Horehound. A hardy perennial that forms a bushy, branching mound 18–24 in. tall and wide. Wrinkled gray leaves are rounded or oval, $1\frac{1}{2}$ in. long, with a musky scent and bitter taste. Both stems and leaves are covered with white hairs. Inconspicuous white flowers are clustered in the leaf axils. Silver horehound, *M. incanum,* has softer, more silvery leaves and grows to 2 ft. or more. Spanish horehound, *M. supinum,* is equally fuzzy but tidier and more compact. Zone 4.

How to Grow

Full sun. Needs good drainage and does well in unamended sandy or gravelly soil. Tolerates heat and drought. Makes a neat bushy clump in dry soil; gets big and floppy in rich or moist soil. Prune or shear to keep it neat. Propagate from seed or divide clumps in spring. Often self-sows but doesn't spread by runners.

Herbal Use

The pungent leaves produce a bitter compound that relieves sore throats and suppresses coughs. Concentrated extract is sweetened with sugar to make horehound drops. Also used as an appetite stimulant and digestive aid. Large doses can be laxative.

Matricaria

Mat-ri-kay′ree-a
Compositae. Composite family

Description

Annuals, biennials, or perennials with finely dissected leaves, sweet or pungent fragrance, and small white and/or yellow flower heads. Only 5 species, native to Eurasia.

■ *recutita* *p. 246*

German chamomile. An annual with very finely divided leaves on slender upright stems 24–30 in. tall. Leaves have a sweet aroma but bitter flavor. The blossoms are 1-in. white daisies with yellow disks that become more prominent and cone-shaped as the blossoms age and go to seed. All zones.

How to Grow

Full sun. Ordinary soil with good drainage. Easily grown from seed sown direct in early spring. Thin seedlings to 6 in. apart. A small patch provides many blossoms if harvested repeatedly.

Herbal Use
A popular and versatile folk remedy. Dried flower heads make a soothing tea, used for mild sleep disorders, stomach ailments, colds, and flu. Also used in antiseptic creams to treat minor wounds, inflammations, and skin irritations.

Melissa
Me-lis′sa
Labiatae. Mint family

Description
Perennials with square stems, opposite leaves, and small flowers borne in whorls. Only 3 species, from Europe and Asia.

■ *officinalis p. 183 Pictured above*
Lemon balm. A hardy perennial that makes a bushy mound if pruned repeatedly or a sprawling patch if left alone. Upright stems 2 ft. tall have opposite heart-shaped leaves with a crisp texture, distinct veins, and toothed edges. Ordinary plants are bright green; there's also a yellow-variegated form. Zone 5.

How to Grow
Full or part sun. Ordinary soil and watering. Propagate by dividing clumps in spring. Looks best if you shear it 2–3 times during the season to renew the foliage and to prevent flowering. The skinny greenish yellow flower stalks look weedy, and the volunteer seedlings are weedy.

Herbal Use
The fresh leaves make a pleasant hot or iced tea or a garnish for other beverages or fruit confections.

Mentha
Men´tha
Labiatae. Mint family

Description
Perennials with square stems, opposite leaves, and small flowers borne in dense whorls, heads, or spikes. About 25 species, native to the Old World. Mints hybridize readily, and there are hundreds of named selections, differing in flavor, foliage, height, and vigor and sold under a babel of names. If you can, visit an herb nursery where you can sniff leaves and observe the plants before choosing which mints to buy.

■ *aquatica*
Water mint, bergamot mint. 'Eau de Cologne', 'Orange Bergamot', and 'Orange' mint are popular selections now assigned to this species. (Formerly they were classed as *M. citrata* or included in *M. × piperita*.) All are similar plants with a wonderful, sweet aroma that lingers on your hands. Leaves are smooth, rounded, and dark green. Smooth dark stems are often floppy and tend to sprawl over adjacent plants. Pale flowers are borne in small heads. Usually grows 1–3 ft. tall. Runners can spread several feet in one year. Zone 5.

How to Grow
Full or part sun; tolerates shade but gets weak and leggy. Prefers rich, moist soil but doesn't require it; grows well in ordinary garden soil with regular watering. Plant in an out-of-the-way spot where it won't matter when the patch spreads, or curb it by planting in a buried bottomless pot or an area confined by adjacent pavement. Grows well in half-barrels or other containers with frequent watering and fertilizing. Shear to the ground in winter. Divide and replant every year or two in early spring. Generally pest-free.

Herbal Use
Fresh or dried leaves make a wonderful hot or iced tea.

■ × *piperita* *p. 184*
Peppermint. A variable mint, usually with many erect stems about 2 ft. tall; oval or oblong leaves with pointed tips, distinct veins, and toothed edges; and pale pink or lavender flowers clustered in small rounded heads at the tops of the stems. It spreads fairly quickly and makes a dense patch. 'Mitcham', 'Blue Balsam', 'Chocolate', and 'Candy' are selections with excellent flavor and fragrance. 'Grapefruit' mint has foliage with less flavor but more substance, and it makes quite a showy display of pink flowers in fall. Zone 5.

How to Grow
Like *M. aquatica*. The cultivars are all propagated from cuttings. Peppermint is a natural hybrid between water mint and spearmint. It doesn't set seed. Seeds that are sold as peppermint seeds have been mislabeled.

Herbal Use
Fresh or dried leaves make an excellent tea, taken for refreshment or to ease indigestion, nausea, sore throats, colds, headaches, or cramps. Oil distilled from the leaves is widely used as a flavoring for candies and confections, beverages such as crème de menthe, and toothpaste and other personal-care products.

■ *pulegium* p. 185
Pennyroyal. A low-growing mint with a strong, penetrating fragrance. The stems branch repeatedly and spread into a dense flat mat of smooth, dark green, oval leaves. In midsummer, weak upright stems 6–12 in. tall hold whorls of small pink or lilac flowers. Makes a good ground cover for damp places or for filling the gaps between stepping-stones. Don't worry; it isn't invasive. Zone 6.

How to Grow
Like *M. aquatica*. Not reliably hardy in zone 6 but sometimes self-sows. Propagate by seed or division.

Herbal Use
Rub fresh leaves on clothing or pet fur to repel mosquitoes or fleas. Leaf tea traditionally was used to induce or allay menstruation and also to induce abortions. Caution: Ingesting pennyroyal essential oil has resulted in fatalities.

■ *requienii* p. 217
Corsican mint. A very dainty plant with tiny bright green leaves and a cool, lingering, crème-de-menthe fragrance. Plant it where you can easily reach out and pet it. The creeping stems, under 1 in. tall, branch repeatedly and root as they go, spreading up to 1 ft. a year. You probably won't notice the tiny lilac flowers. Zone 8.

How to Grow
Part shade. Needs very well drained soil and frequent watering. Grows well between paving stones, over brick walks, or in shallow containers. Makes a mosslike ground cover for a potted shrub or tree. Not reliably hardy, even with good drainage and mulch. Comes true from seed, but it's usually propagated by division.

Herbal Use
Beloved for its fragrance. Though tiny, it's sometimes gathered to use as a tea, flavoring, or garnish.

■ *spicata* p. 185
Spearmint. A vigorous mint that spreads quickly to make a dense patch of many erect stems, usually 2–3 ft. tall, topped in summer with long slender spikes of tiny pale lilac flowers. The toothed leaves are usually dark green and can be smooth or hairy, veined or wrinkled. 'Crispa' has round crinkly leaves. Silver mint is a form with white hairs on the leaves. 'Kentucky Colonel' has wrinkled leaves with excellent flavor. Zone 5.

How to Grow
Like *M. aquatica*.

Herbal Use
Fresh or dried leaves make a tasty tea, enjoyed and used like peppermint tea. Also used as a flavoring for candies.

■ *suaveolens* p. 186
Pineapple mint, apple mint. Pineapple mint is the most ornamental of all mints, with bright green-and-white oval leaves about 1 in. long. It makes a mound about 1 ft. tall and doesn't spread too fast. Pale lavender flowers fill dense elongated heads at the tip of each branch in late summer. Apple mint has larger leaves with a soft hairy texture and a mild fruity scent. More robust, it grows 2 ft. tall and spreads fairly quickly. Zone 5.

How to Grow
Like *M. aquatica* but needs good drainage and tolerates drier soil than most mints.

Herbal Use
The flavor is mild, but the leaves make a pretty edible garnish for beverages or salads.

Monarda
Mo-nar´da
Labiatae. Mint family

Description
Annuals or perennials with square stems, aromatic leaves, and dense clusters of tubular, 2-lipped flowers. Only 12 species, most native to North America.

■ *didyma* p. 187

Bee balm, Oswego tea. A showy wildflower, popular in perennial borders, with moplike heads of tubular flowers that hummingbirds love. Spreads quickly to make a patch of slender
erect stems 2–4 ft. tall. Opposite leaves, oval with toothed
edges, have a pungent minty aroma. Forms a basal mat of
new foliage in fall that's evergreen (or greenish purple) where
winters are mild. Resumes growth in early spring and flowers
in summer. There are several new cultivars selected for red,
pink, purplish, or white flowers; extended bloom; and resistance to powdery mildew, which regularly disfigures or defo-
liates the older cultivars. Zone 4.

How to Grow

Full sun or afternoon shade. Native to damp sites throughout the East and grows best in moist, fertile soil. Doesn't tolerate extreme heat. Give it plenty of space, and expect it to
spread. Divide and replant every few years in early spring.

Herbal Use

Leaf tea traditionally was used as a beverage and was taken
for colds, fevers, intestinal gas, and insomnia and as a worm
repellent.

■ *fistulosa* p. 187

Wild bergamot. A perennial wildflower native to drier sites
and poorer soil than *M. didyma*. It has slightly fuzzier leaves
with a sweeter fragrance, and lavender-pink flowers. New
flower heads form above the old ones, extending the season
of bloom. Grows 2–4 ft. tall. Zone 4. Lemon bergamot, *M.
citriodora,* looks similar but has lemon-scented leaves and
pinker flowers, and it grows as an annual.

How to Grow

Full sun or afternoon shade. Not fussy about soil but does
best with good drainage. Subject to mildew in still, humid
weather, especially if crowded by other plants. Divide and replant every few years. Easily raised from seed.

Herbal Use

Same as for *M. didyma.*

■ *punctata* p. 188

Horsemint. Another native perennial that's easy, showy, and
unusual. Forms a clump of stems 2–4 ft. tall with slender opposite leaves. Whorls of purple-spotted yellow flowers that
look like open jaws nestle among pink petal-like bracts.
Blooms in late summer. Zone 4.

How to Grow
Like *M. fistulosa*. May be short-lived but usually self-sows.

Herbal Use
Same as for *M. didyma*. The essential oil contains thymol, an antiseptic.

Myrica
Mir'i-ka
Myricaceae. Bayberry family

Description
Deciduous or evergreen shrubs or trees, most with fragrant leaves and small, round, waxy, fragrant fruits. Some are nitrogen-fixing. About 50 species, distributed worldwide.

■ *cerifera* *Pictured above*
Wax myrtle. An easy, low-maintenance evergreen for much of the South, especially along the Atlantic coast, where it grows wild. Has a graceful appearance and sways in the wind. The slender light green leaves are smooth and leathery and smell wonderful when crushed. Clusters of small blue-gray berries dot the stems of female plants in fall and winter. Birds like them. Makes attractive hedges and screens that tolerate (but don't require) repeated pruning. Can also be trained into a small tree, up to 30 ft. tall. *M. californica* is a similar plant native to the Pacific coast, with dark blue-purple berries. Both are hardy to zone 7.

How to Grow
Full sun or part shade. Tolerates infertile, sandy, acidic soil and salt spray; thrives in ordinary garden conditions. Space 8–10 ft. apart for hedge. Easy to grow and pest-free.

Herbal Use
Wax from the berries is used to make bayberry candles or, more commonly nowadays, to perfume candles made of paraffin. Root bark historically was used as an astringent and remedy.

■ *pensylvanica*   *p. 122*
Bayberry. Hardier than wax myrtle but just as attractive. The fragrant leaves are deciduous, slightly broader than those of wax myrtle and scalloped around the edge, glossy green in summer and purple from fall to early winter. Forms an irregular spreading mound, usually under 8 ft. tall, with stiff stems that branch freely. Clusters of waxy silver-gray berries on female plants are conspicuous after the leaves drop in fall and last until the birds eat them. Zone 4.

How to Grow
Like *M. cerifera.* Plant 4 ft. apart for hedge. Spreads by suckers, but not very fast. Prune (if desired) in late winter.

Herbal Use
Same as for *M. cerifera.*

Myrrhis
Mir′ris
Umbelliferae. Carrot family

Description
A perennial herb with fragrant ferny foliage. Only 1 species, native to Europe.

■ *odorata*   *p. 188*
Sweet cicely. A hardy perennial. It makes a bushy clump of ferny, finely cut foliage that smells like anise or licorice. Grows about 3 ft. tall and wide. Leaves are dark green all summer, gold in fall. Flat-topped umbels of tiny white flowers in early spring are soon followed by ribbed fruits, 1 in. long, that point up like rockets. Fruits slowly ripen from green to glossy dark brown and are decorative all summer and fall. Zone 4.

How to Grow
Part sun or shade. Likes rich organic soil and constant moisture. One of the best herbs for shady spots such as the north side of a building. Space purchased plants 2 ft. apart in

spring. Mature clumps can be cut apart and reset in fall, or sow fresh seeds in fall to germinate in spring. Long-lived and trouble-free.

Herbal Use

All parts are edible. The sweet, anise-flavored leaves and seeds can be used to flavor applesauce or other cooked fruits. The seeds formerly were used to polish and perfume wooden furniture.

Myrtus

Mir´tus
Myrtaceae. Myrtle family

Description

Evergreen shrubs or small trees with opposite leaves and fragrant flowers. Only 2 species, from the Mediterranean region.

■ *communis* p. 145

Myrtle. A tough, drought-resistant shrub with a rounded habit and dense foliage, very useful for sheared hedges and edgings. Leathery, stiff, bright green leaves are oval with pointed tips, 1–2 in. long. They release a strong but pleasant fragrance when crushed. Sweet-scented white flowers like tiny powderpuffs open over a long season in summer, followed by dark blue berries. Patterned bark is an attractive cinnamon color. The species can grow (slowly) 15–20 ft. tall, but most cultivars are smaller. 'Compacta' grows about 3 ft. tall and wide. 'Microphylla' has smaller leaves and a tighter habit. 'Variegata' has small leaves with white edges. 'Boetica' has thick pointed leaves, closely set on stiff upright stems, and grows 8–12 ft. tall. Zone 7.

How to Grow

Full sun. Ordinary or unamended soil. Needs good drainage. Tolerates dry soil once established. Grows slowly. Shear to shape as desired. Grows well in containers, but avoid overwatering. Keeps growing if placed in a cool sunny location in winter. Subject to mealybugs but otherwise trouble-free.

Herbal Use

Edible berries have been used as seasoning, in tea, and as a remedy for arthritis. Oil from the berries and flowers has been used in perfumes. Leaf tea has been used as an antiseptic, astringent, and mild nerve sedative.

Nashia
Nash´ee-a
Verbenaceae. Verbena family

Description
Perennials or shrubs with aromatic leaves. Only 7 species, native to the West Indies.

■ *inaguensis* *p. 218*
Moujean tea. A tender shrub, usually grown as an annual or in a pot. Grows upright, 1–2 ft. tall, with stiff stems that branch readily. Opposite leaves are small and rounded, with a brittle, crinkly texture. They smell like musky poppy seeds. Occasionally bears small clusters of creamy verbena-like flowers. Zone 10.

How to Grow
Full sun. Needs good drainage and prefers sandy soil. Grows slowly and does well with its roots cramped in a small clay pot. Needs a sunny window and moderate watering in winter. A good herb for training into a standard, espalier, or bonsai. Propagate by tip cuttings. Subject to spider mites and mealybugs.

Herbal Use
Fresh or dried leaves make a pungent tea.

Nasturtium
Na-ster´shum
Cruciferae. Mustard family

Description
Water-loving perennials with smooth foliage and white flowers. Only 6 species, native to Europe and Central Asia.

■ *officinale* *p. 189*
Watercress. A vigorous perennial that spreads underground and by seed to make a dense tangled mat of slender stems and foliage. The crisp, succulent, tasty leaves are pinnately lobed or compound, 2–4 in. long. Tiny white flowers form clusters at the tops of the 4-in. stems, followed by slender pods. Zone 5.

How to Grow
Full or part sun. Needs plenty of moisture and rich, fertile, well-limed soil. Grow it in a boggy corner, along a stream, or

in a shallow clay pot standing in a saucer of water. Sow seeds indoors or out in early spring, or buy a plant to start. Harvest regularly to encourage new growth, and shear off the flower stalks to favor the foliage. Can be grown as an annual.

Herbal Use
Young leaves add a peppery flavor to salads and sandwiches and are rich in vitamin C. Caution: Avoid watercress from water that might be polluted with industrial or agricultural wastes.

Nepeta
Nep'e-ta, ne-pee'ta
Labiatae. Mint family

Description
Perennials or annuals with opposite leaves, sometimes scented, and tubular 2-lipped flowers in shades of blue, purple, pink, or white. About 250 species, most native to dry sites in the Old World.

■ *cataria*   p. 189
Catnip. A Eurasian perennial that has naturalized in many parts of the United States. It makes a lax clump of square-sided stems, usually 2–4 ft. tall. Downy, gray-green leaves are triangular, 1–3 in. long, with toothed edges. Bears spikes of small pale flowers in late summer if you let it but looks better if you shear the tops off before that happens and encourage a fresh crop of foliage. Regular catnip has a bitter, camphorlike fragrance. 'Citriodora' looks similar but has a lemony scent. Zone 3.

How to Grow
Full or part sun. Ordinary soil and watering. Tolerates heat, dry soil, and neglect. Spreads quickly by rhizomes and can be invasive, but not like mints are. Self-sows if you let it.

Herbal Use
Cats are excited by the fragrance, and dried leaves make good kitty toys. Tea made from the leaves and tops helps relieve cold symptoms and is mildly sedative.

■ × *faassenii*   p. 190
Catmint. Prettier than common catnip, this herb has won a place in many perennial borders. It forms a soft mound, 18–24 in. tall and wide, covered with soft, crinkled, gray-

green leaves and a profusion of blue, purple, or white flowers. Blooms for weeks in early summer. There are a few cultivars. One favorite is 'Six Hills Giant', an especially vigorous and showy plant. This species is often listed (mistakenly) as *N. mussinii*. Zone 4.

How to Grow
Full or part sun. Needs well-drained soil. Tolerates heat but not humidity. Give it plenty of space; it's apt to flop over and cover nearby plants. Shear after flowering to encourage re-bloom. Propagate by division in spring.

Herbal Use
Contains the same cat stimulant as common catnip but in smaller quantities. Not traditionally used for tea.

Nicandra
Ny-kan´dra
Solanaceae. Nightshade family

Description
A vigorous upright annual. Only 1 species, native to Peru.

■ *physaloides* p. 246
Shoo-fly plant. A bushy plant up to 5 ft. tall, with many branching stems. Smooth, light green leaves are oval with wavy or toothed edges, 2–6 in. long. Blooms profusely all summer with sky blue flowers like small petunias, 1 in. wide, followed by 5-sided papery husks enclosing small round seed-pods. All zones.

How to Grow
Full sun. Average soil and watering. Grows easily from seed and self-sows eagerly. Makes a good specimen for the garden or in a large pot. Said to repel flies and whiteflies but is subject to grasshoppers, tomato hornworms, and flea beetles.

Herbal Use
Traditionally used to repel flies, and the tea has been used as a hair rinse for head lice. Caution: Considered toxic.

Nicotiana

Ni-ko-she-ay´na
Solanaceae. Nightshade family

Description

Annuals, perennials, and a few shrubs, usually with sticky smelly leaves, tubular flowers with 5 lobes, and round dry pods loaded with thousands of tiny seeds. About 70 species, native to the Old and New World.

■ *rustica p. 247*
Indian tobacco. A tender annual, native to Mexico. Makes a single erect stem, usually 2–4 ft. tall. The large thick leaves are covered with sticky hairs. Small yellow flowers and pea-sized brown seedpods crowd the top of the stem in late summer. Common smoking and chewing tobacco comes from dozens of varieties of *N. tabacum*, another annual species that grows taller with larger leaves. All zones.

How to Grow

Full or part sun. Grows best and makes the biggest leaves in rich, deep, moist soil. Survives even in adverse conditions but makes only small leaves and soon goes to seed. Easy to grow from seedlings started indoors in spring, like tomatoes. Usually doesn't self-sow. Subject to tomato hornworm, Colorado potato beetle, and flea beetles.

Herbal Use

The leaves are very high in nicotine, used as an insecticide in greenhouses and gardens since the 1700s. Native Americans have smoked and chewed the leaves for ceremonial and medicinal purposes. Caution: The consequences of smoking tobacco are well known. Wear rubber gloves when picking and soaking the leaves for a homemade insect spray.

Nigella
Ny-jel´a
Ranunculaceae. Buttercup family

Description
Annuals with feathery foliage and unusual swollen seedpods. About 14 species, native to Eurasia.

■ *sativa* *p. 247*
Black cumin. A delicate-looking annual, 1–2 ft. tall, with many slender stems and finely divided leaves. Single flowers with 5 pale blue petals open in late summer, followed by puffy, papery pods filled with aromatic seeds. *N. damascena*, love-in-a-mist, is more commonly grown, because the flowers and pods are larger and showier in the garden or in dried arrangements. Its seeds are edible, too, but have much less flavor. All zones.

How to Grow
Full sun. Average soil and watering. Doesn't transplant well but starts easily from seeds sprinkled in the garden. Thin seedlings 8–12 in. apart. Harvest the pods as they dry but before they open and spill the seeds. Self-sows eagerly.

Herbal Use
Toasted and ground seeds are used in curries and other dishes in India and the Middle East. Seeds are also thought to repel insects from stored clothing.

Ocimum
Oh´si-mum
Labiatae. Mint family

Description
Annuals, perennials, or shrubs, most with very fragrant foliage, used for flavoring, fragrance, and medicine. About 150 species, native to warm and tropical regions, especially Africa.

■ *basilicum* *p. 248*
Sweet basil, common basil. A tender annual with shiny, wonderfully fragrant leaves. Erect branching stems usually grow 2–3 ft. tall. Opposite leaves are smooth ovals, medium green, 1–2 in. wide by 2–3 in. long, with pointed tips. Small white flowers are arranged in whorls of 6 on slender spikes that top the stems in summer and fall.
     In addition to regular sweet basil, a dozen or more special

strains are readily available from seed. 'Fino Verde' has especially good basil flavor. 'Anise', 'Cinnamon', 'Licorice', 'Lemon', and 'Mrs. Burns' Lemon' all have distinct flavors. 'Lettuce Leaf' has crinkled leaves up to 3 in. wide by 5 in. long. 'Opal' has deep purple leaves with a clovelike aroma. 'Spicy Globe' and 'Dwarf Opal' are two compact forms that make dense basketball-sized spheres of tiny spicy leaves. All zones.

How to Grow
Full sun. Ordinary soil and regular watering. Prefers hot weather. Easy from seed, started indoors 8 weeks before last frost or sown direct. Don't sow or transplant into the garden until the soil is warm. Grows well in containers. Sow 'Spicy Globe' in late summer to grow on a warm sunny windowsill all winter. Generally pest-free but can be ravaged by Japanese beetles. Remove flowers to prolong the harvest of leaves.

Herbal Use
Fresh leaves are a popular seasoning for tomato dishes and many other foods. Pesto is excellent with pasta. Leaf tea relieves nausea, gas pains, and fevers. Used in folk medicine to cure warts and worms and to treat snake and insect bites.

■ *kilimandscharicum* *p. 219*
Camphor basil. A tender shrub, usually treated as an annual. Grows about 5 ft. tall in a single season, with upright branching stems that get quite woody at the base. Opposite oval leaves are gray-green, are covered with white hairs, and have a strong camphor aroma. White to pale pink flowers crowd terminal racemes from summer to fall. Zone 10.

How to Grow
Like *O. basilicum.* Easily raised from seed or cuttings. Sometimes self-sows. Makes an impressive specimen or bushy hedge. Can be trained as a standard.

Herbal Use

Has been grown as a commercial source of camphor. Leaf tea is used in Africa for colds and stomachaches. Dried leaves make insect-repellent sachets for stored woolens.

■ *sanctum p. 249*

Sacred basil, holy basil, sri tulsi. A tender shrubby perennial, usually treated as an annual. Grows erect and bushy, about 2 ft. tall. Medium green leaves are slightly hairy, with smooth or softly toothed margins, rounded ends, and a warm, spicy, clovelike aroma. The flowers are purple or white. There's also a form with purplish stems and foliage. All zones.

How to Grow

Like *O. basilicum.* Can be kept as a houseplant on a warm sunny windowsill in winter if you start from seed in fall.

Herbal Use

A sacred herb in Hindu tradition. Used in cooking and medicine.

■ other basils

'African Blue' basil (p. 218), a hybrid of camphor basil and opal basil, is the showiest and most ornamental basil. It makes a bushy mound about 3 ft. tall and has gray-green leaves with purple veins, purple new growth, and light purple flowers. The leaves have a warm clove/camphor aroma. Propagated only by cuttings.

Tree basil, *O. gratissimum,* is a tender shrub that makes an impressive specimen 4–6 ft. tall. Fuzzy lime green leaves, up to 5 in. long, smell like pennyroyal. Has pale yellow flowers on branched racemes in late summer and fall. The leaf tea is used for colds and fevers, and the leaves are burned to repel mosquitoes.

Oenothera

Ee-noth´er-a
Onagraceae. Evening primrose family

Description

Annuals or perennials with 4-petaled flowers in bright yellow, white, or pink. Some open in the evening, but others are day bloomers. About 80 species, native to the New World.

■ *biennis p. 250 Pictured opposite*

Evening primrose. A hardy biennial, common as a wildflower

along roadsides in the eastern United States. Makes a flat rosette of slender pointed leaves and sends up one or more stiffly erect flower stalks. Usually grows 4–6 ft. tall. At dusk, the pointed buds open in less than a minute, spreading into clear yellow 4-petaled flowers, 1–2 in. wide. The flowers are fragrant all night, then close in the morning or stay open on cloudy days. Keeps growing taller all summer, always blooming at the top. Flower arrangers like the long stalks of seedpods, which dry to a warm beige. Goldfinches like the tiny seeds. Zone 4.

How to Grow
Full or part sun. Ordinary or unimproved soil. Tolerates dryness and neglect. Good for meadows or semiwild landscapes. Easily started from seed and self-sows. Pest free.

Herbal Use
The whole plant traditionally was used in tea for various disorders and poulticed to enhance wound healing. Oil from the seeds is used in Europe (especially England) to treat eczema, asthma, migraines, PMS, and inflammation and for prevention of heart disease and stroke.

Origanum
Oh-rig´a-num
Labiatae. Mint family

Description
Annual or perennial herbs, sometimes woody at the base. Simple opposite leaves may be very fragrant or odorless. Some species have showy flowers. About 36 species, native to Eurasia.

■ *majorana* p. 250
Sweet marjoram, knotted marjoram. A tender perennial, usually grown as an annual. Forms a bushy, branching mound 1–2 ft. tall. Opposite leaves are gray-green ovals, 1 in. long, with soft hairs and a delicious fragrance. Stems are topped with rounded, knotlike clusters of gray bracts that surround inconspicuous white flowers. Makes a good annual edging or a bushy specimen in a pot. Formerly called *Majorana hortensis*. Zone 9.

How to Grow
Full sun. Prefers rich, well-drained soil with plenty of lime. Start seeds indoors 8 weeks before last frost, or buy started plants to set out. Pinch or harvest frequently to promote bushiness. Lives over where winters are mild but may get straggly. Grows well in a container outdoors but must never dry out completely. Doesn't thrive indoors in winter; gets leggy and subject to aphids and other pests.

Herbal Use
Gather leaves before flowering for best flavor. Use them fresh or dried to season meat dishes; add in the last 10 minutes of cooking. Leaf tea is good for colds and headaches and to calm the nerves or settle upset stomachs. Dried leaves are a fragrant ingredient for potpourri or sleep pillows. Essential oil is used in perfumery.

■ × *majoricum* p. 220
Hardy sweet marjoram, Italian oregano. A shrubby evergreen perennial that makes an upright mound 12–18 in. tall. Opposite oval leaves are gray-green, up to 1 in. long. The scent is more penetrating and not as sweet as that of *O. majorana*. Bears small white flowers in terminal clusters in early summer. Considered to be a hybrid of *O. majorana* and *O. vulgare* subsp. *virens*. Zone 7.

How to Grow
Full sun. Well-drained average soil. Must be propagated by cuttings. Can be used as an informal or trimmed edging or grown in a container outdoors.

Herbal Use
Fresh or dried leaves make a tasty seasoning for meat and other dishes. Harvest before flowering for best flavor.

■ *vulgare* subsp. *hirtum* p. 190
Greek oregano. A hardy perennial with a distinct, pungent aroma and flavor. In the fall, creeping stems spread to form

a mat of evergreen foliage. Slightly hairy leaves are pointed ovals about 1 in. long. Sends up leafy stalks about 2 ft. tall in summer, topped with clusters of small white flowers. Often listed as *O. heracleoticum.*

There are several variations within this species; some are attractive, but none has the distinct flavor of Greek oregano. Subsp. *vulgare,* wild marjoram, makes a patch of erect stems 2 ft. tall with pretty rosy-red flowers in late summer. It is commonly sold as oregano, but its leaves are virtually tasteless. 'Aureum' and 'Dr. Ietswaart' are unscented but make attractive mats of creeping stems with cheery golden leaves. Zone 5.

How to Grow

Full sun. Prefers rich, well-drained soil with plenty of lime. Tolerates dry spells. Can be raised from seed, if the source is reliable. The best way to get a fragrant plant is to choose it in person at the nursery, sniffing the leaves before you buy. Renew established plants by dividing and replanting every few years. Cut flower stalks off at the base for dried arrangements and to encourage more leaf growth for culinary use. Plant in a raised bed and mulch with pine boughs to maximize winter survival.

Herbal Use

The best oregano for culinary use in Italian and other foods. Harvest the leaves before flowering. Also used medicinally in Europe for coughs, bronchitis, and respiratory ailments.

■ other species

Several other species of *Origanum* are valued as ornamentals, culinary herbs, or plants of the Bible. *O. dictamnus* (p. 219), dittany of Crete, makes a low, spreading mound of branched stems. It has nearly round leaves 1 in. wide, covered with soft white hairs, and hoplike clusters of greenish bracts surrounding small pink flowers in late summer. Needs excellent drainage and grows best in a terra-cotta pot, hanging basket, or window box. Keep in a sunny window and don't overwater in winter. Leaves have a mild oregano flavor, and flowers are dried for arrangements. Zone 8.

O. onites, pot marjoram, is a tender perennial with bright evergreen leaves about 1 in. long on hairy reddish stems topped with dense clusters of white or pale pink flowers. Forms a dense mat in winter, mounded up to 2 ft. tall in summer. Looks like Greek oregano but is daintier. The fragrant leaves are used as a seasoning and in potpourris and sachets. Zone 8.

O. syriacum (p. 220), Bible hyssop, is a tender shrubby

plant, to 2 ft. tall, with hairy stems, oval gray-green leaves about 1 in. long, and small heads of tiny white flowers. Needs protection from cold but grows well in pots. This is believed to be the hyssop of the Old Testament. The leaves have a pleasant aroma and a good oregano flavor. Also listed as *O. maru* and sometimes as *Majorana syriaca*. Zone 10.

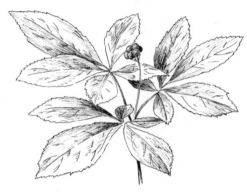

Panax
Pan´ax
Araliaceae. Aralia family

Description
Perennials with compound leaves and thick roots. Only 6 species, native to North America and eastern Asia.

■ *quinquefolius* *Pictured above*
Ginseng. A hardy perennial, native to rich woodlands in eastern North America. The single erect stalk, 1–2 ft. tall, holds 2 or more compound leaves, each palmately divided into 5 finely toothed oval leaflets. Centered between the leaves is a rounded umbel of small white or pale yellow-green flowers in summer, followed by a few bright red berries in fall. The fleshy forked root may resemble a human figurine. Zone 3.

Look closely to distinguish ginseng from wild sarsaparilla, *Aralia nudicaulis* (p. 156), another native perennial that grows in similar settings. Its leaflets are arranged in pinnate, not palmate, position, and its white flowers and dark blue berries are held on a short separate stalk. Its aromatic rhizome makes a pleasant tea or tonic, important in Native American and pioneer medicine.

Another point of confusion is Siberian ginseng, *Eleutherococcus senticosus*. Many of the claims for ginseng's health benefits relate to this hardy shrub from Asia, not to our native ginseng. Siberian ginseng is rarely grown in this country.

How to Grow

Full shade. Prefers soil rich with organic matter and leaf mold. Buy one plant for an interesting specimen. To increase, bury its seeds $1/2$–1 in. deep and be patient. Long-lived and carefree if well sited, but slugs may eat the foliage and rodents eat the seeds.

Herbal Use

Most ginseng is exported to Asia, where it is regarded as a panacea. Root tea or extracts are used as a tonic for fatigue, for reduced work capacity and concentration, and during convalescence. Although much scientific research has been done on this plant, the results are conflicting and inconclusive.

Papaver

Pa-pay´ver
Papaveraceae. Poppy family

Description

Annuals or perennials with showy flowers borne singly on long stalks, lobed or dissected basal leaves, and milky sap. About 50 species, native to Old and New World.

■ *somniferum* p. 251

Opium poppy. A showy annual poppy with beautiful flowers 6–8 in. wide, single or double, in many shades of white, pink, purple, and red. Stiff upright stalks, 2–4 ft. tall, are clasped by blue-green leaves that are round or oval with wavy toothed edges. Egg-shaped seedpods are filled with blue-black seeds. Seed catalogs list many strains selected for especially lovely flowers or interesting pods. *P. rhoeas,* the field poppy or corn poppy, is a European annual often included in wildflower seed mixes in this country. It has red flowers 1–2 in. wide and small pods of edible black seeds. All zones.

How to Grow

Full sun. Average soil. Tolerates dry spells. Doesn't transplant easily, so sprinkle the tiny seeds where you want them to grow, from fall to early spring. Thin seedlings 4–6 in. apart. Usually self-sows. Mass plantings make bold splashes of color.

Herbal Use

Cut the stalks when the pods turn yellow and stand them in an empty vase to dry. Use the seeds to flavor breads, pastries, noodles, and salad dressings, then use the empty seed heads for dried arrangements. The milky sap harvested from immature pods of this plant is the source of opium and morphine, a painkiller that has yet to be replaced by synthetic drugs.

Passiflora
Pas-si-flo´ra
Passifloraceae. Passionflower family

Description
Mostly evergreen vines that climb by tendrils. Large round flowers are fascinating and complex and are sometimes very fragrant. About 350 species, most native to tropical America.

■ *incarnata* p. 191
Passionflower, maypop. A hardy vine that climbs or sprawls 15 ft. or more in a growing season but dies back in winter. Has smooth 3-lobed leaves, tightly coiled tendrils, and very fragrant pale lavender flowers, 3 in. wide. If pollinated, bears egg-sized yellow fruits with numerous seeds in a tasty sweet pulp. Established plants develop tuberous roots. Zone 5, with winter mulch.

How to Grow
Full or part sun. Well-drained or sandy soil. Transplant container-grown plants in spring. Provide a trellis, or let it scramble over adjacent shrubs or other plants. Spreads by suckers but isn't invasive. Cut down frosted shoots in fall and mulch the roots for winter.

Herbal Use
Native Americans poulticed the root for boils, cuts, earaches, and inflammations and used the whole plant in tea as a sedative. Fresh or dried preparations are still used in Europe in sedatives for nervous anxiety and sleeplessness.

Pelargonium
Pel-ar-go´nee-um
Geraniaceae. Geranium family

Description
Perennials, shrubs, and some annuals. True geraniums (*Geranium*) have "regular" flowers — radially symmetric, with all

petals the same. These have "irregular" flowers—with a top and bottom, like a face. Many species have leaves with distinctive shape, marking, or fragrance. About 280 species, most native to South Africa, and hundreds of hybrid cultivars.

■ **scented geraniums** *pp. 221–225 Pictured on p. 366*
These tender perennials are among the most popular herbs. There are dozens of different species and cultivars with a wide range of growth habits; leaf sizes, shapes, and markings; and aromas. You can grow them as summer bedding plants in the garden, in outdoor containers, or as houseplants. Most kinds are valued primarily for their foliage, but some have attractive flowers, too. Specialty nurseries offer the widest selection. The following are highly recommended. All are hardy to zone 10.

P. capitatum 'Attar of Roses', rose-scented geranium, is a compact upright plant, 2 ft. tall, with a rich rose fragrance. Leaves are soft and furry, 1–1½ in. wide, with 3 lobes. May bear small pink flowers in spring. Space 1 ft. apart and prune young plants to make a neat low edging in the herb garden.

P. crispum, lemon-scented geranium, has vertical stems, 1–2 ft. tall, crowded with small rounded leaves that have crinkly toothed edges, brittle texture, and intense aroma. White flowers streaked with pink may bloom in spring or summer. 'Prince Rupert' is the easiest cultivar to grow and is excellent for topiary. It has plain green leaves ½ in. wide. 'French Lace' or 'Variegated Prince Rupert' has beautiful creamy-edged leaves but is subject to various rots and wilts — protect it from rain and never overwater. All forms of *P. crispum* are slow-growing and must be pruned when young to initiate branching. Even with pruning, they tend to be columnar, not bushy, plants.

P. × fragrans, nutmeg-scented geranium, is one of several scented geraniums with sprawling or trailing stems that spread about 2–3 ft. wide. It forms rosettes of blue-green leaves, 1 in. wide, that are rounded and have frilly notched edges, and it bears many lacy sprays of tiny white flowers from early spring to summer. 'Logeei' or 'Old Spice' is similar but more vigorous, with abundant flowers and a spicier aroma. *P. odoratissimum,* apple-scented geranium, has wider leaves with a fresh green-apple aroma and blooms infrequently. *P. parviflorum,* coconut-scented geranium, has rosettes of rounded leaves that are deep green with red edging. It bears tiny, deep pink flowers all year. These trailing plants all grow well in hanging baskets.

P. graveolens, true rose geranium, is a vigorous plant that grows upright and bushy, 3 ft. or taller and just as wide. The

leaves are soft and furry, deeply cleft or notched, 3–4 in. wide. There are many cultivars. 'Lady Plymouth' or 'Silver Leaf Rose' has irregularly shaped leaves edged with cream. 'Rober's Lemon Rose' has gray-green leaves with deep irregular lobes and a lemon-rose aroma. 'Joy Lucille' has fuzzy green glove-shaped leaves with a peppermint-rose aroma. 'Red Flowered Rose' has crimson flowers and deeply notched leaves. 'Mrs. Taylor' bears many small red flowers. 'Little Gem' is slow-growing with plentiful pink flowers. All are excellent accent plants for the garden or can be shaped as topiary or trained into standards.

P. × *nervosum*, lime-scented geranium, is another upright grower, like lemon-scented geranium. It makes a narrow bushy plant about 2 ft. tall. Deep green leaves with a true lime aroma are rounded, up to 1 in. wide, and have sharply toothed edges. May bear pink flowers in spring. 'Toronto' (formerly *P. torento*), ginger-scented geranium, has slightly larger, flatter leaves with a spicy scent. Both need early pruning to encourage branching.

P. quercifolium, oakleaf geranium or pine-scented geranium, has branching stems that grow 2–3 ft. tall and 3 ft. or more wide. The oak-leaf-shaped leaves look glossy, feel sticky, and smell piney or resinous. Pretty, pale pink flowers bloom in spring. 'Village Hill Oak' is more compact, with deeply lobed leaves. 'Fair Ellen' has lobed leaves with bronzy centers. Prune early to train a bushy specimen or accent plant.

P. tomentosum, peppermint-scented geranium, is a large, fast-growing plant, sometimes upright but usually trailing, with stems 4 ft. or longer and lobed leaves up to 6 in. long. The silvery foliage is very fuzzy and pettable and has a strong minty aroma. 'Chocolate Mint' has gray-green leaves marked with chocolate brown and an "after-dinner mint" fragrance. Use either one to cascade over a bank or retaining wall or to fill a large pot.

How to Grow

Full sun is needed for compact growth and best aroma. Shaded plants may get leggy. Use well-drained soil without too much compost or organic matter. Water and fertilize regularly.

Transplant into the garden after danger of frost for use as summer bedding plants. Pinch or prune to encourage branching. If you cover plants with a blanket to protect them from the first mild fall frost, they may live a few extra weeks before severe frost strikes.

All scented geraniums do well in containers on a sunny porch or patio. Vigorous forms can fill a half-barrel or larger planter; small kinds thrive in clay pots. Upright growers can be trained as standards, espaliers, or bushy mounds. Spreading types will spill from a hanging basket or window box. Plants in containers need fast-draining soil and regular watering and fertilizing. Don't let water stand in a saucer under the pot, but don't let the soil dry out completely either.

Most scented geraniums make good houseplants in winter. Keep them in a cool but very bright window and hold back on watering. Use insecticidal soap or horticultural oil to control aphids, mealybugs, spider mites, and whiteflies. Nurseries grow new plants from cuttings. Some kinds root easily at home, but many don't.

Herbal Use

The fragrant leaves are mostly dried for potpourris and sachets but are sometimes used to flavor jellies or cakes. Essential oils are used in perfumery and have antiseptic properties.

Perilla

Pee-ril′a
Labiatae. Mint family

Description

Annuals with upright stems and opposite leaves. About 6 species, native from India to Japan.

■ *frutescens* p. 251

Perilla, shisho, beefsteak plant. An erect bushy annual with branching stems 3–4 ft. tall. Oval leaves up to 5 in. long have a wrinkled texture, deep veins, toothed edges, and a distinct spicy fragrance. Different strains have lime green, reddish bronze, or dark purple leaves that are more or less crinkly or ruffled and have somewhat different aromas. Spikes of small white or pale purple flowers top every shoot in late summer and fall. All zones.

How to Grow

Full sun. Average soil and watering. Sow seeds in fall for germination in spring. Plant it once, and it will reseed itself forever. The purple forms in particular make an easy and colorful addition to annual or perennial flower beds.

Herbal Use

Fresh leaves are used as seasoning in various Oriental dishes. Leaf tea is used in traditional Chinese medicine for upset stomachs and other ailments. Oil from the seeds is used like linseed oil, as a finish for wooden objects.

Petroselinum

Pet-ro-se-lee′num
Umbelliferae. Carrot family

Description

Biennials with thick roots and finely divided leaves. Only 3 species, native to Europe and the Mediterranean region.

■ *crispum*   p. 252

Parsley. An indispensable herb, easy, attractive, and tasty. Usually grown as an annual, it forms a low rosette about 1 ft. tall and wide. Dark green leaves are triangular in outline but divided into many flat or curly leaflets. The foliage stays fresh, attractive, and tasty until hard frost, or all winter in mild climates. Plants bloom in the second year, with small umbels of greenish flowers on leafy stalks 2–3 ft. tall. Most seed catalogs list at least two strains of parsley. The curly-leaf types are attractive and widely used for garnishes, but gourmets insist that the Italian flat-leaf types are more flavorful. All zones.

How to Grow

Full or part sun. Prefers rich, moist, well-drained soil but grows okay in average soil. Soak seeds overnight in hot water to speed germination, which is otherwise slow. Sow indoors 8 weeks before last frost, or buy little plants. Space 12 in. apart in the garden. Makes a pretty edging for beds of annuals or herbs and also grows well in containers. May host green-and-yellow caterpillars of the swallowtail butterfly; grow enough to share with these beautiful creatures. If you let it overwinter and go to seed, it often self-sows. May bloom the first year if you set plants outdoors too soon, while the weather is still cool.

Herbal Use
Use fresh or dried leaves to season salads, soups, and main dishes. It's very rich in vitamin C. Chewing fresh leaves also sweetens the breath. In France, parsley preparations are used for chapped skin, insect bites, and other dermatological conditions.

Pinus
Py´nus
Pinaceae. Pine family

Description
Evergreen trees with needlelike leaves and woody cones. More than 90 species, native worldwide.

■ *strobus* p. 122 *Pictured below*
Eastern white pine. One of the most ornamental pines, with soft blue-green needles 2–4 in. long and slender cones 6–8 in. long. Young trees grow fast and can be sheared to form dense tall hedges. Old specimens eventually reach 75 ft. tall. The many cultivars include dwarf, columnar, and weeping forms. Zone 3.

How to Grow
Full sun. Prefers rich, moist, organic soil. Grows best in its native area — the Northeast, Great Lakes, and Appalachians. Transplant in early spring or fall, and water regularly until established. To encourage more compact growth, break off the top half of new shoots, called "candles," in early summer.

Herbal Use
Preparations of the inner bark formerly were used in cough syrups. The needles make a pine-flavored tea that is rich in vitamin C. Other pines also have herbal uses. Sticky sap tapped from the southeastern longleaf pine, *P. palustris,* is processed into turpentine and rosin. The large tasty seeds from the Swiss stone pine, *P. cembra,* and the Rocky Mountain piñon pines, *P. edulis* and *P. monophylla,* are used in pesto and other herb pastes.

Platycodon
Plat-i-ko′don
Campanulaceae. Bellflower family

Description
A perennial with unusual balloonlike buds. Only 1 species, native to eastern Asia.

■ *grandiflorus* *p. 191* *Pictured above*
Balloon flower. A trouble-free and long-lived perennial that forms a small clump of erect stems, 18–30 in. tall. Leaves are narrow, 3 in. long, with toothed edges. Unique puffy buds open into elegant flowers like 5-pointed stars, 2 in. wide, in shades of violet, blue, pink, or white. Continues blooming throughout the summer if spent flowers are removed. There are compact and double cultivars. Zone 3.

How to Grow
Full sun in northern regions; afternoon shade where summers are hot. Ordinary or better soil and regular watering. Choose a spot and leave it there — it doesn't like to be moved or divided. Easily raised from seed but doesn't bloom for a few years. Very late to emerge in spring; mark the spot to avoid digging and damaging it.

Herbal Use
The root is used in modern traditional Chinese medicine for coughs, sore throats, lung ailments, and dysentery.

Plectranthus
Plek-tran´thus
Labiatae. Mint family

Description
Perennials or shrubs, sometimes succulent, with square stems and opposite leaves. About 300 species, native to the Old World.

■ menthol plant   *p. 225*
Menthol plant, Vick's plant. A tender evergreen perennial that thrives in containers outdoors or as a houseplant. Sprawling stems spread 2–3 ft. or more. Opposite leaves are thick and fleshy, are covered with soft silvery hairs, and have a strong menthol aroma. Leaf size is quite variable, depending on the plant's age and vigor, how much you prune it, and growing conditions. Rarely flowers. This is a common plant, but its specific identity is uncertain. Sometimes listed as a *Coleus*. Zone 10.

How to Grow
Full or part sun. Well-drained or sandy soil. Tolerates dryness; don't overwater. Easily started from tip cuttings. Prune to encourage branching. Quickly fills a clay pot, hanging basket, or window box. Grow it on a sunny windowsill in winter. Start a new plant when the old one gets straggly or bare.

Herbal Use
Rub or pinch the leaves and inhale the menthol to clear a stuffy nose. Also used as a poultice or chest rub for congestion.

Pogostemon
Po-go-stem´on
Labiatae. Mint family

Description
Tropical evergreen perennials with fragrant foliage. About 70 species, native to Southeast Asia.

■ *heyneanus*
Patchouli. A tender shrubby perennial, up to 3 ft. tall and wide, with many branching stems. Opposite leaves are oval with notched edges; are slightly rough, sticky, or hairy; and have an exotic musky aroma. Pale lavender or white flowers appear mostly in winter. *P. cablin* (p. 226) is similar; the two plants are sometimes confused and mislabeled. Very tender to frost but easily grown as a houseplant in all zones.

How to Grow
Full or part sun. Average or rich soil with regular watering. Tip cuttings root easily in water or damp sand. Plant in the garden after all danger of frost is past, or grow it in a container where you can touch it often. Old plants get woody at the base. Root a cutting in summer to start a new plant for the winter windowsill. Subject to aphids, spider mites, and mealybugs.

Herbal Use
Dried leaves are used in potpourris and sachets, especially to scent stored clothing. Essential oil was a popular perfume in the 1960s. The herb is used medicinally in India and China.

Poliomintha
Po-lee-o-min´tha
Labiatae. Mint family

Description
Shrubby perennials with square stems and opposite leaves. Only 4 species, native to the southwestern United States and Mexico.

■ *longiflora*   *p. 226*
Mexican oregano. A bushy plant that thrives in hot, dry summers. Grows about 4 ft. tall and wide in the Southwest but smaller in other parts of the country. Stems are covered with smooth, shiny, oblong leaves about $\frac{1}{2}$–1 in. long. Blooms in summer and fall, with slender tubular flowers in various shades of pink or lavender. Can be pruned to make a hedge or specimen. Zone 8.

How to Grow
Full sun or afternoon shade. Prefers rich, well-drained soil. Tolerates dry spells. Propagate by tip cuttings. Grows well in a container and makes a good winter houseplant.

Herbal Use
Fresh or dried leaves are used like oregano but have a stronger flavor. Good in Mexican food and on pizza.

Polygonatum
Po-lig-oh-nay′tum
Liliaceae. Lily family

Description
Perennials with spreading rhizomes, leafy arching stems, and small starry flowers. About 55 species, native to the north temperate zone.

■ *biflorum* *p. 192*
Solomon's-seal. A woodland wildflower, common in the eastern United States. Forms a patch of erect arching stems 2–3 ft. tall with alternate oval leaves. Pairs of yellow-green flowers dangle from the leaf axils in spring, followed by blue berries in fall. Other species look similar and have similar properties. Compare this with false Solomon's-seal, *Smilacena racemosa,* p. 200. Zone 3.

How to Grow
Part or full shade. Does best in fertile, organic, moist soil. Plant or divide in early spring or late fall. Top-dress with compost every year or two. Long-lived and trouble-free.

Herbal Use
Root tea was used by Native Americans and settlers for indigestion, "general debility," and coughs.

Polygonum
Po-lig′o-num
Polygonaceae. Buckwheat family

Description
Annuals, perennials, or vines, some aquatic. Stems usually have swollen nodes. Leaves are alternate. Flowers are small but sometimes showy. Some species are very weedy, spreading by seed or rhizome. About 150 species, native worldwide.

■ *odoratum* *p. 227*
Vietnamese coriander. A tender perennial, easily grown as an annual and overwintered as a houseplant. Stems rarely exceed

1 ft. tall, but they flop over and spread indefinitely, rooting as they go. Narrow pointed leaves, 3 in. long, are green with a dark triangular blotch and have a strong coriander/cilantro aroma. Rarely blooms, but can bear terminal clusters of small pink flowers in autumn. Zone 8, with winter protection.

P. multiflorum, Fo-ti, is another Asian species that spreads or climbs several feet in a season. It has jointed stems, arrowhead-shaped leaves, greenish flowers, and tuberous roots. It grows well in containers indoors or out and is hardy to zone 6 with protection. The root is highly valued in Chinese medicine.

How to Grow
Part sun. Grows fine with average soil and watering; thrives in rich, damp soil. It looks invasive but it isn't, at least in most parts of the United States, because frost kills it back and it doesn't set seed. Cuttings root easily in water or damp soil. Start a new plant in summer to overwinter indoors.

Herbal Use
Pick fresh leaves anytime. Doesn't dry well. The cilantro flavor is popular in Latin American and Asian cuisines.

■ *tinctorium* p. 253
Japanese indigo. A tender annual that makes a bushy mass of branching erect stems up to 3 ft. tall. Smooth oblong leaves, 3–4 in. long, are thinner than paper and wilt easily in hot, dry weather. Very showy when it starts blooming in late summer, with loose sprays of bright pink flowers that hide the foliage, but it succumbs to the first hard frost. All zones.

How to Grow
Full sun or afternoon shade. Prefers rich, moist soil. Grow it like tomatoes or peppers: start seeds in a warm place indoors and transplant after last frost. Space 12–18 in. apart. Needs regular watering but otherwise carefree. Rarely self-seeds.

Herbal Use
The leaves produce indigo pigment, valued as a permanent blue dye for cotton and other textiles. Important traditionally and still used in Japan and Southeast Asia.

Populus
Pop´you-lus
Salicaceae. Willow family

Description
Deciduous trees with soft light wood, simple leaves, and dangling catkins in early spring. Closely related to willows (*Salix*). About 35 species, native to the north temperate zone.

■ *tremuloides* p. 123 *Pictured above*
Aspen, quaking aspen. A small tree that's very common in cool mountain or northern climates. Glossy spade-shaped leaves dance in the slightest breeze and are fresh green all summer, warm gold in fall. Smooth gray bark is attractive all year. Suckers readily and often grows in clumps, rather than as single trees. Usually doesn't exceed 25–30 ft. tall in cultivation. Zone 2.

How to Grow
Full or part sun. Prefers cool, moist soil but tolerates average sites if watered regularly. Can't take hot, dry weather. Transplant nursery-grown plants in early spring.

Herbal Use
Preparations of the winter buds of this and related species traditionally were used for relieving minor aches and pains, colds and coughs, and externally for sores, bruises, and cuts.

Poterium
Po-teer´ee-um
Rosaceae. Rose family

Description
Hardy perennials or low shrubs with compound leaves and clusters of tiny flowers. About 25 species, native to the Old World.

■ *sanguisorba* *p. 192*
Salad burnet. An easy, attractive, and tasty perennial herb. Evergreen in mild climates, it forms a low mounded rosette of compound leaves with several pairs of scalloped leaflets. Stiff, hollow flower stalks up to 3 ft. tall bear many round heads of scentless pinkish flowers in late spring and summer. Makes a plump specimen or bushy low edging. Sometimes listed as *Sanguisorba minor.* Zone 3.

How to Grow
Full or part sun. Average soil and watering. Easy from seed and self-sows freely if you let it. Tolerates cold and heat but not drought. Cut back after bloom and remove old leaves periodically to keep it tidy. Long-lived and carefree.

Herbal Use
Gather fresh tender young leaves, which taste like cucumbers, for use in salads and as a garnish for food and beverages. Leaves are used as a tonic and astringent to treat diarrhea and internal bleeding. Historically, soldiers drank leaf tea before entering battle, in hopes that bleeding from wounds would be less severe.

Premna
Prem´na
Verbenaceae. Verbena family

Description
Tropical trees or shrubs, some with aromatic leaves or attractive hardwood. About 200 species, native to the Old World.

■ *japonica* *p. 123*
No common name. A deciduous shrub, 3–4 ft. tall and wide, with handsome mahogany-colored bark and shiny dark green foliage. Opposite, oval leaves have a brittle texture. The slightest touch releases an intense fragrance likened to roasted poppyseeds. Sprays of small white flowers appear in summer. Zone 5.

How to Grow
Full or part sun. Average or heavy soil. Tolerates dry spells once established. Needs frequent pruning to encourage branching. Buy a plant; it's hard to root and seeds aren't available.

Herbal Use

The leaves are used as a moth repellent. Roots and leaves of related species are used in Malaysia to treat fevers.

Primula

Prim′you-la
Primulaceae. Primrose family

Description

Low-growing perennials with a rosette of basal leaves and clusters of showy flowers on leafless stalks. About 400 species, native worldwide, mostly in cool climates.

■ *veris* p. 193 *Pictured above*
Cowslip. A hardy perennial, popular as a wildflower in England and Europe. It makes small rosettes of soft, crinkled, oblong leaves about 3 in. long. Blooms for several weeks in early spring, with nodding umbels of sweetly fragrant yellow flowers on 6-in. stalks. Zone 5.

How to Grow

Part sun in spring, shade in summer. Needs fertile soil amended with plenty of organic matter, and a layer of organic mulch. Can't survive where summers are too hot or dry. Once established, it often self-sows, or you can gather ripe seeds and sow them immediately. Divide every year or two in late spring or early summer, after flowering, and reset in freshly enriched soil. Foliage may be attacked by aphids, flea beetles, spider mites, slugs, and snails.

Herbal Use

Tea made from the flowers is used in Europe as a mild sedative and a remedy for common ailments. Flowers are also candied and made into syrups and wines.

Prunella
Proo-nel′la
Labiatae. Mint family

Description
Low-growing perennials with square stems, opposite leaves, and small flowers arranged in dense heads. Most are spreading and can be weedy. Only 7 species, native to the Old and New World.

■ *vulgaris p. 193*
Heal-all, self-heal. A hardy perennial that forms a patch of stems up to 1 ft. tall, topped all summer with dense heads of purple flowers. Opposite leaves are slender ovals, 2 in. long, and have a dark green color. Flowers and leaves have little fragrance. A Eurasian herb, common in lawns and roadsides across the northern United States. Zone 4.

How to Grow
Full or part sun. Average soil and watering. Very easy to grow, except where summers are hot and dry.

Herbal Use
Leaf tea has been used as a gargle for sore throats and mouth sores; taken internally for fevers and diarrhea; and applied to minor wounds, bruises, scratches, insect bites, and the like. Recent research confirms that it has several medicinal properties.

Prunus
Proo′nus
Rosaceae. Rose family

Description
Deciduous or evergreen trees or shrubs with alternate simple leaves, pink or white flowers, and fleshy fruits with one hard seed. Includes cherries, plums, peaches, prunes, and apricots. About 400 species, most native to the Northern Hemisphere.

■ *serotina*
Wild cherry, black cherry. A deciduous tree native to eastern North America, valued especially for its beautiful heartwood lumber and known as the flavoring in wild cherry cough drops. Grows to 50 ft. or more, usually with a slender crown. Oval leaves have fine-toothed edges. Drooping clusters of starry white flowers in spring are followed by tart black cherries, which make good wine or preserves if the birds don't get

them first. The outer bark has an attractive ridged texture; the inner bark is strongly aromatic. Zone 4.

P. virginiana (p. 124) is a smaller tree (to 20 ft.) with broader leaves and showy clusters of bright red sour cherries. Its bark is not aromatic, but it has been used externally to treat wounds. Zone 3.

How to Grow
Full or part sun. Rich, well-drained soil and regular watering. Grows quickly from seed, or transplant purchased plants in early spring. Like all cherries, subject to several fungal and insect problems that are serious in some years and minor in others.

Herbal Use
Tea or syrup from the inner bark was a traditional remedy for colds, coughs, sore throats, and other ailments. Caution: Cherry leaves, pits, and bark can cause cyanide poisoning if consumed in quantity. The amount used in medicinal preparations is safe.

Ptelea
Tee′lee-a
Rutaceae. Citrus family

Description
Hardy trees or shrubs with fragrant flowers and aromatic foliage. Only 3 species, native to North America.

■ *trifoliata* p. 124
Common hoptree. A deciduous tree, 15–20 ft. tall, that's neat, carefree, and easy to grow. The small white flowers have an especially sweet fragrance, like orange blossoms. The healthy green leaves are compound with 3 oval leaflets; when crushed, they release a fragrance that some people enjoy and others call skunklike. Clusters of flat papery pods hang on into winter and rustle in the breeze. A good tree for small gardens. Zone 4.

Don't confuse *Ptelea trifoliata* with *Poncirus trifoliata*, the hardy orange, also in the citrus family. Hardy orange is a shrub or small tree with crooked, thorny, green twigs and glossy, semievergreen, 3-parted leaves. It has very fragrant white flowers and equally fragrant yellow fruits with a fuzzy hard rind and edible but very sour pulp. It is grown as an ornamental and used as a rootstock for common edible citrus. Native to China. Hardy on sheltered sites to zone 6.

How to Grow
Full sun, part sun, or shade. Average soil and watering. Transplant a nursery-grown tree in early spring. Needs little care or pruning and has no serious pests. Grows wild across the central and eastern United States, but is never common.

Herbal Use
Root preparations were used by 19th-century physicians as a tonic for asthma, fevers, poor appetite, and other conditions. Fruits have been used as a substitute for hops in brewing beer.

Pycnanthemum
Pik-nan´the-mum
Labiatae. Mint family

Description
Perennials with upright stems, opposite leaves, and a minty aroma. About 17 species, native to North America.

■ *muticum* p. 194
Mountain mint. A carefree native that makes a bushy clump 2 ft. tall. Opposite oval leaves are softly fuzzy and gray-green and have a pleasant minty aroma. The upper leaves turn silver in late summer and fall, framing the small lilac-pink flowers. *P. incanum* is very similar. *P. virginianum* has shiny slender leaves and abundant clusters of pale flowers. Other species are also desirable. All spread by runners but aren't invasive. Zone 5.

How to Grow
Full or part sun. Well-drained soil. Easy to grow, with no common pests. Increase by division in early spring.

Herbal Use
The leaves make a pleasant mild tea, used by Native Americans for fevers, colds, upset stomachs, and other minor ailments.

Reseda
Re-see´da
Resedaceae. Mignonette family

Description
Annuals, biennials, or perennials with smooth foliage and

stalks topped with clusters of small flowers. About 55 species, native to Europe and Asia.

■ *luteola* *p. 253 Pictured above*
Weld. A hardy biennial. First it makes a flat rosette, 6–12 in. wide, of oblong leaves with wavy ruffled edges. In late spring the second year, it bears hundreds of small greenish yellow flowers on a stalk 2–4 ft. tall. Zone 4.

How to Grow
Full or part sun. Average soil amended with a generous dose of ground limestone. Sow seeds in spring or summer where they are to grow. Cut off the flower stalk after bloom to limit self-seeding.

Herbal Use
Used since ancient times, the leaves and flower stalk give a beautiful permanent yellow dye on wool and other fibers.

Rhus
Roos
Anacardiaceae. Sumac family

Description
A diverse group of deciduous and evergreen trees, shrubs, and vines, including poison ivy and a few other species that cause skin rashes. About 200 species, native worldwide.

■ *typhina* *p. 125*
Staghorn sumac. A carefree native shrub or small tree, 15–25 ft. tall, with excellent red or purplish fall color, crimson fruit clusters that last from fall to spring, and distinctive forked branching that makes an interesting winter silhouette. The

compound leaves and thick twigs are covered with downy hairs. 'Dissecta' and 'Laciniata' have large leaves that are divided into many slender segments, like fern fronds. *R. glabra,* smooth sumac, is a similar plant with smooth twigs and leaves. Zone 4.

How to Grow
Full or part sun. Not fussy about soil. Tolerates heat and drought once established. Pest-free. To make a dramatic clump with tropical-looking foliage, let a plant grow for a few years to get well established, then start cutting it to the ground each year in early spring. This makes it send up vigorous new shoots with unusually large leaves.

Herbal Use
Berries and leaves make a soft pink-beige dye. Staghorn sumac berries formerly were used in cough syrup. Berries of various species are used to make lemonade-like beverages.

Rosa
Ro´za
Rosaceae. Rose family

Description
Roses are the most popular of all flowers and have been grown in gardens since the days of the ancient Egyptians, Romans, and Chinese. There are about 100 species and literally thousands of cultivars. All are deciduous or evergreen shrubs with thorny stems, compound leaves, and an upright, climbing, or trailing habit. Wild rose flowers have 5 petals and many stamens. Garden roses often have many petals. Rose fruits, called hips, have a fleshy hull with several hairy seeds inside.

■ *canina* p. 125
Dog rose. A large rounded shrub, 10 ft. tall and 8 ft. wide, with arching canes, strong hooked thorns, and beautiful blue-green leaves. Blooms in spring. Single flowers, 1–2 in. wide, are white or pale pink and have a mild sweet fragrance. Distinctive drooping hips are orange-red, up to 2 in. long. Because of its size, it is best used in a hedgerow or a natural-style garden. Zone 5.

How to Grow
Full sun. Average soil with good drainage and regular water-

ing. Prune lightly in late winter or summer, or not at all. Easily grown from seed. Often used as a rootstock for bud grafting of hybrid tea roses; sometimes overtakes the grafted plant.

Herbal Use
The most important source of hips for rose hip tea or jam. Fresh hips are rich in vitamin C. Gather them in late fall; cold weather reduces their astringency. Remove the large seeds before using the hips.

■ × *centifolia*   *p. 126*
Cabbage rose, Provence rose. An upright or sprawling shrub, up to 6 ft. tall, with lax bristly canes; thick gray-green leaves, often hairy on both sides; and light pink flowers 3–4 in. wide with a rich, intense perfume. Blooms in midspring. There are many cultivars with larger or smaller flowers in various shades of pink or white. Moss roses are a related group that have a unique mossy growth on the buds that is sticky and fragrant. All are lovely specimens for the spring border. Combine with lavender, catmint, calamint, and other herbs to extend the season of bloom. Zone 6.

How to Grow
Full sun. Rich, well-drained soil with regular watering. Do not prune for the first few years after planting, as it blooms on old wood. Use a hoop or stakes to support the floppy stems. Apply mulch for winter protection. Subject to leafspots and mildew.

Herbal Use
Dried petals are used in potpourri. Rose water and rose oil, prepared from the petals, are used in cosmetics and aromatherapy. Flower extracts are used in preparations for irritated eyes. Petals are edible and can be used as flavoring.

■ × *damascena*   *p. 126*
Damask rose. An upright shrub about 6 ft. tall that can be trained up a column or wall. Arching canes have many large hooked thorns, gray-green foliage, and double pink flowers. Blooms in late spring, with the best fragrance of any roses. There are many cultivars. Among the best are 'Trigintipetala', the Kazanlik rose, used in making attar of roses; and var. *semperflorens*, also called 'Rose des Quatres Saisons', because it flowers recurrently, unlike most of these roses. Zone 5.

How to Grow
Like *R.* × *centifolia*.

Herbal Use
Attar of roses is produced commercially from the Kazanlik rose, in southern Bulgaria. 'Rose des Quatres Saisons' was the favorite rose of the Greeks and Romans, who used the petals to make rose wine, rose water, and rose petal baths and to flavor food.

■ *eglanteria*   *p. 127*
Sweet briar, eglantine. A large rounded shrub, up to 10 ft. tall, with arching canes that are extremely prickly. Wetting or touching the shiny green leaves releases a wonderful apple-like aroma. Has clusters of single pink flowers in spring and oval red hips that last all winter. Also called *R. rubiginosa*. Zone 5.

How to Grow
Full sun. Average soil. Good for a natural shrub border or hedgerow. Can be pruned, but the thorns make it difficult. Easily grown from seed and often self-sows. Has naturalized in California and parts of the Northeast.

Herbal Use
Beloved for its fragrance and described by Shakespeare. The flowers are mixed with honey and used in confections; also used in the Middle East to treat colic and diarrhea.

■ *gallica* 'Officinalis'   *p. 127*
Apothecary rose. A small (3-ft.) shrub with floppy stems, crinkly-textured foliage, fragrant deep pink or crimson flowers 3–4 in. wide in late spring, and brick red hips in summer. 'Versicolor' or 'Rosa Mundi' is a sport with pink-and-white-striped petals. 'Tuscany' or 'The Old Velvet Rose' has rich purple-red petals with a very velvety texture. Zone 5.

How to Grow
Full sun. Rich, well-drained soil with regular watering. Prune in late winter and lightly after flowering. Use hoops or stakes to support the stems. Propagate by digging up rooted suckers in early spring. The foliage is very susceptible to mildew.

Herbal Use
Has a long history of cultivation and use in Europe. Medieval apothecaries produced a fragrant powder by grinding the dried petals and also extracted rose oil from the fresh petals. Dried petals are used medicinally as a mild astringent and sedative.

■ *rugosa* *p. 128*

Rugosa rose, Japanese rose, tomato rose. A bushy upright shrub, usually 4–6 ft. tall, with prickly canes. Large leaves have a coarse, wrinkled texture; are dark green in summer and golden yellow in fall. Single pink flowers 2–3 in. wide bloom throughout the summer and have a superb fragrance. Plump round hips are showy from late summer through winter. There are several cultivars and hybrids. 'Frau Dagmar Hartopp' (often listed as 'Frau Dagmar Hastrup') is especially healthy, hardy, and compact and has beautiful single pink flowers and abundant hips. 'Belle Poitevine' has semidouble rose to magenta flowers, dark foliage, and a bushy habit. 'Blanc Double de Coubert' is vigorous and healthy and has prolific double white flowers, but it usually doesn't make hips. Zone 4.

How to Grow

Full sun. Average soil. Tolerates ocean salt spray and road salt. Easy to grow, with fewer problems than most roses. Makes a carefree hedge or specimen. Prune in late winter.

Herbal Use

Gather the hips after several frosts to make jam or preserves. Add fresh petals to a salad for beauty and flavor. The dried petals are used in potpourri and for making fragrant beads. (Rose-petal beads originally were used to make rosaries.)

Rosmarinus

Ros-ma-ry´nus
Labiatae. Mint family

Description

Evergreen shrubs with slender opposite leaves and small 2-lipped flowers. Only 2 species, from the Mediterranean region.

■ *officinalis* *pp. 145–146*

Rosemary. An evergreen shrub with very aromatic, gray-green, needlelike leaves ½–1½ in. long. Small light blue, lilac, or white flowers form on old wood and last for weeks in winter and spring. Usually makes an upright bush about 4–6 ft. tall, which can easily be trained and pruned into formal shapes or left unpruned as an informal specimen or billowing hedge. 'Tuscan Blue', 'Collingwood Ingram', and 'Blue Spire' are popular upright growers, all with blue flowers.

There are also upright forms with pinkish purple or pale blue-white flowers. 'Prostratus', 'Huntington Blue', and 'Lockwood de Forest' are creeping forms that look striking as ground covers or trailing down a bank or over a wall. They grow less than 1 ft. tall but spread several feet wide. Most rosemaries are hardy to zone 8. 'Arp' is the cold-hardiest cultivar, surviving on protected sites in zone 6. It's an upright, bushy plant with blue flowers.

How to Grow
Full sun. Needs well-drained soil. Tolerates alkaline conditions, heat, and drought. Where hardy outdoors, it makes an excellent specimen, hedge, or ground cover. Plant 2 ft. apart and pinch the growing tips to promote full, bushy growth. Cut back hard only in spring, so the new growth has time to mature and flower the next winter.

In colder climates, you can grow a rosemary for years in a large clay pot or similar container. Put it outdoors before the last frost in spring, and wait until after frost in fall before bringing it back in. Water and fertilize regularly during the summer months. Keep it in a cool, bright room for the coldest months of winter, and don't overwater. Watch for aphids, spider mites, mealybugs, and other houseplant pests in winter.

Herbal Use
Fresh or dried leaves are an excellent seasoning for meat, poultry, potatoes, pasta, soups, and other dishes. Because they are tough, chop them into tiny bits or use whole sprigs that you can remove before serving. Leaf tea soothes an upset stomach. Dried leaves make fragrant sachets.

Rubia
Roo´bee-a
Rubiaceae. Madder family

Description
Perennials with spreading roots, sprawling stems, and whorled leaves. About 40 species, from the Old and New World.

■ *tinctorum (tinctoria)* *p. 194* *Pictured opposite*
Madder. A hardy perennial that makes a dense patch. Prickly stems may stick up 2 ft. or more, but they usually flop over and may spread several feet on the ground. Oblong leaves, 2 in. long, are borne in whorls of 4–8. Established plants, especially in climates with warm summers, bear small white

4-petaled flowers and round blue-black berries. Underground, it makes a tangle of woody roots, thick as a pencil and bright red inside. Zone 4.

How to Grow
Full sun. Grows in any average garden soil but produces the best roots in deep, fertile soil amended with plenty of ground limestone. Tolerates cold, heat, and considerable drought. Pest-free. Propagate by seed or division.

Herbal Use
The roots are an important source of red, orange, and brown dyes, used for thousands of years on cotton, wool, and other fibers. Persian carpets, Indian calicos, the British redcoats, and early American coverlets were all dyed red with madder roots.

Rubus
Roo′bus
Rosaceae. Rose family

Description
Shrubs with thorny stems, compound leaves, and edible berries. About 250 species, native worldwide.

■ *idaeus* p. 128
Raspberry. A hardy shrub native to Europe but common in New England where birds have spread seeds from cultivated patches. Has stems with soft thorns; leaves with 5 wrinkly, toothed leaflets; small flowers with 5 white petals; and very sweet and tasty red berries. Usually grows 3–5 ft. tall. Other

kinds of raspberries and blackberries have similar habit and uses. Zone 4.

How to Grow
Full or part sun. Average soil and watering. Prune in winter or early spring, removing canes that have borne berries. Propagate by digging up suckers. Long-lived and easy to grow.

Herbal Use
Raspberry leaf tea is a popular folk therapy for strengthening pregnant women before childbirth. Tea from blackberry leaves and dried berries is enjoyed for its flavor.

Rumex
Roo´mex
Polygonaceae. Buckwheat family

Description
Perennials with many basal leaves and small flowers clustered on upright stalks. About 200 species, native to temperate climates.

■ *acetosa* p. 195
Garden sorrel. A hardy plant that makes a robust clump of foliage. Starts growing in late winter and continues through the year. Smooth leaves about 5 in. long are shaped like large arrowheads. Slender, branching, 3-ft. flower stalks bear hundreds of small greenish brown flowers in summer. Selected strains have especially large and tender leaves with mild flavor. *R. scutatus,* French sorrel, is a shorter plant with spreading stems and smaller, thicker leaves in irregular lobed shapes. Zone 3.

How to Grow
Full or part sun. Average soil and watering. Easily propagated by division or seed. Carefree, but it can be weedy.

Herbal Use
Chopped leaves are added to soups and salads or nibbled as an appetite stimulant. Traditionally used in Europe to make a nourishing, refreshing tea.

Ruta

Roo´ta
Rutáceae. Rue family

Description
Shrubby perennials with strong-scented compound leaves.
Only 7 species, most native to Europe and the Middle East.

■ *graveolens* p. 196
Rue. A shrubby perennial that grows 2–3 ft. tall. Its smooth
blue-gray leaves are divided, fernlike, into many small segments. Foliage is almost evergreen in mild climates. Clusters
of small yellow flowers are held above the foliage for 2–3
weeks in summer. 'Jackman's Blue' has waxy blue foliage and
doesn't flower, so it remains compact and bushy, $1\frac{1}{2}$–2 ft.
tall. It combines well with the flowers and foliage of other
perennials. 'Variegata' has leaves dappled with cream or white
when young; prune often to force new growth. Zone 5.

How to Grow
Full or part sun. Well-drained ordinary soil. Tolerates hot, dry
weather. Use conifer boughs or other mulch as winter protection in cold zones, and do not uncover too soon in spring.
Prune annually in early spring, cutting back to old wood.
Wear long sleeves and gloves when handling this plant—
touching the foliage, especially in hot weather, gives some
people a rash.

Herbal Use
Historically an important herb, much cited in the old herbals,
and formerly used in cooking, perfumery, and medicine. Now
grown mostly for ornament.

Salix

Say´licks
Salicaceae. Willow family

Description
Deciduous trees or shrubs with simple leaves and separate
catkins of small male and female flowers. Most willows are
fast-growing but relatively short-lived. About 300 species,
nearly all native to cold or temperate climates in the Northern Hemisphere.

■ *elaeagnos* p. 129
Rosemary willow. A deciduous shrub or tree that makes a

graceful specimen or hedge. The long, narrow leaves are dark
green above and covered with woolly white hairs below, giving a wonderful two-tone effect when rippled by the breeze.
Slender twigs are reddish brown in winter. Can make a tree
45 ft. tall if unpruned but is usually pruned to make a dense,
bushy clump 8–12 ft. tall and wide. Many other willows can
be grown as shrubs by cutting them back hard each spring,
and they offer colorful winter twigs, fuzzy catkins in early
spring, and useful stems for making baskets, trellises, or garden ornaments. Zone 5.

How to Grow
Full sun. Not fussy about soil. Tolerates moist or dry conditions. Prune back to the ground every few years to keep it
compact and vigorous. Subject to leaf-eating insects but generally trouble-free.

Herbal Use
Willow stems are used, peeled or with the bark on, to make
a variety of baskets and containers. Willow bark tea was a
traditional remedy for minor pain and fever. It contains salicylic acid, a precursor to aspirin.

Salvia
Sal′vee-a
Labiatae. Mint family

Description
Annuals, perennials, or shrubs with square stems, opposite
simple leaves, and 2-lipped flowers. About 900 species, native worldwide. Many are very aromatic and/or ornamental.

■ *clevelandii* p. 227 *Pictured above*
Cleveland sage. A tender shrubby perennial, up to 4 ft. tall
and wide. The slender gray-green leaves have a pebbled texture and a very strong aroma. Whorls of small, sweet-scented,
lilac-blue flowers open from spring to summer. Native to dry

slopes in southern California, it combines well with rosemary, lavender, and other Mediterranean herbs. Zone 8.

How to Grow
Full sun. Tolerates poor, dry soil and heat. Needs no irrigation after the first year. Prune in early spring to keep it compact, and remove old flower stalks to prolong bloom. Can be grown in a large clay pot outdoors and wintered in a bright window indoors. Don't overwater.

Herbal Use
Fragrant leaves can be used in cooking or dried for potpourri.

■ *dorisiana* p. 228
Fruit-scented sage. A tender shrubby perennial that grows upright and bushy, often reaching 4 ft. or more. The soft, hairy, olive green leaves are heart-shaped, up to 4 in. wide by 7 in. long, and have a strong, sweet, citrusy or fruity aroma. Bright pink flowers, 2 in. long, open in late fall and early winter. Zone 10.

How to Grow
Full sun. Average well-drained soil. Buy a plant to put outdoors after danger of frost, and pinch tips to make it bushy. Does well in containers and makes a good winter houseplant in a sunny window. Tip cuttings root easily in water or damp sand. Subject to aphids, whiteflies, spider mites, and the like but is generally carefree.

Herbal Use
Fresh or dried leaves make a tasty hot or iced tea. Dried leaves make excellent potpourri material.

■ *elegans* p. 228
Pineapple sage. A tender shrubby perennial that grows bushy and upright, reaching 4 ft. or more in one growing season. Foliage and young shoots are covered with soft hairs. Pointed oval leaves are rich green, with a strong pineapple fragrance and flavor. Bears 8-in. spikes of slender red flowers from late summer until frost outdoors, or all winter indoors. Formerly listed as *S. rutilans*. Zone 8.

How to Grow
Like *S. dorisiana*.

Herbal Use
Same as for *S. dorisiana*. In Mexico, leaf tea traditionally was used to calm an upset stomach.

■ *officinalis* *pp. 196, 197*
Garden sage. A hardy perennial, woody at the base, with fragrant gray-green or colored foliage that is evergreen in mild climates but freezes back where winters are cold. Leaves are oblong, 2–3 in. long, with a nubbly texture. Blue-purple flowers on 2-ft. spikes are showy for weeks in early summer. 'Berggarten' has broader, rounded leaves in a pretty shade of blue-green. 'Aurea' has gold foliage, and 'Purpurea' has reddish purple leaves. These are all hardy to zone 5. The lovely variegated cultivars such as 'Tricolor' (white, purple, and green leaves) and 'Icterina' (green and yellow leaves) are hardy only to zone 7.

How to Grow
Full sun. Needs well-drained soil and prefers raised beds. Cut back frozen shoots in late spring, before new growth starts, and remove faded blooms in summer. Divide every few years. Root cuttings to overwinter tender cultivars, or buy new plants in spring. All cultivars grow well in containers for a few years, then need replacement.

Herbal Use
Fresh or dried leaves are used to season poultry, meat, beans, and other dishes and are considered to aid the digestion of fat or rich foods. Leaf tea is a traditional remedy for nervous conditions, gastritis, and sore throats and is used to reduce perspiration. Sage has been valued since ancient times, and modern research confirms that it has many therapeutic properties.

■ *sclarea* *p. 254*
Clary sage. A hardy biennial. Makes a broad rosette of large, crinkly-textured, gray-green leaves the first year. The second summer it sends up several branching flower stalks, 3–4 ft. tall, crowded with papery white, pink, or purplish bracts and small white flowers. The flowers and foliage release a very rich aroma, particularly after a rain. 'Turkestanica' has flowers, bracts, and leaves that are larger than average. *S. argentea,* silver sage, is a similar biennial, grown for its large leaves that are densely covered with silvery hairs. The first-year rosette is a striking accent for the front of a border, but the second-year flower stalk is a disappointment compared with that of clary sage. Zone 4.

How to Grow
Full sun. Ordinary soil and watering. Tolerates heavy soils better than most sages do but can't take extreme heat or humidity. Start seedlings indoors or outdoors the first year; after

that, it usually self-seeds. Transplant volunteer seedlings to their permanent location by midsummer. Individual plants sometimes live a third year if flower stalks are cut before they go to seed.

Herbal Use
Formerly used to season food, wine, and other beverages; leaf tea was taken for upset stomachs. Now the essential oil is used to perfume soaps and cosmetics.

■ other sages and salvias
The genus *Salvia* includes many other outstanding species and hybrids. Some have fragrant foliage, but most of the plants listed below are grown for their flowers more than for their herbal properties. These are very popular plants, readily available at garden centers or from mail-order nurseries. They combine beautifully with the herbal salvias and most other plants in a sunny herb garden.

S. azurea, wild blue sage, grows 3–5 ft. tall and produces wonderful sprays of clear blue flowers from summer to frost. Var. *grandiflora* (often listed as *S. pitcheri*) has larger, light blue flowers. Both are carefree perennials. Zone 5.

S. farinacea, mealy blue sage, is perennial in zone 7 but makes a fine annual in colder zones. It's a bushy plant, 2–3 ft. tall, that blooms and blooms from late spring to hard frost. Cultivars with dark blue, light blue, or white flowers are available from seed catalogs or as bedding plants in spring. *S. guaranitica,* blue sage, grows 3–5 ft. tall and wide and has fragrant dark green leaves and dark violet-blue flowers. It is hardy to zone 8. These two species are native to Texas and the Southwest. *Salvia* 'Indigo Spires' is a hybrid between them. It makes a spectacular display of very dark violet-blue flowers on dozens of crowded spikes that extend 2 ft. above the foliage. It blooms from midsummer until hard frost. Hardy to zone 8, it is sterile and must be propagated by cuttings or division.

S. greggii, cherry sage or autumn sage, is a low bushy plant, about 3 ft. tall and wide. It bears loose clusters of lightly fragrant pink, red, salmon, purple, or white flowers from spring to fall. The small crisp leaves are fragrant and semievergreen. Zone 8.

S. leucantha, Mexican bush sage, doesn't have much fragrance, but it's easy to grow; thrives in hot, dry weather; and blooms nonstop for months. It grows 3–4 ft. tall and has graceful arching stems tipped with long spikes of rosy purple bracts and small white flowers. Zone 7.

Herb lovers make room for two other "sages," even though both are more ornamental than useful. Jerusalem sage, *Phlomis fruticosa,* is a shrubby perennial, good for dry, sunny gardens in zone 7 or warmer. It grows about 4 ft. tall and 6 ft. wide. The thick, wrinkly leaves are gray-green above, woolly white below, and have a mild fragrance when crushed. The stems are topped with a series of ball-shaped whorls of fuzzy buds and tubular 1-in. yellow flowers. Blooms over and over if you cut it back after each cycle.

Russian sage, *Perovskia atriplicifolia,* is a shrubby perennial hardy to zone 5. It has a graceful, airy appearance and grows 3–5 ft. tall. The square stems and coarsely toothed leaves are silver-gray, topped in late summer with tiered whorls of lavender flowers. The foliage has a spicy aroma and could be used in potpourri, but it isn't used in cooking.

Sambucus
Sam-bew´kus
Caprifoliaceae. Honeysuckle family

Description
Shrubs or small trees with pithy stems, compound leaves, clusters of small flowers, and seedy berries. About 20 species, most from North America and Eurasia.

■ *canadensis* p. 129
Elderberry. A hardy native shrub, usually 6–12 ft. tall. The arching stems and stout twigs make an interesting winter profile. Deciduous leaves are compound and have 7 fine-toothed leaflets that turn pale yellow in fall. Large flat clusters of small white flowers are showy for about 2 weeks in summer and are followed by clusters of blue-black berries that weigh down the limbs when they ripen. 'Aurea' has pretty golden foliage and bright red berries. *S. nigra,* European elder, is a similar plant that typically resembles our native elderberry and includes several attractive cutleaf, golden, or variegated cultivars. Zone 4.

How to Grow
Full or part sun. Not fussy about soil if it gets plenty of water. Thrives in heavy, damp soil. Easy to transplant. Remove old shoots and thin suckers in winter to encourage new growth and to keep it tidy. Old plants can be cut to the ground for renewal.

Herbal Use
Flower tea traditionally was used as a diuretic and laxative and to induce sweating and vomiting. Cooked berries make

excellent pie, wine, and preserves. The European elder is valued for its lore as much as for its appearance or properties. It has been surrounded with myth, superstition, and legend since the days of the Druids.

Sanguinaria
Sang-gwi-nay´ree-a
Papaveraceae. Poppy family

Description
A perennial wildflower. The rhizome has bright red sap. Only 1 species, native to eastern North America.

■ *canadensis* *p. 198 Pictured above*
Bloodroot. A hardy perennial that blooms in early spring, before the deciduous trees leaf out. Round white flowers with several petals are about 1 in. wide, on stalks 6–8 in. tall. The large, thick, smooth, blue-green leaves are round in profile, up to 8 in. wide, with irregular lobes around the edge. Both leaves and flowers grow directly from spreading rhizomes, which release a startling red sap when broken. Gradually forms a patch 1–2 ft. wide, and self-sows on suitable sites. Goes dormant by late summer. 'Multiplex' or 'Flore Pleno' is a beautiful form with large, long-lasting, double flowers. It doesn't set seed and can be propagated only by division. Zone 4.

How to Grow
Part sun in spring, shade in summer. Ordinary soil and watering. Divide every few years in early spring. Trouble-free.

Herbal Use
Native Americans traditionally used minute doses of the rhizome to treat fevers, rheumatism, skin burns, and sore throats. Now sanguinarine, an alkaloid from the rhizome, is used in dental products to inhibit plaque formation. Caution: Toxic. Do not ingest.

Santolina

San-to-ly′na
Compositae. Composite family

Description

Shrubs or perennials with pungent foliage and round flower heads. About 18 species, from the Mediterranean region.

■ *chamaecyparissus* *p. 198*

Lavender cotton, gray santolina. A favorite plant for knot gardens or low clipped edgings around rose beds or herb gardens. Grows naturally into a low spreading mound, about 2 ft. tall and 3 ft. wide. The silvery gray, aromatic foliage has a rough, curly texture, like terrycloth. Buttonlike yellow flower heads perch on 6-in. stalks in summer. Hardy to zone 6 if protected.

How to Grow

Full sun. Needs good drainage and air circulation. Subject to root and foliar fungal diseases in wet soil or hot, humid weather. Tolerates poor dry soil and heat. Space 18–24 in. apart for clipped edging, 30–36 in. apart for mass plantings. Older plants get woody at the base and split open in the middle. Cut back hard in spring to renew, or, better yet, replace them with fresh new plants.

Herbal Use

The pungent foliage historically was used to expel worms and as an insect repellent.

■ *virens* *p. 199*

Green santolina. A shrubby perennial, 2 ft. tall and 3 ft. wide. Slender dark green leaves, 1–2 in. long, look like twisted pine needles and have a penetrating, resinous aroma. Blooms in summer, with pale yellow, round flower heads on stalks 6 in. tall. Often combined with gray santolina and used as a clipped edging or a mass planting on dry banks. The form most often sold is now identified as *S. rosmarinifolia* 'Primrose Gem'. Zone 6.

How to Grow

Like *S. chamaecyparissus* but is slightly cold-hardier and also more tolerant of moist soil and humid air.

Herbal Use

Same as for *S. chamaecyparissus*.

Saponaria
Sap-o-nay´ree-a
Caryophyllaceae. Pink family

Description
Annuals, biennials, or perennials with opposite leaves and 5-petaled pink or white flowers. About 30 species, most native to the Mediterranean region.

■ *officinalis* *p. 199*
Soapwort, bouncing Bet. A hardy perennial native to Europe but widespread as a roadside wildflower in the United States. Forms a dense patch of leafy stems 2–3 ft. tall, topped with small clusters of fragrant pale or rosy pink flowers, $\frac{1}{2}$ in. wide. Blooms all summer and into the fall. The foliage is ever-green in mild climates. 'Rosa Plena' has larger clusters of double flowers with a spicy, clovelike fragrance. Zone 2.

How to Grow
Full or part sun. Not fussy about soil; grows in dry sand or wet clay. Spreads by runners, so give it space, or curb it with edging, plant in a bottomless pot, or divide and replant every few years. Easily started from seed or increased by division. No pests or diseases. Lives for decades with virtually no care.

Herbal Use
All parts contain saponins, substances that produce suds when mixed with water. Formerly used as a cleanser, laundry soap, and shampoo and also to increase the foaming of beer. A poultice of the leaves helps soothe irritated skin.

Sassafras
Sas´a-fras
Lauraceae. Laurel family

Description
Deciduous trees with aromatic leaves, flowers, bark, and wood. Only 3 species, one from North America and two from eastern Asia.

■ *albidum* *p. 130 Pictured on p. 398*
Sassafras. A beautiful and popular native tree, 40–60 ft. tall. Young plants often form dome-shaped, suckering colonies with bright yellow-green bark, antlerlike branch forks, and mitten-shaped leaves with 1 or 2 "thumbs." Can mature into a grove or, if suckers are removed, a single-trunked specimen

shade tree. Older trees have thick, furrowed bark and simple oval leaves. In fall, the foliage turns vivid shades of red, purple, orange, or gold. Small yellow flowers open with the leaves in spring, and dark blue berries attract birds in fall. All parts have a rich spicy fragrance. Zone 5.

How to Grow
Full or part sun. Grows best in fertile, moist soil but tolerates poor, dry soil. Difficult to transplant; must be started from seed or grown in containers. Plants dug from the wild rarely survive. Grows fast and needs little care once established. Leaf-eating insects may cause cosmetic but not serious damage.

Herbal Use
The flowers and root bark are made into tea as a traditional spring tonic; also formerly used for bronchitis, high blood pressure, rheumatism, arthritis, and skin problems. The dried leaves are used in gumbo. Caution: Contains safrole, considered carcinogenic. The FDA does not allow use of sassafras in foods.

Satureja
Sat-you-ree´ya
Labiatae. Mint family

Description
Annuals or perennials with square stems and opposite leaves, used medicinally and for flavoring. About 30 species, native to the Old and New World.

■ *hortensis* p. 255

Summer savory. A slender, almost inconspicuous annual. Grows 12–18 in. tall, with narrow gray-green leaves under 1 in. long and a few small white or lilac flowers on top. The leaves and stems have a pleasant mild flavor and aroma. All zones.

How to Grow
Full sun. Average soil and regular watering. Sow seeds in spring where they are to grow, and thin seedlings 3–4 in. apart. Needs no special care. May self-sow.

Herbal Use
Fresh or dried leaves are used to season all kinds of beans and peas, other vegetables, and soups. Leaf tea is used for upset stomachs, sore throats, and other common ailments.

■ *montana* p. 200

Winter savory. A shrubby perennial, about 2 ft. tall and wide. Makes a neat dense mound of glossy evergreen foliage. The tiny pointed leaves are stacked close together on all 4 sides of the stems and make a tidy pattern of squares. They have a spicy aroma and flavor. Abundant whorls of small white, lavender, or pink flowers attract bees in late summer. Zone 5.

How to Grow
Full sun. Needs good drainage. Thrives in dry, sandy soil with an occasional watering. Harvest by trimming back in early summer; stop trimming before it blooms. New growth needs time to mature and harden before cold weather. Propagate by seed or division.

Herbal Use
Same as for *S. hortensis* but has a sharper, more peppery flavor.

■ other species

A few other species of *Satureja* are popular, attractive plants with fragrant foliage. *S. douglasii,* yerba buena, is an evergreen species native to California and the Southwest and valued there for the rich minty fragrance of its rounded leaves. It's a creeping perennial, hardy to zone 8, that also grows well in a hanging basket or as a houseplant.

S. viminea (p. 229), Costa Rican mint bush, is a spreading upright shrub, 2–3 ft. tall. Its small pale green leaves have a unique, intense fragrance like musty pennyroyal. It's tender to frost but grows well in a container and makes a fine winter houseplant. Pinch or prune to keep it bushy. Zone 10.

Simmondsia

Sim-mond´see-a
Buxaceae. Boxwood family

Description
A dryland shrub with leathery evergreen foliage. Only 1 species, native to the southwestern United States.

■ *chinensis* *p. 147*
Jojoba. A spreading shrub, usually reaching 6 ft. tall and 8 ft. wide. Pairs of stiff rounded leaves look like butterfly wings poised above the stems at regular intervals. Stems and leaves have a waxy appearance and dull gray color. Clusters of small flowers are followed by acorn-sized edible nuts. Zone 9.

How to Grow
Full sun. Tolerates poor, dry, alkaline soil and needs no summer irrigation once established. Space 3 ft. apart to make a low-care, low-water-use hedge in dry climates. Grows slowly and can be pruned to make it even denser than normal. Makes an interesting and unusual container plant. Don't overwater.

Herbal Use
Oil from the seeds is used in many shampoos and cosmetics.

Smilacina

Smy-la-see´na
Liliaceae. Lily family

Description
Perennials with creeping rhizomes, leafy arching stems, and terminal clusters of small flowers. About 30 species, native to North America and eastern Asia.

■ *racemosa* *p. 200 Pictured opposite*
False Solomon's-seal. A woodland wildflower that spreads slowly to form wide colonies. Pointed oblong leaves, 4–6 in. long, are arranged alternately on slender arching stems 2–3 ft. tall. Fluffy terminal clusters of tiny white flowers in spring are followed by small round berries that turn red in late summer. Compare this with Solomon's-seal, *Polygonatum biflorum*, p. 192. Zone 3.

How to Grow
Shade. Grows best in deep, loose, acidic, organic soil that is

moist but well drained. Sow seeds outdoors in fall, or space plants 6–12 in. apart. Increase by dividing older plants into clumps with at least 1 bud each. Trouble-free.

Herbal Use
Tea made from the roots traditionally was used for constipation, for rheumatism, and as a stomach tonic. It is seldom used now.

Solidago
Sol-i-day´go
Compositae. Composite family

Description
Perennials with leafy erect stalks and conspicuous displays of gold flowers in late summer or fall. About 100 species, most native to North America.

■ *odora* *p. 201*
Sweet goldenrod. A hardy wildflower of dry open woods and fields. Makes a small clump or patch of erect stems 3 ft. tall. Narrow oblong leaves, 2–4 in. long, are glossy green and have a strong anise or licorice scent when bruised. Blooms over a long season from July to September, with large sprays of tiny, sweet-scented, yellow flowers. Zone 5.

How to Grow
Full sun. Average soil and watering. Propagate from seed or by dividing the crown in early spring. One clump makes a nice accent for a bed or border. It also grows well in a container outdoors. Cut back old stalks in winter or spring. Usually long-lived and trouble-free.

Herbal Use

Leaf tea is a pleasant beverage, traditionally taken for coughs, colds, fevers, upset stomachs, and the like. Leaves and flowers of all goldenrods make a yellow dye. Contrary to popular thought, goldenrods do not cause hayfever, but individuals with allergies to plants in the composite family shouldn't drink this tea.

Stachys
Stay'kis
Labiatae. Mint family

Description

Perennials or shrubs with square stems and opposite leaves. Some kinds are used in medicine or cooking. About 300 species, native to temperate climates.

■ *byzantina* *p. 201* *Pictured above*

Lamb's-ears. A classic edging plant that forms low mats of semievergreen foliage. The ear-shaped leaves, 3–6 in. long, are covered with thick silver fur and irresistibly soft to touch. One plant grows about 8 in. tall and 18 in. wide. Fat stalks about 12–18 in. tall hold scattered pink or purple flowers in late spring or early summer. Many gardeners remove the flowers or choose 'Silver Carpet', a nonflowering cultivar. Lamb's-ears is sometimes listed as *S. lanata*. Zone 5.

How to Grow

Full or part sun in most regions. Tolerates heat but not high humidity. Leaves and stems rot in hot, wet weather. Needs well-drained average soil. Water during long dry spells. Space 12–18 in. apart for edging or small-scale ground cover. Trim back in spring and groom frequently to remove withered or shabby leaves. Divide in early spring or fall. Commonly damaged by slugs and snails.

Herbal Use

Grown mostly for beauty and for fun, but the thick, mildly astringent leaves are sometimes used to dress minor wounds and stop the bleeding.

■ *officinalis* p. 202

Betony. A hardy perennial that forms a low rosette of oval to oblong leaves, up to 5 in. long, with a heart-shaped base and scalloped edges. The foliage is dark green, slightly hairy or rough, and evergreen in mild winters. Flower stalks 2–3 ft. tall hold dense spikes of tubular reddish purple flowers in summer. 'Alba' has white flowers; 'Compacta' is a dwarf form. Zone 4.

How to Grow

Full sun. Average soil and watering. Tolerates dry spells. Propagate by seed or divide clumps in spring or fall. A good specimen for the bed or border, carefree and easy to grow.

Herbal Use

Fresh or dried leaves are used as a sedative in Europe for nervous headache and anxiety. The leaves are also used as a tea substitute and provide a yellow dye for wool and other fibers.

Stevia

Stee´vee-a
Compositae. Composite family

Description

Perennials or shrubs with composite flower heads. About 150 species, native to Latin America.

■ *rebaudiana* p. 229

Sweet herb of Paraguay, sugar herb. A weak and tender plant, neither showy nor easy, but remarkable for the incredible sweetness of its leaves. Lax stems branch reluctantly and grow only about 1 ft. tall. Slender oblong leaves are slightly hairy, with a pronounced midrib. Tiny composite flowers are white, with no fragrance. Pinch them off, or the plant will blossom and die. Zone 10.

How to Grow

Full sun. Needs well-drained soil. Fussy but fascinating to grow. Try planting it in a window box or clay pot on the porch, protected from rain. Avoid overwatering. Goes dormant in winter. Bring it indoors to protect it from frost.

Herbal Use

Stevioside, a compound much sweeter than saccharine, is used commercially in Brazil and Japan but not currently approved by the FDA. Traditionally it was used as a sugar replacement for diabetics and also as a folk contraceptive agent.

Symphytum

Sim´fi-tum
Boraginaceae. Borage family

Description

Coarse perennials, usually with hairy leaves and flowers clustered on curling stalks. About 35 species, native to Eurasia.

■ *officinale p. 202*

Comfrey, knitbone, bruisewort. An indomitable perennial that forms a robust clump of large dark green leaves with a rough hairy texture, easily confused with the first-year rosette of foxglove (*Digitalis purpurea,* see p. 242). Blooms from May to September, with drooping, 1-sided clusters of bell-shaped flowers in shades of white, rose, or purple. Has a deep, thick, mucilaginous root. Zone 3.

How to Grow

Full sun. Average soil and watering. Tolerates dry spells. Be careful where you plant comfrey, as it's difficult to eradicate — any overlooked sliver of root will grow into a new plant. The cautious and easy way is to grow it in a large container, or plant it at a distance from your tended garden.

Herbal Use

Used externally as a poultice, because the leaves and roots contain allantoin, a compound that promotes healing of bruises, wounds, and broken bones. Tea from the leaves and roots formerly was taken for many internal ailments, but internal use is now discouraged because it can cause serious liver damage. If you have extra comfrey, the leaves make good compost.

Tagetes

Tay-gee´teez, taj´eh-tees
Compositae. Composite family

Description
Annuals or perennials with strong-scented leaves, usually opposite and finely dissected. Composite flowers are most often yellow. About 50 species, one from Africa and the rest from Central and South America.

■ *lemmonii* *p. 230*
Mexican bush marigold. A tender perennial with many erect and/or sprawling stems, 3–6 ft. tall. Evergreen foliage has a strong citrus/marigold odor. Dark green leaves are pinnately divided into many narrow leaflets. Bright orange-yellow daisylike blossoms, 1 in. wide, are borne in clusters at the branch ends. Bloom continues all year but is heaviest in winter and spring. Popular in southwestern gardens, combined with rosemaries, lavenders, artemisias, and other Mediterranean plants. Zone 9.

How to Grow
Full or part sun. Ordinary soil and watering. Tolerates dry soil once established. Prune to improve shape and to prevent sprawl. Hard frost will kill it, but it survives mild winters. Trouble-free. Does well in a large pot outdoors in summer but gets too big and leggy as a houseplant.

Herbal Use
The leaves make a pleasant aromatic tea. The leaves and flowers of this and all other marigolds give a range of yellow, gold, and olive green dyes.

■ *lucida* *p. 230* *Pictured below*
Mexican mint marigold. A good substitute for French tar-

ragon in hot climates. The foliage, stems, and flowers have a rich anise fragrance and flavor. Makes a bushy clump of erect stems, usually about 3 ft. tall. Narrow dark green leaves are 1–2 in. long. May be evergreen in mild winters. Single yellow blossoms, about 1 in. wide, top the stems in late summer and fall. Blooms when the daylength gets shorter, like chrysanthemums. Zone 8.

How to Grow
Full or part sun. Average well-drained soil. Harvest leaves whenever you choose. Cut back to the ground and mulch after hard frost. Grows well as an annual and produces plenty of fragrant foliage but few flowers in northern gardens. It doesn't overwinter well indoors, so start from seed or buy a new plant each year.

Herbal Use
Fresh leaves are used as a seasoning. Fresh or dried leaves make a pleasant tea, used medicinally in Mexico for upset stomachs and other ailments. Laboratory results confirm that it has tranquilizing, hypotensive, and anti-inflammatory properties.

Tanacetum
Tan-a-see′tum
Compositae. Composite family

Description
Annuals or perennials with strong-scented foliage and composite flowers. Closely related to *Chrysanthemum,* and some species keep getting shifted back and forth between the two genera. Between 50 and 70 species, most native to the Old World.

■ *vulgare p. 203*
Tansy. A hardy perennial with strong-scented foliage. Forms a clump or mat of basal leaves up to 8 in. long, divided into many flat feathery segments. Blooms in summer, with flat clusters of many flower heads that look like gold buttons, about ½ in. wide. Flower stalks stand 3–4 ft. tall. One plant makes a patch 3–4 ft. wide. Var. *crispum* is prettier than average, with thick, crisp-textured leaves. Zone 4.

How to Grow
Full or part sun. Grows in any well-drained soil. Tolerates poor, dry soil. Spreads fast by underground runners and is in-

vasive in most garden beds. Easily started from seed or propagated by division in spring or fall. Trouble-free.

Herbal Use
In the past, tansy leaf tea was taken for various ailments, and
the leaves were used to flavor a particular kind of cake, but
ingesting tansy is now discouraged. Instead, organic gardeners now brew a tea from tansy leaves and spray it on other
plants to repel insect pests.

Teucrium
Too´kri-um
Labiatae. Mint family

Description
Perennials or small shrubs with square stems, opposite leaves,
and clusters of small 2-lipped flowers. Several species have
aromatic foliage with various medicinal uses. About 100
species, native worldwide.

■ *chamaedrys* p. 203
Germander. A shrubby perennial, 1–2 ft. tall and wide, with
many branching stems and glossy evergreen foliage. Dark
green leaves, about 1 in. long, resemble miniature oak leaves
and release a pungent aroma when rubbed. Clusters of small
purple flowers are showy and attract bees for a few weeks in
midsummer. 'Prostratum' is a shorter plant that spreads by
rhizomes (it can be invasive) and has lighter green leaves.
'Variegatum' has white, cream, or yellow variegation on the
leaves. Zone 5.

How to Grow
Full or part sun. Needs good drainage. Tolerates poor, dry
soil and hot weather. Shear after flowering to keep it compact, and shear or trim to renew plants in early spring. Often
used in knot gardens, because it responds well to pruning.
Also makes a neat edging or mini-hedge around rose beds or
herb gardens. Unpruned, it makes a low mound that combines well with other Mediterranean herbs, heaths and
heathers, or dwarf conifers. Grows well in containers and can
be trained as a bonsai. Propagate by seed or divide plants in
spring. Pest-free.

Herbal Use
Leaf tea has been used like horehound for coughs, sore
throats, and fevers. Until recently germander was used in the

Middle East and Europe as an ingredient in teas to induce weight loss. Caution: Consuming germander is now discouraged because it has been shown to cause liver damage.

■ *majoricum* p. 204
Majoricum. A low, spreading perennial, only 6 in. tall but 1–2 ft. wide. Trailing stems have whorls of needle-thin leaves with a pretty blue or silver color, a lightly felted surface, and a pungent odor, like creosote. The blossoms are quite showy, appearing in snowflakelike arrangements at the tips of the stems in spring and summer. They're raspberry pink with a delightful pineapple scent. Zone 5.

How to Grow
Full sun. Average well-drained soil. Branches readily to form a rounded specimen. Makes a good accent plant in the garden or can be used as a ground cover. Looks especially nice trailing from a window box, hanging basket, or urn. Remains handsome as a houseplant in winter but usually doesn't bloom.

Herbal Use
Grown primarily for its fragrance, which is stimulating to some people and overwhelming to others.

■ *marum* p. 231
Cat thyme. A tender little shrub, under 1 ft. tall and wide, that could be mistaken for a thyme. Has many branching stems and slender blue-green to gray-green leaves. The stems and leaf bottoms are covered with white hairs. When crushed, the foliage releases an intense, biting aroma that can bring tears to your eyes, but some cats find it irresistible. Blooms in summer, with purplish pink flowers in terminal clusters. Zone 8.

How to Grow
Full sun. Needs well-drained soil and tolerates dry spells. Makes an attractive low border where hardy, or a good container plant. Can overwinter as a houseplant in a bright window.

Herbal Use
Now grown for ornament and to entertain cats, but it was taken medicinally in the past. Among other uses, a snuff of the powdered leaves was inhaled to induce sneezing.

■ other germanders
Other species of *Teucrium* are sometimes grown as ornamentals or used as herbs. *T. canadense,* called American ger-

mander, wood sage, or wild basil, is a hardy perennial that tolerates damp soil and part shade. It spreads and fills in fast enough to use as a ground cover or mass planting, but it can be invasive in formal beds. Oval leaves are green above, white below. Masses of white, pink, or purplish flowers are quite showy for several weeks in late summer. Easily raised from seed. Native Americans used the leaves for medicinal teas. Zone 4.

T. scorodonia, wood sage or wood germander, is a hardy perennial with upright, branching stems about 2 ft. tall. The oblong to heart-shaped leaves have a color and texture like sage leaves, but the taste and fragrance are reminiscent of hops. Long, slender, 1-sided spikes of pale yellow flowers top the stems for weeks in late summer. Attractive as a single specimen or in mass plantings. Easily raised from seed. Formerly used to flavor ale, in medicinal teas, and to poultice wounds. Zone 4.

Thuja
Thew′ya
Cupressaceae. Cypress family

Description
Tall evergreen conifers, usually with scalelike foliage arranged in flat fans or sprays. Only 5 species, native to eastern Asia and North America, and hundreds of selected cultivars.

■ *occidentalis* p. 130
American arborvitae. A popular conifer in the Northeast and Upper Midwest, used extensively for hedges, screens, and foundation plantings. The foliage is quite fragrant when crushed. Tiny scalelike leaves are arranged in flat sprays that tilt in all directions. Small cones are brown and woody. There are several cultivars with good foliage color and compact habit. 'Emerald', 'Nigra', 'Techny', and 'Wintergreen' stay rich green all winter and make excellent hedges up to 15 ft. tall. 'Aurea' and 'Rheingold' have yellow, gold, or bronzy foliage and stay under 5 ft. tall. 'Hetz Midget' makes a dense ball of green foliage that eventually reaches 3 ft. tall and wide. Zone 3.

How to Grow
Needs sun; gets loose and leggy if growing in shade. Ordinary soil and watering. Tolerates moist, heavy, or clay soil but not dry or sandy soil. Easy to transplant in spring or fall. Responds well to pruning, but dwarf cultivars don't need it. Sus-

ceptible to bagworms and spider mites but generally trouble-free. Doesn't do well where summers are hot.

Herbal Use
Leaf preparations traditionally have been used for skin diseases, and leaf tea was taken for coughs, fevers, and other ailments. Contains thujone, which is toxic, so internal use is now discouraged. The essential oil is used by industry in soaps, paints, and other products.

Thymbra
Thym´bra
Labiatae. Mint family

Description
Small shrubs with aromatic foliage. Only 2 species, native to the Middle East.

■ *spicata* p. 231
Za'tar. A bushy little shrub, 1–2 ft. tall, that makes many upright stems crowded with narrow, dark green leaves and topped in summer with clusters of pretty pink flowers. The foliage has a spicy fragrance likened to oregano, savory, or thyme. Zone 8.

How to Grow
Full sun. Needs well-drained soil. Does well on sandy sites or in raised beds or containers. Tolerates alkaline soil and dry spells. Trim back old shoots in spring. Can be overwintered as a houseplant. Pest-free.

Herbal Use
This is one of several Middle Eastern plants called za'tar. All are used individually or blended to season a tasty flatbread and other dishes.

Thymus
Thy´mus
Labiatae. Mint family

Description
Perennials or small shrubs with very small opposite leaves and clusters of small white, pink, rosy red, or purple flowers. Some thymes are used for flavoring or fragrance. Others are

valued for their handsome foliage and masses of tiny but colorful flowers. Most are evergreen in mild winters. About 350 species, native to Europe and Asia, and many hybrids and cultivars.

■ × *citriodorus* *p. 204*

Lemon thyme. A bushy, mounding plant, 6–8 in. tall and 18–24 in. wide. The glossy green leaves, about $1/4$ in. long, have a sweet lemony aroma. Forms dense heads of lilac-purple flowers in June and July but doesn't set seeds (because it's a hybrid species). 'Aureus' has leaves edged with gold or yellow; 'Argenteus' has leaves edged in creamy white. Both are pretty while they last, but they tend to revert to the all-green form and are somewhat less hardy than it is. Zone 5.

How to Grow

Full or part sun. Well-drained average soil. Tolerates dry spells. Grows well in containers, indoors or out, if given plenty of light and not overwatered. Prune after flowering and as needed to keep it compact and tidy. Use pine boughs or other loose mulch for winter protection in cold climates, and shear off damaged shoots in spring. Divide and replant every few years.

Herbal Use

Tasty leaves are used to season soups, sauces, chicken, fish, pastries, and desserts and are dried for potpourri.

■ *herba-barona* *p. 205*

Caraway thyme. A low, spreading thyme with relatively long shoots. One plant makes a mat about 4 in. tall and spreads up to 24 in. wide; adjacent plants intertwine to form a thick matted ground cover. The stems are reddish. The needlelike leaves are dark green and smell like caraway when crushed. Dense heads of dark rose-colored flowers are held on short ascending stems in midsummer. 'Nutmeg' thyme is basically the same plant. Zone 4.

How to Grow

Full sun. Average well-drained soil. Plant in raised beds where the climate is rainy or humid. Makes a good ground cover or herbal lawn. Prune, shear, or mow after flowering and in spring. Can be invasive in small beds. Not recommended for containers.

Herbal Use

Fresh or dried leaves add a caraway flavor to beef and other foods.

■ *praecox* subsp. *arcticus* cvs.　*p. 205*

Creeping thymes, English wild thymes. This group includes some of the showiest flowering thymes. All form low mats 3–4 in. tall and 18–24 in. wide. Leaves can be shiny or woolly, needlelike or elliptic, green or silvery. The tiny flowers are borne in generous clusters, starting in early summer and sometimes continuing until September. There are many cultivars. 'Coccineus' has crimson flowers and dark green leaves. 'Alba' has white flowers and bright green leaves. 'Pink Chintz' has pale pink flowers and slightly woolly gray-green leaves. 'Annie Hall' is very flat, with shiny green leaves and bright pink flowers. 'Minor' or 'Minus' forms a compact cushion of very small hairy leaves and has pink flowers; it's great for underplanting bonsai specimens. 'Mayfair' has lemon-scented leaves that are touched with gold in spring and fall. The cultivars named above are often listed in catalogs under the name *T. serpyllum.* All are hardy to zone 4.

How to Grow

Full sun. Need well-drained soil and tolerate dry spells. Make a good ground cover between flagstones and look nice trailing over a stone wall or draping over the sides of a planter box. Shear after flowering. Propagate by division or cuttings.

Herbal Use

Rarely used in cooking but enjoyed for their fragrance.

■ *pseudolanuginosus*　*p. 206*

Woolly thyme. Thyme taxonomy is confusing. This plant used to be listed under the name *T. lanuginosus,* but it may just be a variation of *T. praecox.* Whatever the name, it's unmistakable when you see it. The stems and leaves are thickly covered with silver-gray hairs that sparkle in the sun. It makes a dense, low mat about 3 in. tall and 24 in. wide and has pale pink flowers in early summer. Hardy to zone 5, but only on well-drained sites.

How to Grow

Full sun. Needs better drainage and drier soil than most thymes. It looks beautiful in dry climates but is very susceptible to overwatering, damp soil, and high humidity. Makes a good ground cover in sunny rock gardens and will completely cover large rocks. Crosses readily with other thymes and produces interesting seedlings.

Herbal Use

The leaves are fragrant, but it's planted mostly for fun. Once you've seen this woolly foliage, you have to try growing it.

■ *pulegioides* *p. 206* *Pictured above*
Mother-of-thyme. The most vigorous and fastest-growing thyme. It grows easily from seed, and there are many different forms. Most make a mound about 8 in. tall and 24 in. wide, with glossy, aromatic leaves that are larger and rounder than those of other thymes. Flowers are pinkish, lavender, or purple and make quite a show over a long season. May smell like lemon thyme, common thyme, or oregano. Various forms are sold, often under the name *T. serpyllum*. Zone 4.

How to Grow
Full or part sun. Average soil and watering. Tolerates dry spells. This species has naturalized in parts of the United States and grows wild in meadows and lawns. It makes an excellent ground cover and competes with grass and other plants better than other thymes do. You can walk on it or mow it. Shear after flowering and in spring. Divide every few years. Soon outgrows a container.

Herbal Use
Harvest leaves just before flowering for maximum flavor. Fresh or dried leaves are used for seasoning, in potpourri, and in tea, like *T. vulgaris*.

■ *vulgaris* *p. 207*
Common thyme. A bushy little plant, woody at the base, with many erect, wiry stems up to 12 in. tall. Seedlings are interesting but variable; named cultivars have more reliable flavor and appearance. Most produce showy heads of lilac or purple flowers in summer. 'English' or 'Broadleaf English' is a vigorous plant with smooth, shiny green leaves that have rounded ends. 'French' or 'Narrow-leaf French' is less robust; has narrower leaves with pointed ends; has a silvery, rather than green, color; and has a spicier, more pungent aroma than 'English' thyme. 'Orange Balsam' has leaves that are even narrower and grayer than 'French' thyme and a citrus-thyme aroma. 'Silver' thyme smells like 'French' thyme; it has beau-

tiful variegated green and white foliage but is weaker and less hardy than the other selections. Zone 4.

How to Grow
Full sun. Well-drained average soil. Tolerates dry spells. Individual plants are upright and bushy. Space 6–8 in. apart to make a low clipped edging. Can be trained as a miniature bonsai. Grows well in containers outdoors but gets leggy as a houseplant in winter. Propagate selected forms by division or cuttings.

Herbal Use
Harvest leaves prior to flowering for maximum flavor. They dry and store well. An essential culinary herb, excellent for seasoning a wide variety of meats and vegetables. Thyme leaf tea is used in Europe for various gastrointestinal and respiratory complaints. The essential oil contains 40 percent thymol, an antiseptic used in various over-the-counter products such as Vicks Vaporub and Listerine mouthwash.

Tilia
Till´ee-a
Tiliaceae. Linden family

Description
Deciduous trees with large alternate leaves, fibrous inner bark, versatile white timber, and fragrant flowers. About 45 species, native to the north temperate zone.

■ *cordata* p. 131
Littleleaf linden. An adaptable and attractive tree that forms a dense, fine-textured crown and casts plenty of shade. In Europe, this tree is used successfully for tall formal hedges that are pruned into outdoor "walls." Here, it is grown mostly as a lawn specimen or street tree, up to 50 ft. tall. Leaves are nearly round with a pointed tip, 1½–3 in. long, dark green above and silvery below, turning yellow in fall. Very fragrant flowers dangle in small clusters from the center of a leaflike bract. *T. americana,* American linden or basswood, looks similar but grows larger, up to 80 ft. tall, and has heart-shaped leaves about 6 in. long. Zone 3.

How to Grow
Full sun. Ordinary soil and watering. Tolerates heat (if the soil is moist), alkaline soil, and air pollution. Specimen trees need only routine pruning. Subject to aphids, which produce

messy, sticky honeydew. Japanese beetles may attack the foliage and flowers.

Herbal Use

Europeans dry the flowers to make a fragrant tea, considered helpful for nervous headaches, restlessness, or painful digestion. Bees visit the flowers and make a tasty honey. The inner bark has been used for cordage and basketry.

Tropaeolum

Tro-pee′oh-lum
Tropaeolaceae. Nasturtium family

Description

Annuals or perennials with showy red, orange, or yellow flowers. More than 80 species, native to the mountains of Central and South America.

■ *majus* *p. 255*

Nasturtium. A popular annual that's easy, adaptable, and colorful. The fleshy stems can climb or sprawl 2–4 ft. or more. The leaves are like parasols, with a long stalk attached in the center and a rounded blade up to 6 in. wide. The surface is smooth, almost waxy. The large, long-stalked flowers have a spicy fragrance and come in bright shades of yellow, orange, red, mahogany, cream, and bicolor. Looks cheerful in containers, trailing over walls, or edging annual flower beds or vegetable gardens. Seed catalogs offer several strains, including compact bushy forms and one kind with white-variegated leaves. All zones.

How to Grow

Full or part sun. Ordinary soil and watering. The seeds are large enough that children can handle them easily. Sow direct in early spring, covering the seeds $\frac{1}{2}$ in. deep. Thin to 6–12 in. apart. Subject to aphids but generally carefree. Self-sows readily but isn't an aggressive weed.

Herbal Use
Leaves, buds, flowers, unripe pods, and dry seeds can all be used as seasoning. They have a peppery flavor, good in salads and sandwiches. The leaf juice is antibacterial and has been used to disinfect minor scratches and wounds.

Tsuga
Soo´ga
Pinaceae. Pine family

Description
Evergreen conifers with flat needles and small woody cones. Only 10 species, native to North America and eastern Asia.

■ *canadensis* p. 131
Canada hemlock. One of the most graceful conifers, native to cool moist sites in the Great Lakes, Northeast, and Appalachians. Grows 50–100 ft. tall, with a central trunk and relaxed, spreading branches that sway in the breeze. Short flat needles are crowded on the twigs, forming flat feathery sprays of foliage that stays rich green all year. Small cones are like miniature pinecones. Responds well to pruning and can be shaped into a dense, fine-textured hedge. Var. *sargentii* is a weeping form that spreads wider than tall. There are a few dwarf forms. Zone 4.

　T. caroliniana, Carolina hemlock, has slightly larger needles on all sides of the twigs and stiffer branches. It makes good hedges and is more tolerant of dry air and wind. Zone 5. *T. heterophylla,* western hemlock, makes a beautiful specimen in the Pacific Northwest. Zone 7.

How to Grow
Part shade. Prefers a north or east exposure that provides some sun in summer and shade in winter. Needs cool, rich, moist, well-drained, acidic soil with a thick layer of organic mulch. Water regularly during dry spells. Can't take heat or drought. Space 6 ft. apart for hedges and prune to encourage dense growth. Subject to a few insect and disease problems, some locally serious. Check with a local nursery or extension agent before planting.

Herbal Use
The highly astringent bark was once used as a poultice to stop bleeding, as well as an agent for tanning leather. The leaf tea was used to treat colds, coughs, fevers, and stomach problems.

Tulbaghia
Tul-baj´ee-a
Amaryllidaceae. Amaryllis family

Description
Small perennials that smell like onions or garlic, with small bulbs, grassy foliage, and umbels of 6-petaled flowers. More than 20 species, native to Africa.

■ *violacea* p. 232
Society garlic. A tender perennial that blooms most in summer but repeats throughout the year. The clusters of starry white or lilac flowers are held on 1–2 ft. stalks and make good cut flowers. The garlic-scented foliage is evergreen. Leaves are flat and slender, up to 12 in. long. 'Tricolor' is a variegated form with striped leaves. Zone 9.

How to Grow
Full or part sun. Ordinary soil and watering. Plant a few clumps in the garden, or put one plant in a 6- or 8-in. pot. Grows fine on a winter windowsill. Propagate by division. Easy and trouble-free.

Herbal Use
The Zulus of South Africa plant it around their huts to repel snakes and have used the bulbs as a remedy for tuberculosis and to expel worms. Don't confuse this plant with the edible garlic chives; eating these leaves or flowers can cause vomiting.

Tussilago
Too-si-lay´go
Compositae. Composite family

Description
A low-growing perennial. Only 1 species, native to Europe but widely naturalized in eastern North America.

■ *farfara* *p. 207*
Coltsfoot, coughwort, son-before-the-father. A hardy perennial that flowers in spring, before the leaves appear. Both flowers and leaves grow from a spreading root system. Like dandelions, the flowers are yellow, about 1 in. wide, on scaly 6-in. stalks, and make puffy clusters of winged seeds. The leaves are shaped like a horse's footprint, about 8 in. wide, with slightly lobed or toothed edges. They are dark green above, covered with soft white hairs below, and slightly aromatic. Zone 4.

How to Grow
Full sun. Average soil and watering. Spreads too fast to include in formal beds but can be confined with a bottomless pot, used as a ground cover, or grown in a container. Easily propagated by division. Carefree.

Herbal Use
Tea made from the leaves and flowers was once one of Europe's most popular cough remedies, but internal use is banned today because it can cause liver damage.

Umbellularia
Um-bel-you-lay′ree-a
Lauraceae. Laurel family

Description
An evergreen tree with aromatic foliage. Only 1 species, native to California and Oregon.

■ *californica* *p. 132*
California bay, Oregon myrtle. A dense, round-headed tree 60–75 ft. tall, sometimes with multiple trunks. Alternate leaves are smooth and leathery, 2–5 in. long, shiny green on top and dull below, with a much stronger, more bitter aroma and flavor than sweet bay (*Laurus nobilis*). Clusters of greenish yellow flowers in spring are followed by dark purple fruits in fall. Like miniature avocados, the fruits have 1 big seed inside. Zone 7.

How to Grow
Full sun. Average well-drained soil. Established plants tolerate dry spells. Propagate from fresh seed or cuttings. Young plants need shelter from cold and dry winter winds. Subject to scale.

Herbal Use

Leaves are sometimes used as a substitute for sweet bay and have been used medicinally in tea and poultices. The best use is in potpourri or dried arrangements. Prolonged inhalation of fresh crushed leaves can cause irritation or headaches.

Valeriana

Va-lee-ri-ay´na
Valerianaceae. Valerian family

Description

Herbs or shrubs with variable foliage, small flowers, and strong-scented roots or rhizomes. About 250 species, native worldwide.

■ *officinalis* *p. 208*

Valerian, garden heliotrope. A hardy perennial with erect or floppy stems up to 5 ft. tall, topped in summer with rounded clusters of overpoweringly sweet-scented white, pink, or lavender flowers. Dark green leaves are pinnately compound, divided into many pointed leaflets. Most people think the spreading roots smell like old dirty socks, but the aroma attracts cats. Zone 3.

This plant is often confused with true heliotrope, *Heliotropium peruvianum,* a tender perennial with crinkled dark green leaves and fragrant purple or white flowers; or with red valerian, *Centranthus ruber,* a hardy, drought-tolerant perennial with smooth blue-green leaves and crimson, pink, or white flowers. Both are desirable plants but don't have herbal uses.

How to Grow

Full sun. Average garden soil with regular watering. Spreads by runners and persists for years with little care. Daughter plants formed by the runners are easily lifted and moved. Sometimes self-sows, too.

Herbal Use

One of the best-known herbal sedatives and a leading over-the-counter tranquilizer in Europe. Tea or tincture of the roots is used for insomnia, fatigue, migraine, stomach cramps, and other nervous conditions. Traditional claims of effectiveness have been confirmed by modern clinical studies. Caution: Large or frequent doses can produce headaches or stupor.

Vetiveria

Vet-i-vee′ree-a
Gramineae. Grass family

Description
Perennial grasses that form large clumps. Only 2 species, native to the Old World tropics.

■ *zizanioides* *p. 232*
Vetiver. A tender grass with spreading roots, used in southern Louisiana and in tropical countries to control soil erosion on levees and banks. Forms clumps 3–4 ft. tall of light green grassy leaves that are thin, smooth, and scentless. Rarely flowers in this country. Zone 9.

How to Grow
Full sun. Prefers rich, moist soil but grows okay in average soil with frequent watering. Propagate by division. Where not hardy, it does well as an annual. Planted in the garden after frost, it makes a big clump by fall. Dig it up to gather the abundant fleshy roots, and pot up a division to overwinter indoors. Cut the foliage back and keep it on the dry side, in a sunny window.

Herbal Use
Dried roots retain a very pleasant fragrance, desirable in sachets for perfuming stored linens or clothing. Essential oil is used in perfumes. In India, the oil is used to relieve flatulence, colic, and nausea, and leaf tea is applied externally for rheumatism, lumbago, and sprains.

Viburnum

Vy-bur′num
Caprifoliaceae. Honeysuckle family

Description
Deciduous or evergreen shrubs or small trees with simple opposite leaves and showy clusters of 5-petaled flowers, usually white or pink and sometimes very fragrant. About 150 species, native to the Old and New World, and several hybrids.

■ *opulus* *p. 132*
European cranberry bush, crampbark. A deciduous shrub with lacy clusters of white flowers in May, shiny red fruits in fall and winter, and maplelike leaves that turn yellow, red, or

purple in fall. Usually grows 8–12 ft. tall and spreads 10–15 ft. wide. 'Compactum' grows only half as big—a better size for today's smaller gardens, and produces an excellent display of flowers and fruits. 'Roseum', also called 'Sterile', is the old-fashioned snowballbush that makes fluffy white 3-in. balls of flowers in early May. *V. trilobum,* American cranberry bush, is very similar to European cranberry bush but even hardier. All of these shrubs make excellent specimens or hedges for gardens in cold climates. Zone 3.

How to Grow
Full sun. Thrives in rich, moist soil but grows well in average soil if watered frequently during hot, dry weather. Water before the leaves start to wilt. Stressed plants are more subject to aphids, borers, and diseases. Can't take hot summers. Prune in spring, if desired. Flowers form on new growth.

Herbal Use
Preparations of the bark of both the European and American species traditionally were used to relieve cramped muscles and menstrual cramps. The berries of *V. trilobum* are tart but rich in vitamin C and are sometimes used to make juice or preserves.

■ *setigerum*   *p. 133*
Tea-leaf viburnum. A deciduous shrub from China, grown here mostly for its prolific crops of beautiful red berries. Showier than most flowers, they glisten from midsummer to early winter. The stems are upright, usually 8–10 ft. tall, with opposite oval leaves about 4 in. long and small clusters of white flowers in spring. Zone 5.

How to Grow
Like *V. opulus.* Makes a colorful screen behind mid-height perennials or a centerpiece for a round tea garden.

Herbal Use
The leaves have been used to make a mild tea beverage.

Viola
Vy-oh'la
Violaceae. Violet family

Description
A diverse group of annuals, perennials, and a few small shrubs. Most have characteristic violet-type flowers, but the

leaves and habit are variable. About 500 species, native to the Old and New World. Many of the species are distinguished by minor differences, and they hybridize readily.

■ *odorata*   *p. 208   Pictured above*
Sweet violet. A hardy perennial, long treasured for the intense sweet fragrance of its flowers. Forms tufts or clumps of dark green heart-shaped leaves, 1–2 in. wide, on stalks 4–6 in. tall. The foliage is evergreen in mild winters. Flowers rise from the center of the clump and bloom for weeks in late winter, early spring, and fall. May bloom all winter in a cool bright window or greenhouse, or outdoors where winters are mild. There are many cultivars, with deep purple, blue, lavender, white, or pink blossoms. Most are perfectly hardy in zone 5. The cultivars called Parma violets have double flowers that are especially fragrant, but the plants are harder to obtain and hardy only to zone 7 or 6.

How to Grow
Part or full shade. Prefers rich, organic soil with constant moisture. Spreads fast by runners and can make a solid patch or ground cover. Competes well with grass and will spread into a lawn. Propagate by dividing clumps in spring or fall. Mulch tender varieties for winter protection. Grows well in a container or hanging basket; pot one in fall to enjoy on a windowsill indoors in winter. Subject to spider mites, and slugs often attack the foliage.

Herbal Use
The flowers are edible and can be added to salads or candied (by dipping in sugar syrup) to decorate cakes or other desserts. The essential oil is used in perfumes. Tea from the leaves and flowers has been used in Europe as a mild sedative for asthma and heart palpitations.

Vitex

Vy'tex
Verbenaceae. Verbena family

Description

Deciduous or evergreen shrubs or trees with opposite compound leaves and clusters of small flowers. Both foliage and flowers can be aromatic. About 250 species, mostly tropical, native to Old and New World.

■ *agnus-castus* *p. 147*
Chaste tree, pepperbush. A multitrunked shrub or small tree with a loose, open, umbrella-shaped crown. Usually grows 10–20 ft. tall. The deciduous leaves are palmately compound with 3–9 toothed leaflets. Dark green above and gray-green or silvery below, they release a spicy or peppery fragrance when crushed. Clustered spikes of small lilac or lavender flowers bloom on the new growth from midsummer through fall. Adaptable and easy to grow, it makes a fine lawn or border specimen. Selections with white or pink flowers are also available. Zone 7.

How to Grow

Full sun. Thrives in hot weather. Tolerates poor, dry soil but grows faster with ordinary garden soil and regular watering. May freeze back in cold winters; prune off damaged shoots in spring, and it will recover by summer. A carefree plant with no common pests.

Herbal Use

Historically used by monks and nuns in Europe to allay sexual desire, hence the name "chaste tree." Preparations of the seeds are used traditionally and in modern Europe for menstrual and menopausal disorders and to help reestablish normal ovulation upon termination of the birth control pill. The berries and leaves have also been used as a seasoning.

Withania

Wi-thay'nee-a
Solanaceae. Nightshade family

Description

Perennials or shrubs with 5-petaled flowers and seedy berries. About 10 species, native to the Old World.

■ *somnifera* *p. 233*

No common name in English; called ashwaganda in India. A tender perennial, often grown as an annual. Grows about 2 ft. tall the first summer; gets bigger every year if protected from frost. Upright, branching stems hold oval leaves with a soft, downy texture. Small cream or yellow flowers appear in the leaf axils in early fall, followed by red berries encased in paper husks, like Chinese lanterns. Zone 10.

How to Grow

Full sun. Average soil and watering. Sow seeds indoors, like tomatoes or peppers, and transplant seedlings to the garden after danger of frost. Also does well in a container—it will size itself to the pot. Can be overwintered as a houseplant, but growth slows or stops in winter. Cut it back before it resumes in spring. Subject to flea beetles but generally carefree.

Herbal Use

One of the most important plants in the traditional medicine of India, used there for more than 3,000 years as an invigorating tonic, to overcome weakness, and to stimulate the elderly. The roots are also used as a sedative and an aphrodisiac and are applied externally for rheumatism and inflammation. The leaves are applied to skin lesions, boils, and swelling. Current research indicates that it has "adaptogenic" effects similar to those of ginseng. In Asia and Africa, the berries are used to make a sudsy lather for washing clothes, and the seeds are used to coagulate milk in cheesemaking.

Xanthorhiza

Zan-tho-ry´za
Ranunculaceae. Buttercup family

Description

A low-growing deciduous shrub. Only 1 species, native to woodlands in eastern North America.

■ *simplicissima* *p. 209*

Yellowroot. A hardy native that spreads to make a thicket of upright, unbranched stems about 2–3 ft. tall, each topped with a tuft of glossy foliage. The compound leaves are divided into 3 or 5 toothed leaflets. Dangling clusters of little purplish flowers open in early spring, before the leaves. Zone 3.

How to Grow

Part shade. Thrives in rich, moist soils; prefers damp sites but also grows well in average garden beds if watered regularly. Spreads by rhizomes but not too fast. One plant makes a nice clump, or space several plants 18 in. apart as a ground cover under a deciduous tree. Usually propagated by division in spring or fall. Carefree once established.

Herbal Use

Native Americans and early settlers made tea from the yellow rhizomes and used it as a tonic for jaundice, high blood pressure, colds, cramps, sore mouth or throat, and other conditions. It contains berberine, a compound that has many therapeutic properties, but large doses are potentially toxic.

Yucca

Yuk′a

Agavaceae. Agave family

Description

Robust perennials with evergreen swordlike leaves. About 40 species, native to North America.

■ *filamentosa* p. 209 *Pictured above*

Yucca, bear grass, Adam's-needle. This southeastern native is the most commonly cultivated yucca. It spreads slowly to make a wide patch with many rosettes of sword-shaped leaves 2–3 ft. long. The stiff, branched, 5-ft. stalks of creamy white flowers are very showy in June. Gather the woody pods in fall for dried arrangements. 'Golden Sword' and other variegated forms have pretty gold or cream stripes on the leaves. Plants sold as *Y. filamentosa* may actually be *Y. flaccida* or *Y. smalliana;* it's hard to distinguish these similar-looking plants. Many other yuccas are also desirable garden plants with traditional herbal uses. Look for them at native-plant nurseries. Zone 5.

How to Grow
Full sun. Needs well-drained soil; tolerates poor, dry soil. Tolerates winter cold, summer heat, and wind. Transplant container-grown plants in spring. Established plants form offsets at the base that can be removed and transplanted. The only care required is the removal of old flower stalks and dead leaves.

Herbal Use
Yucca leaves are filled with strong flexible fibers that were used extensively by Native American basketmakers and weavers. Yucca roots contain saponins, compounds that make a suds in water. Native Americans used the roots of several species for soap and shampoo, and they mixed pounded yucca root with lard or other grease to rub on sores and sprains.

Yucca roots have also been used as a fish poison. Adding chopped roots to a dammed-up stream or pool stuns or suffocates the fish, making them float to the surface where they are easy to catch. The stunned fish are perfectly safe to eat.

Zanthoxylum
Zan-tho-zy'lum
Rutaceae. Citrus family

Description
Deciduous or evergreen shrubs or trees armed with prickles, spines, or thorns. Most have aromatic bark, leaves, and/or fruit, and various parts of several species are used for flavoring food and as home remedies. About 200 species, native worldwide.

■ *americanum*   p. 133
Prickly ash. A shrub or small tree native to the Northeast and Upper Midwest. Usually grows 15–25 ft. tall, with several trunks that are armed with stout thorns. The glossy, dark green, compound leaves have several pairs of oval leaflets. Small yellow-green flowers bloom in spring, before the leaves expand. Seedpods ripen in summer. Zone 4.

How to Grow
Full sun. Not fussy about soil. Grows fast on damp or dry sites. Spreads by suckers to make a thicket. Easy to grow, with no common pests or diseases, but devilish to prune.

Herbal Use
A tea or tincture of the bark traditionally was used to treat rheumatism, digestive problems, colds, coughs, lung ailments, and nervous problems. The fresh bark was chewed to relieve toothache.

Zingiber
Zin´ji-ber
Zingiberaceae. Ginger family

Description
Tropical perennials with fragrant rhizomes, leafy stalks, and showy flowers. About 85 species, most native to Asia.

■ *officinale* *p. 233*
Ginger, true ginger. A tender plant, usually grown in pots in this country. Upright leafy stalks, about 2 ft. tall, grow directly from the thick spreading rhizomes. The leaves are slender, about 1 in. wide and 6 in. long, with a glossy, almost iridescent surface; bright green color; and a gingery aroma when crushed. Flowers emerge from conelike spikes on short stalks separate from the leaves. Potted plants rarely bloom. Zone 9.

How to Grow
Part sun outdoors, a sunny window indoors. Prefers rich, moist soil with frequent watering and fertilizing. Ginger is fussy but rewarding to grow. You can start with a piece of fresh rhizome from the grocery store (make sure it has an "eye," or bud). Bury it partway in a small pot of fresh potting soil, and keep it in a very warm place (75° F or warmer) until it sprouts. Move to larger pots as it grows, and put it outdoors in summer. Harvest and use the rhizome in fall, or bring the pot indoors in fall to protect it from frost, and withhold water while it is dormant in winter. Subject to slugs, grasshoppers, and most common houseplant insect pests.

Herbal Use
Ginger has been valued as a flavoring and medicine for thousands of years in China and India. The pungent rhizome is used fresh or dried in curries, condiments, baked goods, beverages, and candies. It stimulates the appetite and induces sweating. Ginger tea is a traditional remedy for colds, stomachaches, and nausea. Recent clinical trials have focused on using ginger as a treatment for motion sickness, with generally positive results.

Appendices

Further Reading

Medicinal Herbs

British Herbal Compendium, vol. 1. P. R. Bradly, ed. Dorset, England: British Herbal Medicine Association, 1992.

The Complete Medicinal Herbal. Penelope Ody. New York: Dorling Kindersley, 1993.

The Family Herbal. Peter and Barbara Theiss. Rochester, Vt.: Healing Arts Press, 1989.

A Field Guide to Medicinal Plants: Eastern and Central North America. Steven Foster and James A. Duke. Boston: Houghton Mifflin, 1992.

Herbal Emissaries: Bringing Chinese Herbs to the West. Steven Foster and Chong-xi Yue. Rochester, Vt.: Healing Arts Press, 1992.

Herbal Medicine. Rudolf Fritz Weiss; tr. from German by A. R. Meuss. Beaconsfield, England: Beaconsfield Publishers Ltd., 1988.

Herbal Medicine Past and Present, 2 vols. J. K. Crellin and J. Philpott. Durham, N.C.: Duke University Press, 1989.

Herbal Renaissance. Steven Foster. Layton, Utah: Gibbs Smith, 1993.

The Honest Herbal: A Sensible Guide to the Use of Herbs and Related Remedies, 3rd ed. Varro E. Tyler. Binghamton, N.Y.: Pharmaceutical Products Press, 1993.

Medicinal and Other Uses of North American Plants. Charlotte Erichsen-Brown. New York: Dover Publications, 1989.

Out of the Earth: The Essential Book of Herbal Medicine. Simon Y. Mills. New York: Viking, 1992.

Potter's New Cyclopedia of Botanical Drugs and Preparations, 8th ed. R. C. Wren; rev. by E. M. Williamson and F. J. Evans. Essex, England: C. W. Daniel Co., 1988.

Cooking with Herbs

The Complete Book of Spices. Jill Norman. New York: Viking, 1991.

Cooking with Herbs. Susan Belsinger and Carolyn Dille. New York: Van Nostrand Reinhold, 1984.

Cooking with Herbs. Emelie Tolley and Chris Mead. New York: Clarkson N. Potter, 1989.

Cooking with Herbs and Spices, rev. ed. Craig Claiborne. New York: Harper & Row, 1970.

Geraldine Holt's Complete Book of Herbs. Geraldine Holt. New York: Henry Holt, 1991.

The Herb Garden Cookbook. Lucinda Hutson. Houston: Gulf Publishing, 1992.

The Herbal Pantry. Emelie Tolley and Chris Mead. New York: Clarkson N. Potter, 1992.

Herbs: Gardens, Decorations, and Recipes. Emelie Tolley and Chris Mead. New York: Clarkson N. Potter, 1985.

Herbs in the Kitchen: A Celebration of Flavor. Carolyn Dille and Susan Belsinger. Loveland, Colo.: Interweave Press, 1992.

Kitchen Herbs. Sal Gilbertie. New York: Bantam, 1988.

Recipes from an American Herb Garden. Maggie Oster. New York: Macmillan, 1993.

Recipes from a French Herb Garden. Geraldine Holt. New York: Simon & Schuster, 1989.

Recipes from a Kitchen Garden, vols. 1 and 2. René Shepherd. Felton, Calif.: Shepherd's Garden Publishing, 1987 and 1991.

The Sage Cottage Herb Garden Book: Celebrations, Recipes, and Herb Gardening Tips for Every Month of the Year. Dorry Baird Norris. Chester, Conn.: Globe Pequot, 1991.

Planning and Planting an Herb Garden

The Book of Garden Design. John Brookes. New York: Macmillan, 1991.

Classic Garden Design: How to Adapt and Re-create Garden Features of the Past. Rosemary Verey. New York: Random House, 1989.

Garden Paths: Inspiring Designs and Practical Projects. Gordon Hayward. Charlotte, Vt.: Camden House, 1993.

Garden Style. Penelope Hobhouse. Boston: Little, Brown, 1988.

Herb Garden Design. Faith H. Swanson and Virginia B. Rady. Mentor, Ohio: Herb Society of America, 1984.

Landscaping with Herbs. James Adams. Portland, Oreg.: Timber Press, 1987.

Planting in Patterns. Penelope Hobhouse. New York: Harper-Collins, 1989.

Taylor's Guide to Garden Design. Boston: Houghton Mifflin, 1988.

Taylor's Guide to Gardening Techniques. Boston: Houghton Mifflin, 1991.

Using Herbs in the Landscape. Debra Kirkpatrick. Harrisville, Pa.: Stackpole Books, 1992.

Growing Herbs

Artistically Cultivated Herbs. Elise Felton. Santa Barbara: Woodbridge Press, 1990.

The Essence of Herbs: An Environmental Guide to Herb Gardening. Ruth D. Wrensch. Jackson, Miss.: University Press of Mississippi, 1992.

The Harrowsmith Illustrated Book of Herbs. Patrick Lima. Charlotte, Vt.: Camden House, 1986.

Herb Topiaries. Sally Gallo. Loveland, Colo.: Interweave Press, 1992.

Herbs. Simon and Judith Hopkinson. Chester, Conn.: Globe Pequot, 1989.

Herbs: How to Select, Grow and Enjoy. Norma Jean Lathrop. Tucson: HP Books, 1981.

The New England Herb Gardener. Patricia Turcotte. Charlotte, Vt.: Countryman Press, 1991.

The Potted Herb. Abbie Zabar. New York: Stewart, Tabori, & Chang, 1988.

Southern Herb Growing. Madalene Hill and Gwen Barclay. Fredericksburg, Tex.: Shearer, 1987.

Texas Gardener's Guide to Growing and Using Herbs. Diane M. Sitton. Waco, Tex.: Texas Gardener Press, 1987.

Fragrant Products, Gifts, and Crafts

Aromatherapy: The Encyclopedia of Plants and Oils and How They Help You. Daniele Ryman. New York: Bantam, 1993.

The Book of Potpourri. Penny Black. New York: Simon & Schuster, 1989.

Gifts from the Herb Garden. Emelie Tolley and Chris Mead. New York: Clarkson N. Potter, 1991.

Herbal Treasures. Phyllis V. Shaudys. Pownal, Vt.: Storey Communications, 1990.

Natural Fragrances: Outdoor Scents for Indoor Uses. Gail Duff. Pownal, Vt.: Storey Communications, 1989.

Potpourri: The Art of Fragrance Crafting. Louise Gruenberg. Norway, Iowa: Frontier Cooperative Herbs, 1990.

The Potpourri Gardener. Theodore James, Jr. New York: Macmillan, 1990.

Potpourri, Incense and Other Fragrant Concoctions. Ann Tucker Fettner. New York: Workman 1977.

General

The Golden Guide to Herbs and Spices. Julia F. Morton. New York: Golden Press, 1976.

Magic and Medicine of Plants. Reader's Digest. Pleasantville, N.Y.: Reader's Digest Association, 1986.

Plants for People. Anna Lewington. New York: Oxford University Press, 1990.

Rodale's Illustrated Encyclopedia of Herbs. Claire Kowalchik and William H. Hylton, eds. Emmaus, Pa.: Rodale Press, 1987.

Directories

Gardening by Mail, 4th ed. Barbara Barton. Boston: Houghton Mifflin, 1994.

The Herb Companion Wishbook and Resource Guide. Bobbi A. McRae. Loveland, Colo.: Interweave Press, 1992.

Herb Gardens in America: A Visitor's Guide. Karen S. C. Morris and Lyle E. Craker. Amherst, Mass.: HSMP Press, 1991.

Herb Resource Directory. Paula Oliver, ed. Available from Northwind Farm Publications, RR 2, Box 246, Shevlin, MN 56676.

The Herbal Green Pages. Maureen Rogers, ed. Available from The Herb Growing and Marketing Network, 3343 Nolt Rd., Lancaster, PA 17601.

Periodicals

The Business of Herbs, Northwind Farm Publications, RR 2, Box 246, Shevlin, MN 56676.

The Herb Companion, 201 E. Fourth St., Loveland, CO 80537.

Herb Quarterly, Box 548, Boiling Springs, PA 17007.

The Herbal Connection, 3343 Nolt Rd., Lancaster, PA 17601.

HerbalGram, P.O. Box 201660, Austin, TX 78720.

Herban Lifestyles, 84 Carpenter Rd., New Hartford, CT 06057.

Potpourri from Herbal Acres, Box 428, Washington Crossing, PA 18977.

Mail-Order Herb Nurseries

Many of the following nurseries and seed companies are small businesses that need to charge a small fee for their catalog. Send a self-addressed stamped postcard to ask how much the catalog costs. The price is often refundable with your first order.

Plants

Adventures in Herbs
P.O. Box 23240
Mint Hill, NC 28212

Companion Plants
7247 N. Coolville Ridge Rd.
Athens, OH 45701

Goodwin Creek Gardens
P.O. Box 83
Williams, OR 97544

The Herbfarm
32804 Issaquah–Fall City Rd.
Fall City, WA 98024

Lily of the Valley Herb Farm
3969 Fox Ave.
Minerva, OH 44657

Logee's Greenhouses
North St.
Danielson, CT 06239

Rasland Farm
Rt. 1, Box 65
Godwin, NC 28344

Sandy Mush Herb Nursery
316 Surrett Cove Rd.
Leicester, NC 28748

Shady Acres
7815 Hwy. 212
Chaska, MN 55318

Well-Sweep Herb Farm
317 Mt. Bethel Rd.
Port Murray, NJ 07865

Wrenwood of Berkeley Springs
Rt. 4, Box 361
Berkeley Springs, WV 25411

Seeds

Chiltern Seeds
Bortree Stile
Ulverton, Cumbria, England LA12 7PB

The Cook's Garden
Box 65
Londonderry, VT 05148

The Flowery Branch
P.O. Box 1330
Flowery Branch, GA 30542

Le Jardin du Gourmet
Box 75
St. Johnsbury Ctr., VT 05863

Nichols Garden Nursery
1190 N. Pacific Hwy.
Albany, OR 97321

Park Seed Co.
Cokesbury Rd.
Greenwood, SC 29647

Richter's
P.O. Box 26, Hwy. 47
Goodwood, Ont. L0C 1A0, Canada

Rosemary House
120 South Market St.
Mechanicsburg, PA 17055

Seeds Blum
Idaho City Stage
Boise, ID 83706

Shepherd's Garden Seeds
30 Irene St.
Torrington, CT 06790

Sunrise Enterprises
P.O. Box 330058
West Hartford, CT 06133

Thompson & Morgan
P.O. Box 1308
Jackson, NJ 08527

The Thyme Garden
20546 Alsea Hwy.
Alsea, OR 97324

Photo Credits

Allen Armitage: 160B, 239A

Rita Buchanan: 100-101, 104-105, 106-107, 108-109, 118A, 122A, 124A, 125A, 128A, B, 130A, B, 131A, 136A, 137A, 138B, 141B, 146A, 147A, 152B, 154A, B, 155B, 156A, B, 159B, 160A, 162A, 165A, B, 166A, 168A, 169B, 170A, 171A, 173A, B, 174B, 183A, B, 184B, 186B, 188A, B, 190B, 192B, 194B, 195A, 196A, B, 199B, 201B, 203B, 206B, 219A, 222A, B, 223B, 230B, 232B, 237A, 241A, 242B, 243B, 244B, 245A, B, 247A, 248B, 249B, 253A, B, 254A

David Cavagnaro: 200B, 230A, 246B

Michael Dirr: 112A, 113A, 117B, 122B, 125B, 178A

Tom Eltzroth: 121A, 137B, 140A, 142B, 146B, 172A, 179A, 204B

Derek Fell: 181B, 189B, 200A, 209B, 232A, 255B

Steven Foster: 114A, B, 115A, 116A, 124B, 131B, 132B, 133B, 143B, 145B, 148-149, 150B, 152A, 157B, 164B, 169A, 170B, 171B, 175A, 176A, 180B, 184A, 185A, 187B, 189A, 192A, 193B, 201A, 202A, 207B, 208A, 212A, 217B, 219B, 231A, 236B, 238A, 239B, 241B, 246A, 249A, 250A, B, 251A

Pamela Harper: 121B, 144B, 147B, 150A, 161B, 168B, 187A, 191B, 209A, 234-235, 242A

Dency Kane: 98-99, 102-103, 112B, 151A, 155A, 158A, 161A, 166B, 175B, 177A, B, 181A, 182B, 185B, 186A, 191A, 194A, 197B, 198A, 202B, 205A, 213B, 214B, 218A, B, 220A, 221A, 224A, 225B, 226A, 227A, B, 228A, B, 229A, 231B, 233B, 236A, 248A, 251B, 252B, 254B

Tovah Martin: 163A, 204A, 210-211, 215A, B, 216B, 221B, 224B, 225A

Jerry Pavia: 123A, 237B

PhotoSynthesis: 116B, 117A, 129A, 134-135, 136B, 139A, B, 163B

Holly Shimizu: 113B, 120A, 123B, 129B, 132A, 140B, 141A, 142A, 144A, 145A, 159A, 167B, 172B, 176B, 179B, 207A, 212B, 213A, 214A, 226B, 238B, 240A, B, 244A

Lauren Springer: 120B, 126A, 127A, 133A, 151B, 182A, 193A, 197A, 205B, 206A

Steven Still: 115B, 162B, 190A, 199A, 203A, 252A

Joseph G. Strauch, Jr.: 178B, 180A, 198B, 229B, 247B, 255A

Andrew Van Hevelingen: 110-111, 118B, 119A, B, 126B, 127B, 138A, 143A, 153A, B, 157A, 158B, 164A, 174A, 195A, 208B, 216A, 220B, 223A

Janet Walker: 167A, 217A, 233A, 243A

Index